D0713756

Etruscan Myth,
Sacred History,
and Legend

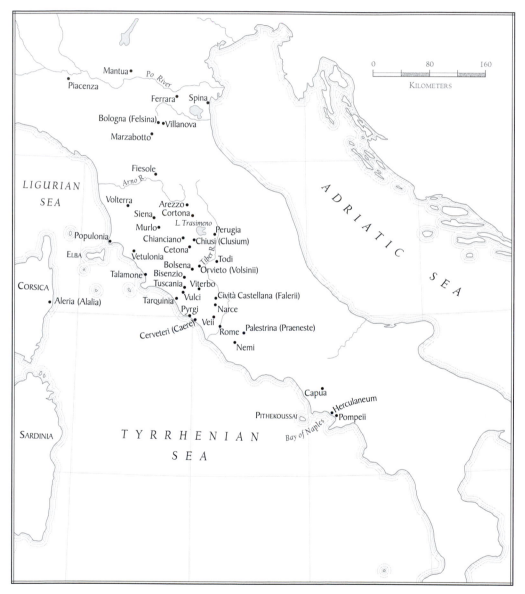

Frontispiece. Etruscan Italy.

Nancy Thomson de Grummond

Etruscan Myth, Sacred History, and Legend

University of Pennsylvania Museum of Archaeology and Anthropology
Philadelphia, PA

Copyright © 2006
by University of Pennsylvania Museum of Archaeology and Anthropology
3260 South Street • Philadelphia, PA 19104

All Rights Reserved

First Edition

Library of Congress Cataloging-in-Publication Data

De Grummond, Nancy Thomson.
Etruscan myth, sacred history, and legend / by Nancy Thomson de Grummond.
p. cm.
Includes bibliographical references and index.
ISBN 1-931707-86-3 (alk. paper)
1. Mythology, Etruscan. 2. Etruscans. I. Title.
BL740.D4 2006
299'.9294--dc22

2006019622

Photograph Credits: Araldo De Luca Archive, Plate V; Bibliothèque nationale de France, VI.38, X.12; Bildarchiv Preussischer Kulturbesitz/Art Resource, NY, VI.9, VII.1, VIII.17; British Museum, ©Copyright The Trustees of the British Museum, II.3, II.16, V.11, V.2, Plate I ; Giovanni Colonna, IV.3, VI. 26; Copenhagen, Ny Carlsberg Glyptotek, V.13; DAI (Deutsches Archäologisches Institut), II.12, V.42 (Felbermeyer, 65.61R), VIII.2 (Nachlass Körte, 31.1697), X.1 (Schwanke, 85.1929), X.7 (Schwanke, 81.4335), X.9 (Schwanke 83.436), X.10 (Schwanke 85.1913), X.11, X.14 (Schwanke, 85.1913), X.16 (Schwanke, 82.565), X.23 (Rossa 75.172), X.24 (Singer 71.428), X.25 (Schwanke, 82.648), X.26 (Schwanke 85.1913), X.29 (Schwanke, 85.1875); Nasher Museum of Art at Duke University, II,15; Kunsthistorisches Museum, Vienna, VI.28; The Metropolitan Museum of Art, New York, VIII.6; Ministero per i Beni e le Attività Culturale: Soprintendenza Archeologica dell' Emilia Romagna, IV.5; Soprintendenza per i Beni Archeologici della Toscana, V.12, V.38, VII.22, X.21, X.27, X.28, Plate II, Plate VII, Plate VIII; Soprintendenza per i Beni Archeologici del Lazio, I.2, II.4, II.8, V.43, VI.12, VI.14, VI.22, VI.23, VI.24, VIII.4, VIII.11, VIII.18, IX.3; Soprintendenza per il Patrimonio Storico, Artistico et Etnoantropologico, Modena e Reggio Emilia, V.2; ©Photothèque des Musées de la Ville de Paris/Fitamant, V.23; Scala/Art Resource, NY, IV.2; Staatliche Antikensammlungen und Glyptothek, Munich, VI.15, VI. 10; Rosa Staneva, I.6; Toledo Museum of Art, Purchased with Funds from the Libbey Endowment, Gift of Edward Drummond Libbey, 1978.22, VI. 11, VIII.5; Vatican Museums, V.31, VII.6, IX.2, X.20, Plate III, Plate IV, Plate VI.

Printed in the United States of America on acid-free paper

for carole law trachy
who believes in Etruscan myth

NANCY THOMSON DE GRUMMOND is M. Lynette Thompson Professor of Classics at The Florida State University. She specializes in Etruscan, Roman, and Hellenistic art and archaeology, with a particular concentration on Etruscan myth and religion. She serves as director of excavations at the Etruscan/Roman site of Cetamura del Chianti under the auspices of the FSU Archaeology Programs in Italy. Her publications include *A Guide to Etruscan Mirrors* (1982) and *The Religion of the Etruscans* (editor and author, with Erika Simon, 2006).

Contents

Illustrations

TABLES

ON CD-ROM

AN ARCHIVE OF IMAGES OF ETRUSCAN MYTHOLOGY
    226 Images

COLOR PLATES

Chronology and Abbreviations

Chronology

All dates are BCE (Before the Common Era=Before Christ, BC)
Early Etruscan (1000/900-450)
    Villanovan (1000/900-750/700)
    Orientalizing (750/700-600)
    Archaic (600-450)
Middle Etruscan
    "Classical" (450-325/300)
Late Etruscan
    "Hellenistic" (325/300-1st cent. BCE)

Abbreviations

In this book the abbreviations of the names of journals, serials, and reference works are based (with a few exceptions) on those used by the *American Journal of Archaeology* as listed in *AJA* 104 (2000): 10-24 (online version at http://www.ajaonline.org/shared/s_info_contrib_7.html).

The following abbreviations are used so frequently that it is appropriate to list them separately here:

Brunn-Körte	Brunn, E., and G. Körte 1872-1916. *I rilievi delle urne etrusche*. 3 vols. Berlin: G. Reimer.
CSE	*Corpus Speculorum Etruscorum*
ES	*Etruskische Spiegel*, ed. E. Gerhard, G. Körte, and A. Klügmann. 5 vols. Berlin, 1840-97.
ET	H. Rix, *Etruskische Texte*. 2 vols. 1991. Tübingen: Gunter Narr.
LIMC	*Lexicon Iconographicum Mythologiae Classicae*
LPRH	*Les Étrusques, Les plus religieux des hommes, XIIes Rencontres de l'École du Louvre*, eds. F. Gaultier and D. Briquel. 1997. Paris: La documentation française.
TLE	*Testimonia Linguae Etruscae*, ed. M. Pallottino. 2nd ed. 1968. Florence: "La Nuova Italia."

Preface

To date no comprehensive account of Etruscan mythology has been published. The subject is elusive and difficult, because no Etruscan mythological textual narratives from antiquity have survived. Instead, to learn about the myths, we study representations in art, evidence from archaeological sites, and indirect accounts of Etruscan lore in Greek and Roman texts. In fact some scholars are quite unaware that an Etruscan mythology exists, while others know that it exists but claim that it is not really Etruscan. For the latter, Etruscan myth is to be understood as a reflection of Greek mythology, which was indeed known and influential among the Etruscans. But what is erroneous about such an approach is that there is a tendency to recognize first what is known and familiar (i.e., the Greek material) and to turn away from and ignore the representations that cannot be explained easily.[1] But it is precisely there that we should look to find the most authentic Etruscan mythology, and there is really a large body of neglected material.

A second mistake scholars make in regard to Greek myths represented in Etruscan art is to search for renderings that coincide with standard versions of the myths in Greece. When these are not found—and sometimes the variations can be quite astonishing—the Etruscans are thought to be ignorant or careless and the scholar feels his job is done by showing what the story ought to be and how it deviates from the "true" myth.[2] In actuality, myths from Greece itself[3] and from other cultures of the world—e.g., of Mesopotamia, Egypt, or India—frequently show variations from place to place or from time to time (i.e., synchronically or diachronically), and to be understood, each myth should be studied within its own temporal and spatial context.

The obsession with finding Greek myths in Etruria is so pervasive that one respected scholar has recently concluded, "It appears to have been the *historical vocation* [italics added] of the Etruscans to integrate Greek mythology and the concomitant iconography into the traditions of the indigenous Italic peoples."[4] Such a view, sympathetic in intent to the Etruscans, draws upon a common valid scholarly position that stresses that they were "intermediaries" between Greece and Rome and even for Europe in general.[5] Undeniably they participated fully in the evolving civilization of the ancient Mediterranean, receiving, transforming, and transmitting cultural cargo just as surely as did the Greeks or the Romans, but the Etruscans themselves most certainly did not feel that they had a particular calling or duty in history to pass on Greek culture to their neighbors. And if this is the most we can say about their treatment of mythology the result is quite impoverishing for the study of the Etruscans.

In this work I propose to avoid the mistake of approaching the Etruscans by way of the Greeks, that is, from what is essentially a framework imposed from outside, and instead to go straight inside to Etruria to try to understand what myths the Etruscans told or depicted and why they did so. Then from that vantage point we may look outside—not just to Greece, but also to the Near East and especially to Rome, with whom the Etruscans had a shared body of Italian experience and religious practice. In this regard, when comparisons are made with other cultures, the emphasis will be placed on a comparative mythology that recognizes the differences as well as similarities in the existing traditions and does not simply track influences from one direction or another. In doing this, I do not intend to ignore Greek and Roman artistic and literary sources that may shed light on Etruscan mythology, but I hope to sift these sources to show what is truly consistent with internal Etruscan evidence and what is of dubious value. As much as possible the aim is to identify what is uniquely Etruscan in the surviving mythological material.[6] In line with my approach, I avoid using technical terms from Greek or Latin that are loaded with meaning from their cultural context in Greece or Italy, a practice that is fairly common in Etruscan studies and is used by some of the best scholars.[7] Throughout the book I attempt to use the Etruscan names of mythological characters whenever they are known (as derived directly from inscriptions), in contrast to the widely observed and sometimes misleading convention of converting the names into Greek or Latin.[8]

This policy may bring disappointment to those who want to start by asking which Etruscan gods corresponded to the various gods of Greece or Rome and who are looking for stories or deities that have a clear, familiar identity. To a certain extent such an exercise is successful, and the reader can consult Table I, listing the Greek and Roman deities who were syncretized with those of the Etruscans. But the various discussions of these gods in their relevant chapters will show how very different the Etruscan deities could be. It is important to remember that Etruscan gods did not inhabit an Olympus, but dwelled instead in particular houses of a 16-part sky. Their cosmos was radically different from that of the Greeks; in addition to the major deities spread through the skies, it featured dozens of other spirits who were little known, if at all, outside of the Etruscan pantheon. Thus readers may be baffled by the content of Chapter III, on creation, time, and the universe according to the Etruscans, and its accompanying Table III, which attempts to illuminate the identity of these many vague spirits known sometimes only by Etruscan names, or else by Latin names that were translations from the Etruscan. But no chapter of the book is more important for understanding the problematic nature of Etruscan mythology. Readers will take away from it, I hope, a healthy caution in making generalizations about Etruscan myth.

This book, then, is planned to demonstrate that the Etruscans did have a mythology of their own, whereby they narrated stories that had a sacred character and helped to explain why the universe was as it was, as well as how to approach the gods by means of prescribed rituals. With the word *myth*[9] I refer to a body of stories (or individual stories) known to the Etruscans about divine and extraordinary beings, embracing some of the standard themes of world mythology such as creation, the pantheon, the mother goddess, intermediary spirits, the hero, the Underworld, and afterlife. As is often the case in myths of all cultures, these stories were told and transmitted anonymously, having a life apart from literary renderings. Further, as Mircea Eliade has noted,[10] myth cannot be separated from the "sacred history" of a people, and accordingly I have included that designation within my title, as well as the word *legend*, which refers to stories that may have a core of historical truth to them. For the Etruscans these are rather important inclusions, since much of their native mythology relates to their prophets, figures of interest for acts that seem to be part of their history and destiny. Indeed prophecy is so important to an understanding of Etruscan myth and sacred history that I have felt it appropriate to place a chapter on prophets at the beginning of this book, before creation, which is normally the opening theme in books on myth from around the world.

During the writing of this book I have become aware of the usefulness of the term *mythologem* employed by mythographers,[11] referring to an over-all theme having multiple constituent parts. The word *mytheme* is something else again, referring to a micro-unit or motif in a myth. For example, an "oracular head" would be a mytheme or single motif (see Figs. II.10-16), whereas the scene in which other motifs are grouped around the oracular head (a prophet who interprets, an assistant who records, an inquirer who has come to learn the prophecy) may be referred to as the mythologem. Given that so many Etruscan myths are known from art and the precise narrative content of the scenes often eludes us, use of this term allows recognition of many myths at a certain level and allows comparison with other similar scenes. In turn, comparison with other scenes can elucidate or add details to the mythologem.[12] This methodology is frequently employed in this work.

To return to the opinions of Eliade, I also agree with him that it is unfortunate that many scholars treat the word *myth* as if it meant *fiction*, since in fact the mythology of a culture often reveals deeply felt beliefs and truths for the members of that society. As far as the Etruscans are concerned, their favorite stories are often closely linked to the rituals of their highly developed religious practice, and thus the relationship between myth and ritual, again a common concern in world mythology, becomes one of the recurrent themes of this book. Also made visible are Etruscan attitudes about politics and in particular about their society; attention will be given to statements about gender and the human body made through myth and art. I hope that this account will provide a new window on the Etruscans through which some of their practices and associated beliefs may be better understood.

How To Use this Book

Etruscan Myth, Sacred History, and Legend is intended to serve a number of different categories of readers. Of course it is hoped that authorities and students involved with front-line research on the Etruscans will find these pages worth consulting. Classicists who study and teach the mythology of ancient Greece and Italy may look here for comparative material, and scholars of world myth may be interested not only in the comparanda but also in the methodology used to investigate myth that must be studied without the illumination of local written narrative (a problem more common than one might suppose in myths around the world). In addition, the work should be relevant for the general public and students who have recently begun the study of ancient Mediterranean and classical civilizations. Given the wide range of readership anticipated, I have included a number of topics to help in introducing the Etruscans: an overview of their geographical setting; a review of the often-discussed question of the origin of the Etruscans and of their general chronology, especially as it relates to the development of myth; a consideration of our written sources, with a short discussion about what is known of the Etruscan language (largely through inscriptions); and discussion of the media in art that are most useful for the study of Etruscan myth, especially engraved bronze mirrors. Most of these matters will be covered in the introductory chapter.

Etruscan inscriptions provide important primary information, and they are cited frequently in these pages. The Etruscans normally wrote from right to left, but modern scholarship reverses the order and the letters so that the inscriptions may be read from left to right. Since Etruscan orthography varies a great deal, sometimes it is necessary to choose one spelling and be consistent in using that even though reference may be made to an inscription that contains a different spelling. As for citing the Etruscan inscriptions themselves, I have used long-established scholarly conventions for transliterating the alphabet, which means retaining Greek forms for the letters *theta* (Θ), *phi* (φ), and *chi* (χ) and using ś for the Etruscan sibilant written like a Greek *sigma* turned on its side.[13] All other letters are in the Latin alphabet.

In the Bibliography and in each chapter I have cited relevant but by no means exhaustive bibliography. For fuller bibliographical coverage in particular one may consult the splendid reference tool, the *Lexicon Iconographicum Mythologiae Classicae* (*LIMC*); the articles are written in English, German, French, or Italian, but whatever the language the corpus of illustrations is invaluable. Often I have incorporated *LIMC* references into the notes (though not into the Bibliography); many more could be added. For a critical treatment of modern scholarship on Etruscan mythology, beginning in the 19th century, the reader may wish to start with the Appendix, Studying Etruscan Mythology,[14] which also includes reference to some of the recent works on Greek and Roman mythology in art.[15]

The illustrations are intended as a starting point for the study of Etruscan myth. These images are really our primary sources and they have been carefully selected to give a wide range of information. Also, each of the illustrations is annotated so that one may thumb through these sources and read a succinct account of each individual work apart from its treatment in the text. Black and white illustrations are numbered in sequence within each chapter. The color illustrations, referred to by continuous plate numbers, are contained in the compact disc accompanying this text. All images are Etruscan unless otherwise indicated. Provenance is listed whenever known.

A special feature of this publication is the inclusion of an *Archive of Images of Etruscan Mythology* on a compact disc (version 1.0). Inside the CD are all relevant illustrations from the book, arranged in alphabetical order according to mythological character. To increase the usefulness of the *Archive*, supplementary images not in the book have been added to the CD, mostly of works carrying inscriptions confirming the identity of the individuals represented. For the most part the supplementary images are not discussed in the book; I have attempted to insert images that are easily identifiable but at the same time enlarge one's view of particular gods, goddesses and heroes. All images illustrated are provided with a basic reference citation, usually from the *Lexicon Iconographicum Mythologiae Classicae*; those from the interior of the book are also referred to by their figure or plate number. As elsewhere here, figures known from Greek mythology are included when they are closely parallel to the Etruscan gods or heroes or when they are relevant for the understanding of those Etruscan figures. In all cases where the Etruscan name or form of the name is known, it is used for the heading of the file on that particular character. Further instructions for the usage of the CD are included in its Introduction and Table of Contents.

Acknowledgments

A draft of this book was written during the teaching of a tutorial on Etruscan myth at Florida State University (fall 2002), and I wish to thank warmly the students who took part in that seminar and provided meaningful responses to the text.[16] I gained many insights from their class reports related to various themes recurring in Etruscan mythological scenes, and some of their results have been incorporated here. My study of the material began in 1966 when I was a graduate student at the University of North Carolina at Chapel Hill, and I took a seminar on the Etruscans conducted by Emeline Hill Richardson. I subsequently gave numerous courses at Florida State devoted to this subject in whole or in part. Of special importance to me was my collaboration with Cheryl Sowder, who enrolled in my first seminar on Etruscan myth (1977) and subsequently wrote the bulk of the chapter on Etruscan Mythological Figures in my book *A Guide to Etruscan Mirrors* (1982: 100-28). In my opinion it is still the best concise introduction to mythology that is purely Etruscan. Another student in that class, John Elliott, went on to write his dissertation on topics related to Etruscan myth and to publish an article on the Etruscan wolf god (Elliott 1995). Also during this period I was encouraged by my colleague at Florida State University, Carole Law Trachy, to believe that one could actually write an entire book on this subject. It is a joy to dedicate to her this work, finished 30 years later, as a tribute to her faith and inspiration.

I wish to acknowledge also a seminar on Etruscan myth given when I was visiting professor at the University of North Carolina at Chapel Hill in 1990. I have kept and regularly consult all of the term reports written in that course by the following students: Lia Fazzone, David Frauenfelder, Peter King, Christopher Mc-Donough, Anne Chapin, Andrew Walker, and Carol Washington. In recent years at FSU, I have had the benefit of using a report compiled by Julia L. Borek on the intermediary spirits of Etruria, on the whole a baffling array of deities unknown in Greece or Rome (see Chapter VII). Wayne L. Rupp has shared with me his many stimulating ideas on the syncretism of Roman and Etruscan mythological figures.

I am very grateful indeed to the following individuals for help in securing photographs: Francesca Boitani, Maria Bonghi Jovino, Sylvia Diebner, Lorenzo Galeotti, Alessandra Nistri, Marco Sala, Maurizio Sannibale, Nikola Theodossiev, and Alex Truscott. Jacquelyn Clements made the drawings in IX.4, X.4, X.5, X.6, and X.15, and Jeffrey Shanks created the diagram of the Etruscan cosmos in Fig. III.3. I wish to express my appreciation to John Wilkins for putting the final touches on this image. Warmest thanks to Alba Frascarelli for allowing me to publish her handsome drawing in Fig. VIII.21. McKenzie Lewis performed essential tasks in creating the CD, and I relied on Peter Krafft, as I have many times in the past, for his skillful preparation of the map I needed. Above all, my thanks go to Gabriele Colantoni for his labors in helping me to obtain photos and in digitizing images from various sources, thus contributing in a most important way to the overall usefulness of the illustrations and the appearance of the book.

Many of the ideas on prophecy have been presented at conferences (Rome, Ann Arbor) and at lectures for the Archaeological Institute of America, and I am grateful to audiences that responded with enthusiasm, good sense, and helpful critical suggestions. I would like to thank the following for inspiration, assistance, and gentle criticism at various stages of the creation of this book: Larissa Bonfante, Elizabeth Colantoni, Lynda Davis, Francesco Roncalli, Francesca R. Serra Ridgway, Svetla Slaveva-Griffin, and Kathryn B. Stoddard. Two scholars especially have influenced me at every turn: Jean MacIntosh Turfa, who asked me many challenging and detailed questions; this text has been enormously improved as I have attempted to answer them; and Erika Simon, who seems to have gone before me in almost every pathway of Etruscan myth I traveled. Her rich and creative interpretation of the core material available in representations in art has helped frame the dialogue for this discipline and has brought in many startling insights and convincing conclusions; that I may disagree with her arguments from time to time is an indication of the problematic nature of Etruscan myth, of how much need there is for debate that will winnow out the superfluous, and of how much work still needs to be done to come to a greater understand of this intriguing corpus of evidence.

Introduction

Introducing the Etruscans: Geography and Chronology

The Etruscans are well known as the first great civilization of the peninsula of Italy, worthy forerunners of the Romans as well as of the Christian culture of the Middle Ages and the humanist flowering of the Renaissance. Because most of their books have not been preserved, we have relatively little documentation of their history, but they are well known from the archaeological record. In terms of geography, we are studying the central part of the Italian peninsula (Frontispiece), where Etruria—the Etruscan territory—is traditionally described as bounded by the Arno River on the north and by the Tiber River on the east and south. The coast of Etruria is washed by the Tyrrhenian Sea; on that coast lay some of the most important Etruscan cities—Tarquinia, Cerveteri (ancient Caere), Vulci, Populonia—while others were inland or farther north, such as Orvieto, Chiusi, Arezzo, Perugia, Volterra. Veii was the Etruscan city closest to Rome. It is important to note that in fact from a very early date the Etruscans inhabited and controlled extensive areas outside of this central territory, as far north as Bologna and as far south as the Bay of Naples. At one point in its history (6th century BCE) Etruscan influence spread the length and breadth of the boot of Italy; thus from time to time we shall refer to sites outside of Etruria proper that provide evidence for the subject of Etruscan myth.

The presence of the Etruscans in Italy is first evident around the 10th century BCE. There are various theories about the origin of this people, who spoke a language unrelated to the other languages of ancient Italy, almost all of which may be classified securely as Indo-European.[1] As will be reviewed in Chapter IX on Foundation Myths and Legends, the Greek historian Herodotus (*Histories* 1.94; 5th century BCE) recorded a legend that the Etruscans came from Asia Minor and were related to the Lydians. This tradition was denied, however, by another Greek author, Dionysios of Halikarnassos, writing around the end of the 1st century BCE for readers living under the early Roman Empire. He declared that the Etruscans themselves believed that they had never immigrated but that they had always been in Italy. Both theories are tantalizing, but modern scholars, having weighed the evidence and found it inconclusive, stress that until new information appears, it is best to abandon speculation. The trend in scholarship is to concentrate instead on what we *can* document, that is, the development of Etruscan civilization within Italy. Archaeological evidence shows continuity in material culture from the earliest prehistoric Etruscan period into historic times on many of the major sites of the great Etruscan cities. While foreign influences, sometimes very strong, may be perceived, there is no evidence of a break or abrupt change that would justify an argument for a large migration or invasion of the type implied by the account of Herodotus.

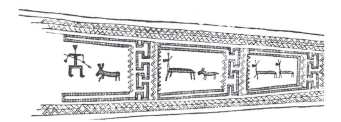

I.1 Bronze sword scabbard from Tarquinia (cemetery at Poggio Impiccato, grave 1), 9th–8th century BCE. Tarquinia, Museo Archeologico Nazionale. After Hencken 1968a:fig. 106. Incised design of hunter and animals, found in an elite burial of an Etruscan warrior; engraving on scabbard, panel 1, may show a hero using a spear to fight a boar; panel 2, a stag chased by a dog; panel 3, two deer, perhaps from other hunts of the warrior.

The study of Etruscan mythology relates in chronology to the period when they first began to write and to represent the human figure in art,[2] probably in the 8th century, and continues into the 1st century BCE, when their civilization was absorbed into the Roman Empire. The customary chronological sequence for studying the Etruscans and their art is as follows:

Early Period (1000/900-450 BCE)

The earliest phase of Etruscan culture may be subdivided into the Villanovan era (1000-750/700; a prehistoric period, also referred to as the Iron Age), the Orientalizing era (750/700-600), and the Archaic era (600-450). The earliest representations of humans and animals occur in the Villanovan, but thus far little mythological content has been recognized. Scenes of hunting incised on bronze, for example on a sword scabbard from Tarquinia, show the hunter and his prey (here a boar; Fig. I.1) but such scenes may be generic rather than the story of some particular heroic hunt.[3] There are actually a good many Villanovan scenes that show little stick figures in action, reflecting a native development within Italy.[4]

But the best candidate for mythical subject matter in the earliest Etruscan period occurs on a bronze burial urn from Bisenzio, near Lake Bolsena, dated to the end of the 8th century BCE (Fig. I.2).[5] Decorated with bronze figurines, it features

I.2 Bronze ash urn from Bisenzio (cemetery of Olmo Bello, Tomb 22), ca. 725–700 BCE. Rome, Museo Nazionale Etrusco di Villa Giulia. Photo: Soprintendenza per i Beni Archeologici del Lazio. On the lid of the urn a large beast is leashed by a chain attached to its neck, surrounded by seven ithyphallic males dancing around in a circle, some with raised spears. The shoulder of the urn carries several other figures, including one leading an ox, perhaps a ritual element.

on the lid of the urn an encounter between an enchained wolf-like monster and a group of naked, ithyphallic warriors who dance around it in a clockwise circular motion, some waving their spears. They wear head coverings such as a pointed hat or crested helmet. The scene has a strongly ritual character, further indicated by the presence on the shoulder of the vessel of a man leading an ox, probably for sacrifice. The ritual may be related, as often in mythology, to a particular story, but there are few further clues to the myth in this particular representation. Shortly we shall encounter this same mythologem—wolfish monster, chain, warriors, and sacrifice—in a series of funerary urns of the Hellenistic period that tend to confirm the theory that the Bisenzio urn shows one of the earliest-known local Etruscan myths.

The designation of Orientalizing refers to a wealthy age when great influences from the older cultures of the Eastern Mediterranean (e.g., Egypt and Assyria) came into Italy, especially under the impetus of visitation by the Phoenicians and of colonization by the Greeks on the Bay of Naples, all actually beginning in the 8th century. During this epoch rich burials found at Tarquinia, Cerveteri, and elsewhere suggest the hypothesis, supported by literary sources, that some Etruscans held the status of kings and princes. Literary tradition places the first Etruscan king of Rome, Tarquinius Priscus, as emigrating from his native city of Tarquinia at the end of the 7th century BCE.

Images of foreign gods appear on imports and in local adaptations of these works of art, and perhaps images of native gods as well. A particular favorite is the winged goddess, internationally known, who is sometimes referred to as Lady of the Beasts; she occurs on Etruscan silver relief plaques in the Vatican, attended by leaping wolf cubs, an appropriate motif for a work from Italy (Fig. V.31).[6]

Pictures with true narrative content are quite recognizable now, though inscriptions rarely tell the viewer who is represented. These images occur on pottery, some created as incisions in the clay (a native technique) and some in the Greek imported style of painting in red or brown on the light clay background of the vase. The city of Cerveteri seems to have been a center for the production of vases decorated with narrative scenes. Located in the south of Etruria near the seacoast, Cerveteri may well have developed this interest through foreign contacts, and scholars determined to make identifications invariably connect such scenes with some Greek mythological subject: a warrior and a woman dressed completely in the Etruscan fashions of the 7th century showing affection for one another are suggested to be Helen and Menelaos or a Trojan female prisoner entreating a Greek (Fig. I.3)[7]; a musician with a 7-string lyre who accompanies armed dancers is said to be Orpheus playing for the Argonauts (Fig. I.4); a grand, mantled lady with a three-headed serpent is identified as Medea (Fig. I.5).[8]

I.3 Detail from painted crater from Cerveteri, necropolis of Monte Abatone, 680–660 BCE. Cerveteri, Museo Archeologico Nazionale. After Bonfante 1975:fig. 41. Lady and warrior; she caresses his face affectionately. Both wear local Etruscan fashions—he the diamond-shaped belt and she the long back braid.

I.4 Detail from painted amphora, ca. 670 BCE. Würzburg, Martin von Wagner Museum (coll. Fujita). After Martelli 1987:262–63. Musician, perhaps Urphe, the Etruscan Orpheus, with the 7-stringed lyre (heptacord) accompanying five dancers with swords and spear. Mask or head in the field next to the musician.

I.5 Detail from painted amphora, 660–640 BCE. Amsterdam, Allard Pierson Museum. After Bonfante 2003:fig. 5. A lady or goddess in a heavy mantle confronts and controls a three-headed dragon; two more single-headed serpents follow.

In the last case, we must ask, if this is Medea, why does the dragon have three heads, who are the other two single-headed serpents, and where is the Golden Fleece? Just to help us keep open to other possibilities, it is worth looking at a similar confrontation of a lady and a three-headed dragon from another land on the periphery of Greek culture, Thrace (Fig. I.6, found at Letnitsa, Bulgaria; the image dates to the 4th century BCE).[9] Her identity is unknown, but the composition has been interpreted as showing the mythologem of the virgin offered to the dragon who tames the beast and wrests away his control of some force of nature (often waters). The image thus may be related to fertility and productivity as well as marriage (another scene in this Thracian series shows a couple having intercourse), and provides a very different model from the story of Medea.

It remains possible that the Etruscans thought of this dragon-tamer as being named Medea, but if she is, the story is quite removed from what we know in Greece, and by labeling it so schematically we limit it and risk ignoring the nuances that might be telling a very different story. When we do in fact have inscriptions on these early mythological scenes, the information they provide can be downright astounding. There is a "Medea" from early Etruria. She has been described as the earliest known image of Medea, but her story is difficult to identify (Fig. I.7). A scene incised on a pitcher made of local Etruscan bucchero, again from Cerveteri,[10] shows a robed figure labeled Metaia, standing before a figure shown in half-length as if rising up from behind or out of a basin. Six youths march toward the pair, bearing a great length of fringed cloth inscribed *kanna* (which has been interpreted to mean "gift"). On the far left of the scene are two boxers and on the far right is a winged figure with arms raised upward (to support something?), labeled Taitle, logically translated as Daidalos. It is possible to see mythemes from the story of Medea, such as the use of a cauldron for rejuvenation (plausible), or, in the *kanna*, the Golden Fleece (unconvincing), or in the boxers, a contest of the Argonauts on the island of Lemnos (but how does that relate to the cauldron scene?). Taitle's role remains unexplained,[11] but it is worth noting that he is located almost under the handle of the pitcher, and his pose may be at least partially explained as depicting a supporting function.

There is a likelihood that this is a story told in Italy that will never be matched in any account of Greek mythology. Scholars have been so tantalized by the prospect of identifying the details of this "incunabulum" of Greek myth that they have always started with the preconception that the story can be explained by consulting and patching together Greek literary texts. If we start with the images themselves, a different interpretation may be proposed. This could be read as a mythologem, one in which a male figure goes through a ritual of bathing (the possibility that the figure is female cannot be ruled out) and then receives a new garment (the *kanna*),

I.6 Thracian gilt silver plaque from Letnitsa (Bulgaria), ca. 350 BCE. Lovech Museum of History. Photo: Rosa Staneva. A lady or goddess with short hair, breasts not indicated (a virgin?), holding a mirror, confronts and controls a three-headed dragon.

at some transitional moment in life or death. The boxing scene could be part of his initiation taking place before the bathing. The hero boxes, bathes, and is adorned. The Metaia figure then appears as the mistress who oversees the ritual. There is no way to prove that this is the connection between these three scenes, but it is worth considering that the Etruscan owner may well have read it in this way and valued it for its reference to his own situation.

J.G. Szilágyi[12] has written eloquently of the possibility that early Etruscan representations of myth, even if containing figures paralleling Greek characters, most likely had a local meaning. His observations were derived especially from his study of the extensive corpus of painted vessels known as "Etrusco-Corinthian," dating

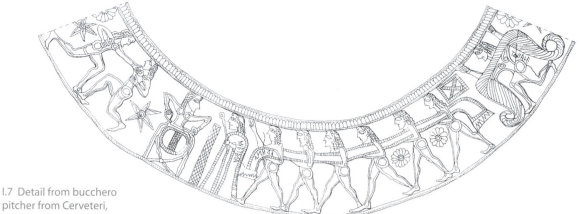

I.7 Detail from bucchero pitcher from Cerveteri, 630 BCE. Rome, Museo Nazionale Etrusco di Villa Giulia. After Bonfante 2003:fig. 4. Incision made before firing shows a pair of boxers on far left. The next scene shows the figure of Metaia, dressed in a mantle and holding a scepter; in front of her a pillar (?) and a vessel from which a figure, perhaps male, seems to emerge. Six youths march toward them carrying a great length of fringed cloth labeled *kanna*, "gift." On far right is a winged figure, Taitale, with legs spread and arms raised.

from a period between about 630 and 550 BCE. He repeatedly questions whether types such as the centaur or the human-headed bull referred to by scholars as the Minotaur were understood by the Etruscans as belonging to Greek stories, and equally significantly cites various figures from the corpus of decorated vases that have no Greek parallel. A male figure lying on a bed with his arms bound and with a panther hovering nearby surely belongs to a narrative, but the story cannot be identified (Fig. I.8); Szilágyi also cites a Master of Birds who occurs on several vases (e.g., Fig. I.9), wearing an Etruscan kilt-like garment and balancing birds on his own wings or holding them by the neck.[13] The recurrence of the figure suggests that he is more than decorative and that he probably had a real role in the Etruscan *immaginario* (corpus of images) of this period.

These Etrusco-Corinthian vases show a continuity from the Orientalizing period into the next phase of Early Etruscan culture, the Archaic. The term *Archaic* refers to the beginnings of an evolving trend in naturalism in the representational arts. In this era there is a continuation of influence from Greece and the Near East as Etruscan ideas about the gods and their worship take a distinctive shape.

Richardson declared the Archaic to be the period when "The Gods Arrive in Etruria," noting that real cult images are first seen in the 6th century.[14] Some of these are identifiable because they take on standard attributes or appearances known in Greece: the Etruscan war goddess Menrva wears the aegis and Gorgon head of Athena (Fig. V.2). But others show the Etruscan tradition, and critical interpretation is needed; for example, a god holding a thunderbolt would be quickly equated with Zeus, except that he is shown as beardless and youthful (Fig. IV.2). Instead he could be one of a number of gods who throw lightning in Etruria.[15] As it turns out his iconography is in fact consistent with that of Tinia, the Etruscan counterpart of Zeus, who is frequently shown (unlike Zeus) as young and beardless.

With cult and votive images, we see new media becoming important for the study of Etruscan myth, in particular the abundant small bronzes that were used as votive offerings. This is also the period when the earliest Etruscan mirrors appear,

I.8 Detail from Etrusco-Corinthian amphora, 630–580 BCE. Rome, Museo Nazionale Etrusco di Villa Giulia. After Szilágyi 1992, 1998:fig. 3. A nude, bearded male figure lies supine on a bed, his arms extended in front of him and upward to display bonds around his wrists. An overly large panther (perhaps not part of the narrative) paces nearby and looks out at the viewer. A male figure approaches from the left carrying an animal, perhaps a rabbit. The story is unknown.

I.9 Detail from Etrusco-Corinthian alabastron from Vulci, 630—580 BCE. Vulci, Museo Etrusco. After Szilágyi 1992, 1998:fig. 35. A winged figure, evidently male, has his legs bent in the scheme used in ancient art to indicate rapid movement. The head is unusual, featuring a crescent-shaped profile with sparse hair along the side of his face (escaping from a cap?). He is probably in flight, as indicated by his large wings. He is attended by two birds perched on his wings and seems to hold a third bird by the neck.

I.10 Bronze mirror from near Orvieto, ca. 500 BCE. Minneapolis, MN, Minneapolis Institute of Arts. After CSE, U.S.A.:1.26a. The Etruscan sun god, known as Usil, rises from the waves, juggling balls of the sun.

a striking example of which is provided by the mirror showing the god of the sun, Usil, rising from the sea (Fig. I.10).[16] The sun is shown as a juggler, tossing balls with fire streaming from them, perhaps indicating a perception of the storms that occur on the sun periodically sending up great plumes of fire. Much more information about the significance of the mirrors will be provided below.

Middle Period (450-325/300 BCE)

This period has sometimes been referred to as the "Classical" Period, using a name from Greek art and archaeology, but this constitutes a misnomer for what occurs in Etruscan territory in the 5th and 4th centuries, and many Etruscan scholars now simply use the century designations instead.[17] Here we recognize this period with a neutral term that places it midway in Etruscan culture.

The Greek term "Classical" is based on the notion (sometimes itself challenged) that the "highest and best" period in the art of mainland Greece is the 5th century, with the 4th century close behind; with this was associated a style that was "noble" and "simple," with perfect balance in representation of the human figure and idealization of the images of gods and men. A good many of the conventions of this style were adopted by the Etruscans, but their own points of emphasis were inserted and most Etruscan art of this period cannot be mistaken for Greek. This is a fairly important point for our subject since a quite large number of Etruscan mythological representations belong to this period. The deviations from the style should not be taken to indicate that the Etruscans did not understand the Greek models; rather they are consistent with the fact that the Etruscans' concepts of mythological beings—their anatomy, clothing, and posture—were sometimes quite unlike the Greeks'. Some good examples of this point may be found in scenes that show figures unknown in Greece, such as the engraved bronze mirror in the Metropolitan Museum of Art (Fig. VII.10) with the characters Prucnas, Zipunu (also called Zipna), and Thalna[18]; it shows some of the conventions of the "Classical" style, though with a tendency to stylize such forms as the breasts of the goddess Zipunu and to use local clothing details such as Etruscan pointed-toe shoes.[19]

Late Period (325/300-1st century BCE)

The Late Etruscan Period is sometimes called "Hellenistic," another term borrowed from Greek archaeology with a result that is not particularly satisfying; the word literally means "Greekish" and was coined to describe the period after Alexander the Great conquered much of the known world and spread Hellenic culture far and wide. As can be seen from the chronology outlined above, the Etruscans had a lively interest in Greek culture from an early date and certainly this Late period is no exception; and there is indeed interest attached to the study of Greek myth in Etruria in this period. But it is more important to identify first the local developments and concerns, and see how art and iconography were evolving in Etruria itself. For example, this is the period when we see hundreds of representations of the spirit named Lasa, carrying her perfume jar (Fig. VII.25), seemingly connected with Etruscan rituals of anointing and adornment.

Of considerable significance for understanding the Late Period is the fact that the Etruscans were conquered by the Romans during this period, city by city, and in art and religion there is evident a blending of these two Italian cultures. It is worth asking how this acculturation affected the depictions of myths in Etruria, and in particular to see how and why there is a new concern with themes of the Underworld and afterlife, sometimes showing a pessimism and preoccupation with the fate of individuals as well as the Etruscan people as a whole.   It is the great period of Charu and Vanth, Etruscan spirits who escorted the deceased to the afterlife, representing death as alternatingly terrifying and comforting (Fig. X.16; cf. Ch. X).

The Sources

Fundamental to the problem of Etruscan mythology is the lack of written sources. The Etruscans did have some kinds of literature, such as sacred texts, history and drama, seemingly not as varied and extensive as the writings of the Greeks and Romans, but what there was has almost totally vanished. We rely on Greek and Roman authors for the information that the Etruscans once had a rich tradition of written religious lore, books that dealt with omens from the gods and with the nature of the universe. This body of literature was known in Latin as the *Etrusca disciplina*, the Etruscan discipline or doctrine. They had special writings on the Underworld that the Romans called the *Libri Acheruntici*. Still other books were said to have been written by their prophets, legendary or mythical figures named Tages and Vegoia in Latin. But since none of these books has survived in Etruscan, and all we have is offhand references or fragmentary quotations from them in Latin or Greek, our knowledge of their contents and their information about the gods is frustratingly limited.

The original Etruscan writings that we do have are almost all in the form of short inscriptions. Estimates vary as to the number of Etruscan inscriptions known, but it is safe to say that there are more than 11,000 known, and new ones are constantly being discovered and/or published for the first time.[20] Great progress has been made in the translation of Etruscan, and it is generally agreed by experts that the language is non-Indo-European (non-IE), an important point for mythographers who have long cherished the idea that Indo-European (IE) speakers in some remote past told myths that later radiated with the evolving languages across the world from India to Iceland.[21] Of course there is some overlap of mythology between the IE Greeks and Romans and the non-IE Etruscans. Also intriguing are the comparisons between Etruscan and Scandinavian myth, a matter that has been little investigated so far but which will be referred to from time to time in these pages.[22] The theorists need not be embarrassed over these connections, since an equally valid method of transmitting myths by "diffusion" may be recognized, i.e., cultural contact between peoples of unrelated ethnicity. On the other hand, the distinction between IE and non-IE serves as a salutary reminder that the Etruscans may have had very different thought patterns than their IE neighbors.

Many of the surviving Etruscan inscriptions can be read with some confidence (it is a popular misconception that Etruscan has not been deciphered), and they tell us the names of the gods, which gods are associated with one another, and something about how these gods were worshipped. These inscriptions will be frequently referenced in this book and can be read fairly easily in the illustrations if one has knowledge of the Greek alphabet; unlike Greek, however, the Etruscan inscriptions are normally written and read from right to left.

Several inscriptions on works of art seem to have genuinely narrative content, such as on a mirror from Volterra that shows the remarkable theme of Hercle (=Herakles/Hercules) as an adult nursing at the breast of the goddess Uni (=Hera/Juno), in which a few lines seem to declare what action is going on (Fig. V.14): *eca : sren : tva : iχnac : hercle : unial : clan : Θra : sce*, "This image shows how Hercle, the son of Uni, was adopted (?)."[23]

Obviously such inscriptions are short, and it remains safe to say that thus far there is no true extended textual narrative of myth in the Etruscan language. The longest and most famous of Etruscan writings is the text written in ink on linen cloth now in the National Museum in Zagreb; the linen strips were found wrapped around an Egyptian mummy collected by a Yugoslavian traveler in 1848/49. It is assumed that the Etruscan linen book—the Roman equivalent was the sacred *Liber Linteus*—was carried to Egypt by an emigrating Etruscan and then later discarded, to be recycled for the mummy. These bizarre "Zagreb mummy wrappings," with about 1,200 words surviving, contain a sacred calendar of which a good bit can be understood, if not literally translated, and include the names of a number of gods. From this we learn which gods were worshipped together and which days were cultic for various deities. The vocabulary includes the word for "gods" in Etruscan, *eiser* (also spelled *aiser*),[24] as well as the names of gods who are recognizable—e.g., Nethuns, Uni, Thesan (goddess of the dawn)—and who are not otherwise known, such as the elusive pair (or group) Śi and Śeu. But so far no true mythological accounts have been recognized here.[25]

Also worth mentioning is the remarkable inscribed lifesize bronze model of a sheep's liver, used in interpreting the will of the gods, found near Piacenza in northern Italy (Fig. III.1-2).[26] Its upper surface is divided into 40 "cells" or houses (there are 16 along the periphery) inscribed with the names of the deities that controlled each area. The liver gives numerous clues about gods known from other sources, as well as the names of some that are otherwise quite unknown. It may be studied in combination with a fascinating Latin text that describes the heavens as having 16 divisions, evidently reflecting Etruscan doctrine, written down in Latin centuries later by Martianus Capella; together these sources reveal much about the Etruscan pantheon (see Table III and Fig. III.3).[27]

The evidence that the Etruscans did tell mythological stories comes mainly from their art. There is a quite rich body of material in their representations of deities, spirits, heroes, and heroines in such media as carved gems, engraved bronze mirrors, and painted vases and frescoes, as well as sculptures on temples and funerary receptacles such as sarcophagi and ash urns. Still, much remains unknown; stories told in representations in art often assume that the viewer already knows the story, and without a written narrative taking place in time it is difficult to reconstruct the sequence of action.

The engraved mirrors[28] have been especially useful, because they sometimes include inscriptions to identify the personages represented, and they are quite numerous, often providing more than one image of a particular myth. They are frequently studied by reference to line drawings, which are easily created and are more legible in details than photographs. Since the mirrors have been used extensively to illustrate Etruscan myth, it is important to keep in mind their context. Their iconography is no doubt influenced by the fact that they were used mostly, if not exclusively, by women; a widely credited hypothesis is that they were often bestowed as wedding gifts. The mirrors were so important to their owners that they were regularly taken to their graves, and so far in excavations no other find spot besides the funerary one has been recorded. In studying the mirrors, then, it is worth remembering that they were relevant for marriage and the funeral, in daily life and in the afterlife.

Another specialty medium is that of engraved gems made to be set on a ring worn on the finger or around the neck (e.g., Fig. VI.38).[29] Hundreds of these miniature works of art have survived (usually measuring only about 1 cm in height), carved in intaglio, often with a single mythological figure or a pair in the tiny field, and an identifying inscription. Just as the mirrors seem intended for a female clientele, so do the gems appear to have been made often for males, possibly because the seals cut on them were utilized by men who needed to mark control of possessions or trade items. There are many prophets, heroes, and gods—Tarchon and Tages, Achilles and Ajax, Hercle, the Seven who fought at Thebes, as well as priests, unnamed warriors, and horsemen. There are nevertheless female personages whose names appear on the gems—Atlnta, Elinai, Menrva, Turan—and also a good many whose names do not appear but are recognizable (e.g., Europa, Artumes).

A third category of art that is very important for the study of myth is Etruscan wall painting.[30] There are relatively few scenes of true mythological narrative but especially in the Etruscan Middle and Late periods numerous representations of the gods and monsters of the Underworld (see Chapter X).

Methodology: Concerning Greek Influence

Obviously a major obstacle in the study of Etruscan myth is the "Greek problem." The Etruscans had the good taste to love Greek art and seek to acquire it, especially in the form of brightly painted vases, imported into Etruria by the thousands during the 6th and 5th centuries BCE. These often have representations of Greek myths that no doubt appealed to the Etruscans. Some have even argued that there was an "Etruscan taste" anticipated by Greek artists when they made products to be shipped to Italy. The Etruscans sometimes imitated these scenes in their own art, or adopted ways of representing their major gods from Greek art. These practices have led some to say that there is no Etruscan mythology, only Greek mythology in an Etruscan phase.

It is certainly true that the Etruscans had a pantheon in which some of the major gods were assimilated to the major gods of Greece and Rome. Table I demonstrates some of these equivalences, which should be consulted always, however, with the *caveat* that there may be very important differences between the counterpart gods. Tinia, the chief Etruscan deity, had much in common with the Greek Zeus and the Roman Jupiter, as well as the Norse Odin. He ruled the sky and was very potent because of his control of lightning, sometimes being represented in art enthroned with the thunderbolt, in a Greco-Roman style (Fig. IV.14). But as noted earlier, he was also commonly represented as a youthful unbearded god (Fig. IV.6, 8-9), in contrast to the heavy, mature figure of Olympian Zeus. We shall see in Chapter IV that he differed from the Greek god in some important ways, beginning obviously with his name.

Other major deities have their similarities to and differences from their Greek and Roman counterparts, and looking at these comparisons will help us to define the nature of deity in Etruria. It is also instructive to look at some of the stories that do come from Greek mythology and see how the Etruscans changed these in accordance with their own tastes, needs, and beliefs. As already noted, sometimes the stories are radically different from the ones told in Greece. The Minotaur, for example, is shown in Etruria as slain by Hercle, the Etruscan Herakles (Fig. VIII.14),[31] rather than by Theseus, the hero of Athens. Theseus's role in Etruscan mythology was not political as in Greece and was restricted mainly to the story of a trip to the Underworld (a mytheme that virtually obsessed the Etruscans). But

I.11 Ash urn with relief sculpture, 2nd century BCE. Florence, Museo Archeologico Nazionale. After Brunn-Körte: 3.9.4. A wolf-monster emerges from a well head as a bearded man wearing a fine mantle pours a libation from a sacrificial patera. The creature attacks one youth as another attempts to restrain him with chains.

Hercle was always a versatile and popular figure, a true god in Etruria. He was a god of water and he had various adventures that are totally unknown in Greece, for example the abduction of the lady Mlacuch, a myth that seems to be purely Etruscan (Fig. VIII.16).

Further, and most important of all, there are some Etruscan stories that are completely non-Greek, for example, the stories of the Vipinas Brothers told on mirrors and ash urns and in wall paintings (Figs. II.5-6; see Chapter VIII especially), and the myth of the youthful soothsayer Pava Tarchies (Fig. II.2). The latter is discussed with several other purely Etruscan prophet figures—Lasa Vecuvia, Cacu, and Umaele, in Chapter II.

In addition there are some Etruscan myths for which we have no inscriptions and simply do not know who the characters are. Most conspicuous of these is the hostile encounter between a noble or royal warrior and a wolflike creature that emerges from a well head, seeking victims and itself subject to attack (Figs. I.11-12). We have already noted an early version of the story that appears on a Villanovan ash urn (Fig. I.2). The scene occurs much later on several sculptured burial urns of the Hellenistic period from Perugia and Volterra; unfortunately there are no inscriptions to give us a clue about the identity of the principal figures, but it is helpful to see the figure of the goddess Vanth included (Fig. I.12), for her appearances are almost always associated with death. The wolf itself was commonly associated with death and the Underworld,[32] and the fact that it quite literally comes up from below, through the well head, adds further to the mythologem. Further, there is normally a struggle in which the adversaries are depicted attempting to chain the beast around the neck (Fig. I.11), and in which it is implied that it will be sacrificed (the tilting of a sacrificial patera over its head; the presence of short knives for slitting the throat). A mature, bearded figure, sometimes wearing a pointed conical hat (not unlike those on the Bisenzio urn), appears to be a leader or king who combats the creature. The menace is great, and very likely the fiend takes its own victims.

I.12 Terracotta ash urn with relief sculpture from Perugia, 2nd century BCE. Perugia, Museo Archeologico Nazionale. After Brunn-Körte:3.10.5. A figure with a wolfskin cap and animal paws emerges from a well head as a kingly figure pours a libation from a sacrificial patera. Bare-breasted winged Vanth in the background. The monster attacks one youth, as soldiers prepare to retaliate.

How can this mythological representation be explicated? In a way we have a test case here, because several different methodologies have been attempted. The first we may dismiss quickly: the "literary reference," which has been used to explain this as a real event that took place at Volsinii, described by Pliny the Elder (*NH* 2.140). "Historical record exists of thunderbolts being vouchsafed in answer to certain rites and prayers. There is an old story of the latter in [Etruria] when the *monstrum* (prodigy) which they called Olta came to the city of [Volsinii], when its territory had been devastated; it was sent in answer to the prayer of king Porsina."[33] Cited in the 19th century by Brunn and Körte[34] as providing an explanation, the idea has led to repeated reference to the scene as the "Olta episode," but it is time to discard this connection. There is a kingly figure who could be equated with King Porsina, but little else is relevant in the passage. Above all, Pliny does not mention a wolf or a chaining action; the word *monstrum* can refer to any kind of prodigy. Further, in the urns there is no lightning. So the two bodies of evidence about Etruscan myth and religion show very little intersection.

Another approach is to note that the scene clearly shows elements of ritual. Not only do we have the patera and the well head, which both frequently show sacred connections, but it seems that there is an impersonation of a wolf in Fig. I.12, for the figure emerging has a human head and is dressed in a wolf skin. It may be that the urns record an actual ritual that was used by the Etruscans in a funerary context.[35] The mythologem may then constitute a story relating to a performance in which the climax showed the conquest of death.

So the scene can be interpreted as a native Etruscan myth and ritual. But inevitably there is also the common methodology of comparing the theme to Greek myth. An intelligent and provocative analysis is made by Erika Simon, who notes the Greek story of King Sisyphos, who chained up Thanatos (Death) in an attempt to deceive Hades.[36] The beast then could be identified as the Etruscan Thanatos (though Thanatos in Greece does not seem to have been represented as a wolf). The use of comparative mythology brings out yet another striking parallel, with the evil Norse wolf Fenrir, brother of the Underworld goddess Hel. Fenrir was bound by the gods with a chain, not without casualties, for he bit off the hand of Tyr, the brave and wise warrior son of Odin. The action was successful and Fenrir remained bound until the end of the world, the so-called twilight of the gods, when he burst his bonds and came to battle with the gods.[37] In this case the bound Underworld wolf takes on great cosmic significance, probably going beyond the Etruscan theme.

A number of other mythological figures were quite unknown in Greece and are often ignored by scholars specializing in classical myth, who are prone to recognize mainly what they already know or else what they can find justification for in some Greek text. The hazards of seeking textual authority have recently been dramatically exposed by J. P. Small in her book *The Parallel Worlds of Classical Art and Text* (2003). In fact, as she notes, it is rare to find that a text and an image in art truly coincide, and it is preferable to study these two "worlds" as developing independently. She refers only to Greek art and literature, but the lesson applies in Etruria as well.

Some scholars show contempt for Etruscan representations of Greek myths that diverge from the standard versions known in Greece and believe that the Etruscans have got it "wrong."[38] In fact, Greek myth itself, whether in image or text, has some amazingly varying and contradictory accounts, and these are considered not errors, but only (and rightly) variants. For example, the preferred version of the myth of Helen of Troy says that after Paris stole her away and the Greeks fought the Trojan War to get her back, she returned to her husband Menelaus at Sparta. But another and extraordinary Greek version has her marry the greatest of the Greek warriors, Achilles, and live happily with him on the island of Leuke.[39]

One may compare the equally surprising representation of Helen, called Elinai in Etruria, on an Etruscan mirror (Fig. IV.14), where she sits enthroned and turns to the right to shake hands with Agamemnon as Menelaus watches. On the left Paris seems to strut beside her, receiving a wreath from the Etruscan goddess Mean, who has been identified as a deity of victory. It looks as if the bitter enemies, Greeks and Trojans, are here coexisting in peace. This Etruscan myth of harmony among the great rivals should not be taken as erroneous any more than the Greek story of Helen and Achilles. Myth is allowed to vary according to geography and chronology, and on the basis of other factors as well, such as political, ritual, or personal considerations. The idea of one scholar that the Etruscans violated "mythological fact" is to be rejected because it is at odds with what is characteristic of the phenomenon of mythology in general.[40]

Methodology: The Internal Combinatory Method

One way to approach the problem of interpreting Etruscan mythic images is to review the methodology used by scholars attempting to translate the Etruscan language. Generally fruitless has been the attempt to translate Etruscan by declaring it to be "really" some other (known) language. Called the "etymological method," this approach led scholars to declare alternately that Etruscan was really Hebrew, Latin, Greek, Armenian, Basque, Finno-Ugric, Dravidian.[41] While lexical and orthographic insights might be obtained by studying bilingual inscriptions and shared vocabulary, especially between Latin and Etruscan and between Greek and Etruscan, such research never led to a satisfactory program for deciphering the Etruscan language.

Instead, Pallottino has stressed the importance of combining and studying internal evidence.[42] The combinatory method involves making "an accurate archaeological estimate" of the "character, meaning and chronology" of a particular object or monument having an Etruscan inscription, making conjectures from that internal evidence, and then checking the reliability of the hypothesis by applying the results to other, commensurate Etruscan objects or monuments. In this way a group of inscriptions can be assembled that have a similar semantic field and grammatical parallels, within an appropriate chronological and/or geographical setting and with a comparable archaeological context. Thus they help to elucidate each other. The technique does not have to be exclusive; certainly to be taken into account are reliable etymological comparisons made from, for example, glosses and bilingual inscriptions. Also helpful is the process of comparing formulas that tend to run parallel from one culture to another (for example, Greeks, Romans, and Etruscans all had a formula for making an offering to the gods: "So-and-So, the son of So-and-So, dedicated me to the god So-and-So").

The "combinatory" rather than the "etymological" method should be the first approach used in analyzing Etruscan mythological iconography. The mirrors have lent themselves to this process especially well because they automatically supply a comparable archaeological context and frequently have defined parameters of place and date. Thus I have analyzed a group of mirrors of similar style and date (Figs. VII.17-19)[43] as having a semantic field of love, fertility, and prosperity, probably associated with marriage, in which the "vocabulary" is provided by personifications of health, good will, and other abstract entities having a "grammar" of relationships in which they may kiss and embrace to show their harmonious relationships.

The results do not exclude comparisons from outside Etruria (the Greeks had formulaic representations of personifications affectionate with one another; Roman personifications supply comparative material), but the starting point was the combining of the Etruscan objects with the same mythologem. And the final step in this process is to see if the hypothesized semantic field and its details may be applied to another Etruscan mirror of around the same time (Fig. VII.20). The reader will see that the results are surprisingly different from those obtained by someone who was using an "etymological method" and attempting to show that an Etruscan scene is "really" Greek.

There is no need to extend further a comparison between studies of language and art. Indeed, some of the data is quite nonverbal, especially regarding gesture and posture and to a certain extent, attributes. Often, signification conveyed by a gesture or pose is difficult both to understand and to put into words. The problem is both social and cultural, as K. Thomas has made clear: "We no longer speak the body language of the past and much of it has to be painfully reconstructed. We cannot intuitively know that when Charlemagne pulled his beard he was expressing grief or that for Quintilian the slapping of the thigh meant not exhilaration, but anger."[44] Even in the present as we travel from country to country, we may find significant variations creating not a language barrier, but a "gesture barrier." Desmond Morris and his colleagues carried out an experiment in which they displayed

20 different gestures to individuals living in different localities of Western Europe. The results were amazingly varied.[45] In quite recent times Americans learned that a gesture made by their President as a display of support for the University of Texas was quite offensive to Europeans, who regarded the hand position as an insult with sexual content.[46]

Some gestures do seem to mean the same thing today as they did in antiquity. Bending one's arm to hold up an inclining head is readily understood as signifying depression or lament: Figs. V.22 in the lower zone, VIII.1, VIII.3, IX.3). Alan Boegehold has labeled such gestures as "Generally Understandable."[47] A good example is his "knuckles under the chin," indicating in Greece and modern-day America, as he demonstrates, that the individual is paying attention and thinking. The gesture occurs in Etruscan scenes especially in a context of prophecy (Fig. II.2) and seems to me to have overtones of meditating on the portentous message. A variant on this gesture, also showing meditation, is the act of raising a finger or a writing instrument to the chin or lips (Figs. II.10-11). Within the mythologem of prophecy there are other details of pose and gesture that are consistent: the raised leg of the prophet, probably indicating his attempt to get in touch with the spiritual world (Fig.II.9), and the upraised, pointing finger, displayed by one who is speaking and explaining the prophecy (also "Generally Understandable"; Fig. VII.10).[48]

We can deduce the meaning of other gestures by the combinatory method. An upraised hand, palm outward but relaxed, sometimes with two fingers projecting, also seems to indicate that someone is speaking (V.22, V.32, VI.32). The hypothesis is strengthened by comparative material amassed by Boegehold as far flung as Greek vase paintings, illustrated mss. of the comedies of Terence, a 17th century manual of speaker's gestures, and a photo of that former actor, Ronald Reagan, addressing Andrei Gromyko.[49] The gesture of flinging an arm above one's head as if to shade the eyes at the sight of someone divine or something too bright to behold directly (Figs. IV.13-14, VI.4) seems to be consistent with the motif in Greek art identified by Jucker as *aposkopein*, "to gaze intently."[50]

The results are not always consistent with Greek formulas, however, and in the end it is best to start with and return to the internal evidence. A gesture in which a female uses one hand to touch or pull up a garment from the shoulder or head is commonly recognized in Greece and in Rome as indicating that she is a bride or wife. It occurs so widely in Etruria, however (Figs. V.5, V.19, V.21), and is used by such a variety of individuals, even males (Fig. V.28), that it is safer to think of it first as a gesture of simply displaying one's physical worth. Of course, it can be used as appropriate for a bride, a wife, or a female who is interested in marriage (Fig. II.11, V.13, VI. 15). Similarly, touching the chin of another person, documented in Greece as a gesture of affection or of supplication,[51] need not have either of those meanings in Etruria (Figs. I.3, V.25, VI.8).

A recurring problem in Etruscan iconography is that found in the numerous Etruscan mirrors and reliefs on ash urns that are of a formulaic and standardized production, belonging to the Late period. Helen Nagy has laid out the parameters of the discussion in her treatment of a mirror in Seattle (Fig. V.21),[52] showing how gestures may migrate from one individual to another or become so stylized that we can no longer perceive their meaning. The late Lasa and Dioskouroi mirrors are particularly representative of this phenomenon (Figs. VII.25, VIII.19), but equally important is a series of compositions so fluid and elusive that it is hard to find a common denominator for them (Figs. IV.9, V.10, V.20, V. 32, VI.7, VI.29, VI.31, VI.32, VIII.15). In general we can note that they normally have a group of four or five figures seated or standing, with subtle interaction among the characters. They have been referred to in German as the *Kranzspiegel* group, or in English as the Spiky Garland mirrors,[53] after the stylized wreath that encircles the medallion with the figured scene (e.g., Fig. V. 20). But this term is not completely appropriate since some of the wreaths show a different kind of framing vegetation (Fig. IX.3) and some show no wreath at all (Fig. V.21).

This category of mirrors sometimes has inscriptions that label the individual figures but baffle the modern observer with their deviations from Greek mythology. I would urge caution in concluding that the inscriptions are "garbled" or "haphazard,"[54] for it may be that we simply do not understand the local Etruscan context. Nagy has made a significant contribution in regard to the scenes that show the bare minimum of four figures, unlabeled and lacking in attributes, which she characterizes as "emblematic," i.e., rather like a logo image that symbolizes rather than narrates.[55]

Many gestures and postures continue to elude. Why does Turan pull up her mantle and hold it in her mouth (Fig. V.5) and thus conceal part of her face? Why do Etruscan babies often raise one arm straight up in the air (Figs. IV.11, V. 5)? Why does a youth involved in an erotic encounter grasp tightly a plant rising in front of him (Fig. VIII.11)? Why do figures in a bridal or fertility context, usually females, hold up a leafy bough (Figs. V. 18, VII.14, VII.15)? There are various other gestures, used only once or twice, and thus impossible to interpret by the combinatory method.

On the whole, however, I feel that much of the language of gesture in Etruscan art is generally understandable, accessible from the point of view of common sense; but it is fluid, and one should not insist that a particular meaning applies in all cases. The Etruscan approach is quite unlike the elaborate codification of gesture recorded in Italy in the 19th century by Andrea de Jorio at Naples.[56] Thus, the methodology recommended here is not meant to create prescription, but rather description, with appropriate and logical interpretation, of the gestures studied.

The Usages of Myth

Mythographers frequently discuss the purposes or functions of myth and some of the categories they have devised for world mythology are certainly applicable to Etruscan material. In fact Etruscan myth, like that of other cultures, may have satisfied several needs at one time. Representations of lovemaking and feasting and dancing obviously would have had a value for entertainment (Fig. VI.1), but Etruscan themes showing couples in union or brides preparing for marriage (Figs. II.11 and II.13) demonstrated serious Etruscan social values as well. The importance of caring for children was a recurrent theme; mirrors have many representations of the nurturing of babies (Figs. IV.14-15; V.5-6). Mythographers recognize the existence of "charter myths,"[57] which may provide an archetypical representation of some kind of activity, whether social or religious. The myth of Pava Tarchies, showing the youth scrutinizing a liver as others look on and listen (Fig. II.2), may well be such a charter, establishing the origin and authority of the religious technique of seeking knowledge from looking at the entrails of animals.

Table I. Etruscan Deities: Their Greek and Roman Parallels

	Etruscan	Greek	Roman
"Olympian" Deities	Aplu	Apollo	Apollo
	Artumes/Aritimi	Artemis	Diana
	Fufluns	Dionysos	Bacchus
	Laran	Ares?	Mars?
	Mariś		Genius?
	Menrva	Athena	Minerva
	Nethuns	Poseidon	Neptune
	Sethlans	Hephaistos	Vulcan
	Tinia	Zeus	Jupiter
	Turan	Aphrodite	Venus
	Turms	Hermes	Mercury
	Turnu	Eros	Cupid
	Uni	Hera	Juno
	Vei	Ceres?	Demeter?
Cosmic Deities	Cavtha		Daughter of the Sun?
	Cel	Gaia	Terra Mater
	Culśanś		Janus
	Thesan	Eos	Aurora
	Usil	Helios	Sol
	Tiv	Selene?	Luna?
Hero Gods	Hercle	Herakles	Hercules
	Tinas Cliniiar	Dioskouroi	Dioscuri
Underworld Deities	Aita	Hades	Pluto
	Charu(n)	Charon	Charon
	Phersipnai	Persephone	Proserpina

The equivalences listed here are of a general nature. There are often significant differences between the Etruscan deities and their Greek and Roman counterparts.

Probably a very large percentage of Etruscan myth is of direct religious significance[58]; many stories, whether local Etruscan or imported Greek myths, seem to reflect Etruscan ritual concerns. For example, the Etruscans had an elaborate lore about the meaning of lightning bolts, depending on their size, color, and location in the sky, all to be judged and interpreted by a priest. The many representations of the lightning bolt in art—whether being held, thrown, or already landed (Figs. IV.1, 7-8; V.1)—probably reflect this interest. Similarly, there seem to have been Etruscan rituals in regard to eggs, symbolic of fertility and rebirth, and thus the story of the Egg of Helen, nourished by foster parents Leda and Tyndareus, which was popular with the Greeks of southern Italy, was appealing to the Etruscans (Fig. VI.16-19). [59] The Etruscans also carried out ritual acts with the hammer and nails, and myths in which these instruments were utilized were also beloved, as for example when the Etruscan death demon Charu swings his hammer to seal the death of an individual (Fig. X.13; cf. Chapter X on the difference between Charu and the Greek ferryman Charon). Another instance of the instrument is found in a scene with Athrpa (Fig. V.30), evidently a counterpart to the Greek deity of fate Atropos, but the Etruscan goddess does not use an instrument for weaving as did the Greek fates, Atropos, Clotho, and Lachesis. Instead she plies hammer and nail to affix the head of a boar and seal the fate of the lovers Turan and Atunis (=Aphrodite and Adonis) and Atlenta and Meliacr (=Atalanta and Meleager), in both of whose stories the boar played a fatal role. Finally we mention the hundreds of mythological representations of actions at an altar, especially on funerary urns from Volterra, often alluding to sacrifice, even of humans, though this point is controversial. Often the story is unknown.[60]

Recent studies by Pairault Massa and Menichetti have attempted to analyze Etruscan mythology as reflecting political concerns.[61] Certainly this function appears commonly in world mythology and it would be no surprise to find it in Etruria as well. An ever-increasing number of Etruscan mirrors and other objects are being recognized as having some connection to prophecy. While many of these no doubt relate to prophecies of a personal nature, very likely some have a larger political or social context. It is well known that in the ancient Greek and Roman world prophecy was often connected with political acts. (Inquiries are recorded such as: "Should we go to war?" "Shall I be king?"[62])

Unfortunately we are so ill informed about Etruscan history and politics that it is difficult to be precise on this topic. But a good example of the hypothesized political function of myth is provided by the Etruscan depiction of the Greek myth of the Seven against Thebes, which could have been read as providing a lesson in regard to the sad results of internal civil conflict (Fig. IV.3).[63] This scene was set up on the back of a famous Etruscan temple at the port city of Pyrgi and would have been visible to those approaching from the nearby city of Cerveteri (Caere); its message to avoid rebellion against the government would have been patent. (The mythoritual theme of lightning was also displayed here, since the chief god, Zeus/Tinia, was shown in the act of punishing an impious rebel with a lightning bolt.)

The Nature of the Gods

A final and very important problem in studying Etruscan mythology lies in the nature of the gods themselves. As noted, we do know the Etruscan word for "god," *ais*, pl. *aiser*, but many aspects of the Etruscan deities can only be called mysterious. Before representation of anthropomorphic forms began in Etruria, the gods were probably conceived of as vague essences. For the Romans, scholars once proposed the Latin term *numen* as expressing the emanating power or vitality of a god, present and active even if no image of the god were shown. Without taking a stand on the question of whether this is a correct usage of the term,[64] we may note that this concept of vague and ambiguous forces really does seem applicable to Etruscan gods. They occurred in groups, sometimes with baffling names that have been preserved in Latin translations. For example the Di Involuti, the "Shrouded Gods," were immensely powerful; their appearance, names and precise number are unknown. Both they and the Di Consentes, the "Counseling Gods," 12 in number, were consulted by the Etruscan chief deity when he was preparing to throw lightning. Gatherings of the gods, which are sometimes clearly councils, are ubiquitous in Etruscan art; it may be that Etruscans did not intend for these scenes to have great narrative extension, but merely to demonstrate the concord of the gods when it came to the affairs of men.

Some deities are at times doubled (see the twin figures of Turms, the Etruscan Hermes, in Fig. VI.13) or even tripled, as in the case of Mariś. An Etruscan mirror shows a ritual scene (Fig. V.5) in which three infants, all named Mariś, are being dipped into a great vase, perhaps as some kind of initiation. Here each of the babies has an extra name: Mariś Isminthians, Mariś Husrnana, and Mariś Halna. A second mirror, in which Menrva has her breast bared to nurse the little fellows, shows only two babies (Fig. V.6), omitting this time Mariś Isminthians. What characteristic or sphere of influence is indicated by these extra names may only be conjectured (cf. Chapter V).

Further, some Etruscan divinities changed sex. Thalna (Figs. VII.7-10), Alpan, Leinth, Lasa, Evan, Achvizr, all of whose names are quite unknown in Greek myth, are sometimes represented as male and sometimes as female. Even Greek gods could change sex in Etruria: Artumes is represented at least twice as male (Figs. V.32-33).

As the leading Etruscan scholar Massimo Pallottino once succinctly remarked, "The Etruscan conception of supernatural beings was permeated by a certain vagueness as to numbers, sex, attributes and appearance."[65] Our task will be to observe the great variety of possibilities for these elusive Etruscan divinities, at the same time attempting to identify their salient characteristics and understand their interactions with one another and with their human worshippers.

The Prophets

The religion of the Etruscans, like that of the Hebrews and Christians, was based on divine revelations. They constantly consulted sacred books equivalent to those of the Bible, and in this respect the Etruscans were quite different from the Greeks and Romans. The Etruscan stipulations for inter-action with the gods were handed down by the gods themselves and recorded in that body of sacred teachings known as the *Etrusca disciplina*. We have numer-ous references to the utterances of Etruscan prophets and priests, who derived their authority from scripture and who communicated the will of the gods, either in a general way or for some special occasion.[1] These prophets were represented in Etruscan mythological art, with the great majority of images ocurring in the Middle Etruscan period, from ca. 400 to 300 BCE.

Tages

The most important Etruscan prophet is the intriguing figure referred to by the Romans as Tages, said to be the son of Genius and the grandson of Jupiter (in Etruscan, Tinia).[2] His Etruscan name, as we shall see, may have been Tarchies. Ci-cero, writing around 44 BCE (*de Divinatione* 2.23), and other ancient authors[3] tell how the whole of the *Etrusca disciplina* was revealed by Tages to a mortal named in Latin as Tarchon, the founder-hero for whom the major Etruscan city of Tarquinia was named.[4] Tarchon was a priest as well, of the type known as an *haruspex*, a soothsayer who practices haruspication, divining the will of the gods by looking at the organs of sacrificed animals. He wrote down all that he learned from the prophet in a question and answer form, putting the answers in what John the Lyd-ian (6th century CE) calls "a very different form of writing," so that the sacred information would be esoteric, accessible only to those who had secret skills and knowledge.

The story of Tages is as follows: one day a peasant (or, in another version, Tarchon himself) was ploughing in the fields of Tarquinia, when the ploughshare went deeper than usual, and suddenly a child sprang forth from the furrow. He seemed to be a newborn, but he had teeth and other signs of mature age, and the "wisdom of an elder." The astonished ploughman raised a cry to summon others, and soon "all of Etruria" came together in that spot. The wise child then revealed many things to his listeners (one version says he transmitted the information by singing), and these were written down. According to one story, the child then dis-appeared and died the same day. In another version, Tarchon took the child home and kept him "in sacred places," continuing to learn from him (John the Lydian,

II.1 View of sacred area, Building Beta, Pian di Civita, Tarquinia, 9th–8th centuries BCE. After Bonghi Iovino 2001:fig. 35. The view shows the channel leading from an altar in Building Beta and emptying into a cavity in the bedrock. Nearby was found the sacred burial of a boy who had suffered from deformation of the skull. The finds may relate to the myth of Tages, the boy who emerged from a furrow in the ground and revealed the mysteries of the Etruscan ritual code.

de Ostentis 2.6.B). Yet another interesting detail relates that Tages taught the art of haruspication to the Twelve Peoples of the Etruscans (Festus 492.6.8), a reference with strong political overtones, since our best evidence of the Twelve Peoples suggests that this was a confederation of Etruscan city-states who bonded together and met periodically for religious and political purposes.[5] Thus the sacred history of Tages has all the characteristics of a "charter" myth, since it provides a paradigm for the acquisition and usage of divine revelation, valid in both religious and political contexts across the Etruscan states.[6]

It is now possible that the actual physical context that validated and perhaps even inspired this paradigmatic myth has been discovered at Tarquinia: excavators from the University of Milan have unearthed a sacred area of a very early date (9th–8th centuries BCE) that features an altar and a channel for liquid sacrifice leading toward a conspicuous cavity in the earth, measuring ca. 80 cm in diameter (Fig. II.1).[7] Nearby were found buried the bones of a boy of special status, furnished with a tiny bronze pendant (a protective amulet?) and showing evidence in the deformation of his skull that he may have suffered during his short life from epilepsy. The ancients believed that epilepsy was a divine disease[8] and so the incoherent raving of a person having a seizure was actually a message from the gods. Thus in this rather small area of ancient Tarquinia were found combined the hole which may have related to the "deep ploughing" that brought forth Tages and then nearby the child who could have done the sacred singing that contained the arcane messages that had to be entrusted to Tarchon.

The writings of Tages were preserved in what the Romans called the *Libri Tagetici,* literally the "Books of Tages," which contained further subdivisions, such

II.2 *Bronze mirror from Tuscania.* Florence, Museo Archeologico Nazionale, ca. 300 BCE. After Torelli 1988:fig. 1. Pava Tarchies scrutinizes a liver in the presence of the lady Ucernei and the bearded Avl Tarchunus, who is meditating. On far left is Rathlth, a personification of the location, and on far right is Veltune, perhaps equivalent to Tinia/Jupiter and the grandfather of Pava Tarchies. Over the left shoulder of Pava Tarchies, a sunburst; upper exergue, goddess of the dawn with four-horse chariot to indicate the day on which the ritual takes place; lower exergue, unidentified winged male figure who acts as support for the sphere.

as the *Libri Haruspicini*, "Books of Haruspication" and *Libri Acheruntici*, "Books of Acheron," or perhaps better "Books of the Underworld." Tages had given instructions on how to read the entrails of animals, how to interpret lightning and thunder and earthquakes, how to lay out a city using the plough, and how to have greater success in agriculture.

The connection with the reading of animal entrails is especially interesting in relation to what is probably a representation in art of Tages. We know from a number of pieces of evidence that the Etruscans were particularly impressed with the power of the liver to transmit messages from the gods. An important Etruscan

II.3 Carved gem, 4th century BCE. London, British Museum. Photo: Trustees of the British Museum. A prophetic head emerges from the ground (probably Tages) as meditating figure (left, probably Tarchon) and peasant (right) observe.

bronze mirror from near Tarquinia (Tuscania) dating to ca. 300 BCE shows precisely an act of haruspication using the liver (Fig. II.2).[9] Here a youth labeled in Etruscan as *Pava Tarchies* (translated, according to some as "Child Tages") stands in a ritual pose with his left leg lifted and holds delicately in his left hand the liver of an animal, which he scrutinizes. He wears the characteristic hat of an Etruscan priest, with twisted, pointed peak, later used traditionally by Roman priests and called in Latin the *apex*. On the left, listening intently is another male figure, bearded and likewise with a priest's hat, but this time set as if hanging from the head rather than fully in place. He leans upon a staff and holds his hand up to his chin in a gesture that signals study or meditation. He is labeled *Avl Tarchunus*, very likely an Etruscan version of the Latin name Tarchon.[10] Experts have interpreted this scene as a representation of Tarchon being instructed by Tages, as in the part of the myth where Tarchon takes the child home with him and continues to learn from him. After he becomes fully adept in the art of haruspication, he may place the priest's hat firmly upon his head. There are three other figures in the mirror scene, one of whom, Veltune, on the far right, may be the equivalent of Jupiter and thus the grandfather of Pava Tarchies.[11] He stands—bearded, dignified, wearing boots, and holding a spear—as he watches the proceedings. The other male figure on the left, labeled Rathlth and carrying a laurel branch, has been identified as a personification of the sanctuary where the haruspication took place.[12] The female figure, Ucernei, occurs only on this mirror and otherwise is quite unknown. She seems to play a key role in the scene, however, as she stands next to Pava Tarchies and reaches out toward the liver. She exemplifies one of our greatest problems in studying Etruscan myths, our sheer lack of information. One interpretation makes her the wife of Avl Tarchunus, and regards the scene as a consultation by the pair.[13]

II.4 Carved sardonyx, 4th century BCE. Rome, Museo Nazionale Etrusco di Villa Giulia. Photo: Soprintendenza per i Beni Archeologici del Lazio. A prophetic figure emerges from the ground (probably Tages) as bearded man (probably Tarchon) reaches toward him. The emerging figure shows the didactic gesture of the pointing finger.

There are other scenes in art that may represent the story of Tages. Especially interesting is a series of carved gems of the 4th century BCE used as seals that show a head or entire body popping up out of the ground, as one or more figures attend. A version in the British Museum seems to show a rustic peasant pointing toward the head and a meditating figure, presumably Tarchon, leaning upon his stick and listening (Fig. II.3).[14] Yet another carved gem shows a large figure bending over a smaller figure emerging from the ground, perhaps Tarchon helping Tages come up out of the furrow (Fig. II.4).[15] The Tages figure points a finger in a didactic gesture familiar in Etruscan prophecy scenes (cf. Figs. II.14-15).

Cacu

A second story about a prophet of Etruria, Cacu, is also known from Etruscan works of art and quite dimly from Roman literature.[16] A bronze mirror dating to ca. 300 BCE and closely contemporary with the Pava Tarchies mirror comes from Bolsena, near Orvieto; the latter city is considered to be identical with the ancient Volsinii, religious capital of the Etruscans where the League of Twelve Peoples was said to meet.[17] The mirror reveals a representation of a long-haired youth labeled Cacu (Fig. II.5), who plays the lyre and presumably sings as his message is studied by a boy at his feet named Artile. The child holds a folding tablet or diptych upon which is written something in a script that is definitely "a different form of writing" and is probably meant to be a secret text read only by the initiated. The pair

II.5 Bronze mirror from Bolsena, ca. 300 BCE. London, The British Museum. After Bonfante 1990:fig. 18. The seer Cacu plays his lyre, attended by the boy Artile, who holds sacred tablets. Caile Vipinas (left) and Avle Vipinas (right) approach to attack; satyr or Silenus peers over rocks; in lower exergue, an unidentified child swings a stick.

is approached by two soldiers, one with drawn sword and the other with a shield, and it is evident here and in other descriptions or representations that their intention is to catch the prophet Cacu and force him to reveal his secret knowledge to them. Perhaps they plan to steal the sacred text held by Artile. The soldiers are labeled as Avle Vipinas and Caile Vipinas, a pair of Etruscan hero-brothers, looking like twins, who are quite prominent in Etruscan myth and legend. (They are mentioned in Latin literature as Aulus and Caelius Vibenna; cf. Ch. VIII below). This myth is also represented on ash urns of the Etruscans (Fig. II.6), showing not only the prophet and his assistant but also a female figure who seems to lament, along with Artile, the outcome of the whole matter. Scenes on some urns make it clear that the singer ends up captured and led away.

Late Roman writers note a figure named Cacus having a sister, Caca, who betrayed him and assisted his captor and was later turned into a goddess of the hearth (Servius, *ad Aeneid*. 8.190; Lactantius, *Div. Inst*. 1.20.36). The female figure here could be the prophet's sister, though there are no signs that she has betrayed him. The existence of a Cacus and a Caca, a male and a female with similar name, has an Etruscan ring to it. There is a good bit of evidence in early Italy for divinities having both a masculine and feminine aspect.[18]

Otherwise, the rest of the stories told by the Romans about Cacus, in which he is a warrior or monster and his captor is Hercules (e.g., Virgil, *Aeneid* VIII.255-349), differ radically from the story presented on the mirror and on the ash urns. The story in Vergil in which the monster steals the cattle of Hercules and ends up choked to death by the hero (discussed fully in Chapter VIII) demonstrates the

II.6 Ash urn from Chiusi, 2nd century BCE. Berlin, Staatliche Museen. After Brunn-Körte:1.85.3. Cacu plays his lyre as one of the Vipinas brothers menaces (right); Artile and female figure (Caca?) laments on left.

theme of triumph over an irrational evil, in this case personified by Cacus. (Indeed, the Latin word may well be derived from the Greek adjective *kakos*, which means "bad."[19]) But the themes of the Etruscan story are rather the power of prophecy and the acquisition of secret knowledge by the twinned heroes.

Lasa Vecuvia

The Etruscans had a famed female prophet, too, known from representations in art and references in Latin literature. The Romans refer to a prophetess they call the Nymph Begoe or Vegoia,[20] who revealed the nature of creation to a certain Etruscan named Arruns Veltymnus, perhaps from Clusium (i.e., Chiusi) and whose texts are known as the *Libri Vegoici*, "Books of Vegoia." She is also mentioned as the author or source of books on lightning kept in a Temple of Apollo, evidently that on the Palatine Hill in Rome.

Vegoia's myth of creation will be discussed in the next chapter, but here we may look at some of the representations of this goddess/spirit. She is labeled on mirrors and on a gold ring bezel of the 4th century BCE (Figs. II.7-8), where she is referred to in Etruscan as Lasa Vecu or Lasa Vecuvia, a name that may have been translated into Latin as Nymph Begoe. The word Lasa[21] seems to have a generic meaning such as "nymph" or perhaps better, "spirit" (a Lasa may also be male; see Chapter VII), and the word Vecu or Vecuvia thus becomes her particular name. She is shown on one mirror as an attendant of the goddess Menrva (Fig. II.7); we do not know the subject of the scene, but Menrva seems to consult her or give her

II.7 Bronze mirror, ca.
300–275 BCE. Rome,
Museo Nazionale
Etrusco di Villa Giulia.
After ES:1.37. Menrva
(left), converses with the
winged prophetic spirit
Lasa Vecu.

orders as the winged Lasa stands with some kind of instrument or plant in her hand; some have suggested this may be a small thunderbolt, inasmuch as Menrva, in Etruria, had the power to throw thunderbolts (Fig. V.1). On another mirror, Lasa Vecuvi(a) is shown near an image of Tinia holding the thunderbolt. Finally, on the ring bezel (Fig. II.8) she appears with another nymph/spirit (unnamed), in a landscape with a sunburst above. She has been said to be looking into a mirror, perhaps related to her powers of prophecy, since the mirror is demonstrably an instrument of foretelling the future in Etruria.[22]

Other Prophets: Chalchas

These three prophetic figures—Tages, Cacu, and Lasa Vecuvia—are obviously purely Etruscan figures. Some of the motifs associated with them may be found also in themes from Greek art translated into an Etruscan context. Thus the Greek

II.8 Gold ring bezel from Todi, ca. 300 BCE. Rome, Museo Nazionale Etrusco di Villa Giulia. Photo: SAEM n. 103772. Lasa Vecuvia (left) looks into a mirror; nude female attendant (right); sunburst above.

priest Calchas[23] (spelled Chalchas in Etruscan), who served Agamemnon in the Trojan War, appears on a famous and beautiful Etruscan mirror in the Vatican (Fig. II.9) interpreting the will of the gods, not from the actions of snakes and birds as he does in the *Iliad* (2.308-329) but from studying a liver, in that quintessential Etruscan act of haruspication. In addition, the seer is depicted here as winged and therefore divine, unlike the mortal Calchas in Greek myth. He bends intently over the liver in the Etruscan ritual pose, the same as that used by Pava Tarchies, with

II.9 Bronze mirror from Vulci, ca. 400 BCE. Vatican, Museo Gregoriano Etrusco. After *ES*:2.223. The winged seer Chalchas, in characteristic prophesying pose with left foot raised, scrutinizes a liver. On the table, entrails. Behind his foot, a ritual pitcher.

his left leg propped up and the liver poised in his left hand for proper scrutiny. The scene unfortunately contains no clues to the content of his prophecy. While it is tempting to think of the Greek military context (Calchas advises Agamemnon how to appease the gods so that the Greeks may sail for Troy), this Etruscan representation completely omits the consultant and it is better not to speculate.

Urphe

Another prophetic figure from Greek mythology with an interesting career in Etruria is the Thracian singer and seer Orpheus.[24] There are only two certain occurrences of his name in Etruscan inscriptions (*ET* Cl 5.11, Pe 5.8), but it is likely that he appears four or five times on Etruscan mirrors and at least twice on Etruscan gems. Most striking is an image on a mirror from Chiusi dating to around 300 BCE (much damaged) with a youthful head appearing on the ground, the hair streaming, which is labeled Urphe (Fig. II.10), obviously the Etruscan form of the name Orpheus. It is well known that in the Greek myth Orpheus was torn apart, but that his head continued to sing after his death, as it floated down a river. The information that the chanting of the head produced oracles is presented

II.10 Bronze mirror from Chiusi, ca. 300 BCE. Siena, Museo Archeologico. After Maggiani 1992:fig. 2. Head of Urphe appears (lower left) at the feet of the soothsayer Umaele, who holds a ribbon attached to a net or bag for the head. Alpunea (right) records the prophecy; couple in between, probably consulting the oracle for a marriage prophecy. Reclining couple in the upper exergue; winged female in the lower exergue. Not all the inscriptions on this mirror are clear, and it is not possible to tell which names belong with which figures. The couple in the exergue may be Turan and Atunis.

only in one late Greek author, Philostratos, writing in the 3rd century CE (*Life of Apollonios* 4.14; *Heroicus* 5.3), but is supported by three Greek vases of the 5th century BCE, which show a head popping out of the ground as Apollo and/or Muses stand by.[25]

The Talking Head

But the rendering of the prophetic head has a completely different setting in Etruria. The example with the head labeled Urphe may be compared with another very similar mirror, uninscribed but better preserved, from Castelgiorgio, near Orvieto (Fig. II.11). Here the head seems to provide its prophecy as a scribe (on the right) displays the oracular message written on a tablet. (The inscription seems to be garbled Etruscan and cannot be translated; perhaps it is another instance of

II.11 Bronze mirror
from Castelgiorgio.
Paris, Louvre. After *CSE*
France:1.1.2a. Scene of
prophecy showing the
same mythologem as
Fig. II.10. Head (probably
Urphe) appears lower
left; assistant with bag,
left, probably Umaele;
male recorder of proph-
ecy (right); couple in
between, probably seek-
ing a marriage prophecy;
upper exergue, naked,
reclining female figure
makes gesture of a bride
displaying herself.

esoteric prophetic writing.)   He seems to meditate, his stylus to his lips, as others turn their eyes toward him. Included in this scene and in others with a similar talking head is a couple, probably to be interpreted as bride and groom, since the female holds up her mantle in the displaying/revealing gesture often utilized by brides and wives in classical antiquity. The implication is that the head can reveal prophecies that have to do with the married life of the couple—how many children they may have, what sort of prosperity they may enjoy. The motif of the prophecy for the married couple is well known from Roman literature, for example from poem 64 of Catullus, where the Fates sing of the consequences of the marriage of Peleus and Thetis. It may be argued[26] that the cycle of Roman paintings in the Villa of the Mysteries at Pompeii (ca. 50 BCE) also shows wedding prophecies; a bride is shown amid various motifs of prophetic significance, including a mirror and tablets to record the prophecy, and a mask or head of Silenus that seems to speak (Fig. II.12).

II.12 Roman wall paint-
ing, Villa of the Myster-
ies, Pompeii, ca. 50 BCE.
Photo: DAI. Married
couple of Bacchus and
Ariadne (right), with ad-
jacent scene of reading
an oracle by looking in a
vessel (*lekanomanteia*).
A mask of Silenus is held
up, probably to pro-
nounce the prophecy.

The identification of this subject with the couple is rather important, as it may help separate representations of Tages, whose head pops out of the ground, leading to someone writing his words down, from those of an Etruscan Orpheus that have a similar bodiless, active head.

Scholars find this motif of the speaking head in traditions around the world. An intriguing parallel is provided by the Norse figure of Mimir, the god of memory who had his head cut off, smeared with herbs for preservation, and taken home by the principal Norse deity Odin, who consulted it to find out secrets about the future.[27] There are several others in Etruscan art and religion, once again associated with prophecy: they include the head of Silenus, the old drunken follower of Dionysos (Fig. II.13), who appears with a bride, just as does the head of Silenus in the Villa of the Mysteries; the head of the gorgon Medusa, sometimes shown emerging from the ground (Fig. II.14), and the head of a goddess with goat's skin and horns (Fig. II.15), apparently identical with the goddess called Juno Sospita in

II.13 Bronze mirror, 325–300 BCE. Berlin, Staatliche Museen. After *ES*:2.212. Adorning of bride, with prophetic head of Silenus (above).

II.14 Bronze mirror possibly from Cerveteri, 3rd century BCE. Brussels, Musées Royaux d'Art et d'Histoire. After Lambrechts 1978: p. 25. Scene of Pherse (left) and Menrva (right) holding the head of Metus (=Medusa); prophetic head (reflection of Medusa?) emerges below. Pherse assumes the role of an interpreter, with left leg raised and right hand extended in a pointing gesture.

Il.15 Bronze mirror cover, 3rd century BCE. Durham, NC, Duke University Art Museum. Photo: Museum. Etruscan version of the reunion of Odysseus and his wife or perhaps his nurse. Oracular head of "Juno Sospita" in the middle of the scene. Odysseus, with left leg raised in the prophecy pose, makes a gesture explaining the message.

Latium.[28] The latter had an oracular shrine at the Latin city of Lanuvium. These all show differing physiognomy and are easily separated from the talking heads of Tages and Orpheus.

Alpunea and Umaele

On the Chiusi mirror (Fig II.10) there are some other notable inscriptions naming the individuals. The couple is inscribed but unfortunately the names are not clear and tell us little further, though the figure with the inscribed tablets on the right, here rendered as female, is labeled Alpunea, a most interesting name, very close to that of Albunea, known in Latin religion and myth as a Sibyl (female prophet) who had an oracular sanctuary at Tivoli, near Rome.[29] We may assume

II.16 Carved gem from Chiusi, 4th century BCE. Cast of gem with image reversed, as on a sealing. London, The British Museum. Photo: © Copyright by Trustees of the British Museum. Head emerges from bag (right, of Urphe?), consulted by Turms.

here a syncretism of Latin and Etruscan prophetic religion. But most intriguing of all is the name assigned to the standing male figure on the left, Umaele,[30] which has defied all attempts to relate the figure to a counterpart in Greek or Roman mythology. Umaele appears here and on the Castelgiorgio mirror as a guardian of the head, holding in his hand a ribbon attached to a tube-shaped sack with a reticulate pattern that dangles down next to him. Evidently the head is normally kept in the bag, and then is extracted for prophetic moments. Other Etruscan mirrors show the bag expanded, as if something is contained within it; one Etruscan gem of the

II.17 Bronze mirror from Castelgiorgio, ca. 300 BCE. London, The British Museum. After *ES*:5.34. Umaele consults a liver, as Turms (left) and Alpnu and Aplu (right) observe; upper exergue, Thesan, goddess of the dawn with chariot, indicates the day of the ritual.

4th century actually shows a head sitting on top of the bag, evidently just emerging (Fig. II.16). Here Turms, often present in prophetic scenes, listens to the message of the oracular head.

Umaele appears in a second type of prophecy scene, on another mirror from Castelgiorgio (Fig. II.17). Here he assumes the pose for the reading of entrails, with his left leg up and his left hand out. Others around him seem intent on the extended hand; even though this part of the design is damaged, it is logical to conclude that he held out a liver and was practicing haruspication in the manner of Pava Tarchies and Chalchas.[31] Thus though we have no certain identity for this figure Umaele, it is clear that he plays a significant role in Etruscan mythology about prophecy. The pose with one leg conspicuously lifted, repeated in the other two liver scenes, is surely a ritual motif, and may help the seer to receive his vision. It is interesting that in Celtic myth a prophet often stands on one foot and closes one eye as part of the moment of inspiration.[32]

With Umaele we may close this chapter, observing that the themes of prophecy in Etruria seem to be immensely popular, especially around Orvieto (Volsinii) in the 4th and 3rd centuries BCE, and that they are displayed in scenes that are purely Etruscan—the myths of Tages, Cacu, and Lasa Vecuvia—as well as those that have a connection with Greek figures rendered in the Etruscan interpretation—Calchas, Orpheus, Silenus, Medusa—and with Latin prophetic figures such as Albunea and Juno Sospita. Until further evidence appears, Umaele, with the head in a bag, eludes classification.

III

Creation, Time, and the Universe

In this chapter we shall consider what the Etruscans thought about the beginning of the universe and about the end of their own nation, as well as how they conceived of the place of the gods in the universe.

Creation

We know the Etruscans had at least one myth regarding creation, but as usual the evidence is quite meager. Lasa Vecuvia, mentioned in the previous chapter, was reported to have made a prophecy regarding creation and the consequences for those who failed to observe the order of the cosmos.[1] The story comes from a Latin text, evidently translated from Etruscan, in which the goddess is called Vegoia, and it is narrated that she made her revelation to a certain Arruns Veltymnus. The name Veltymnus is remarkably similar to *Veltune* on the Etruscan mirror with the story of Tages (Fig. II.2), and may show that this Arruns, sometimes identified as a priest or a prince,[2] had some special connection with the god Veltune (i.e., Jupiter/Tinia). The prophecy in Latin does make specific reference to Jupiter, characterizing him as a god of boundaries. The text begins with the origin of the sea and sky and relates how Jupiter had worked out boundaries in Etruria; for those who violated these confines, disastrous consequences were predicted, including storms, whirlwinds, drought, hail, and mildew. The myth may be quite ancient, but it seems to have been first written down in this version at a time when the Romans were threatening to take over Etruscan lands in the late 2nd and 1st centuries BCE.[3] It therefore puts great emphasis on how Jupiter made boundaries sacred. An interesting detail of the passage is its reference to the Etruscan theory of time in periods (*saecula*), about which we will say more soon:

> [Prophecy] of Vegoia to Arruns Veltymnus: Know that the sea was separated from the sky. But when Juppiter claimed the land of Aetruria for himself, he established and ordered that the fields be measured and the croplands delimited. Knowing the greed of men and their lust for land, he wanted everything proper concerning boundaries. And at some time, around the end of the eighth *saeculum*, someone will violate them on account of greed by means of evil trickery and will touch them and move them. . . . But whoever shall have touched and moved them, increasing his own property and diminishing that of another, on account of this crime he will be damned by the gods. If slaves should do it, there will be a change for the worse in status. But if the deed is done with the master's consent, very quickly the master will be uprooted

and all of his family will perish. The ones who move [the boundaries] will be afflicted by the worst diseases and wounds and they will feel a weakness in their limbs. Then also the earth will be moved by storms and whirlwinds with frequent destruction, crops often will be injured and will be knocked down by rain and hail, they will perish in the summer heat, they will be felled by mildew. There will be much dissension among people. Know that these things will be done when such crimes are committed. Wherefore be not false or double-tongued. Keep this teaching in your heart.[4]

The passage aims to teach proper respect to those who might violate the divine laws of the god of territories, and thus is largely didactic and even political. There is reference to class distinctions and the role they might play. As far as the sequence of creation, however, we learn relatively little. We do not hear how the sea and sky became separated, or how land emerged, but only that Jupiter took Etruria and thus must have made the Etruscans his own people.

Time

The reference to the eighth *saeculum* (sometimes translated as "century," but the word is vague, and means rather "generation, age, period of time") is of particular interest. Again, we do not have a specific narrative that tells how the sacred history of the Etruscans unrolled, but we get clues from various writers that they believed that their nation would last for ten (or according to one author, eight) such *saecula*.[5] A *saeculum* was calculated in the following way: when the Etruscan nation was founded, the first person to be born set the terms for the *saeculum*. When that person died, the period was ended. For the second *saeculum,* the first person born would again provide the reference from which the beginning and end of the period were fixed, and similarly for the subsequent periods. Given that this was the method of calculating, it is a little odd that it is reported that each of the first four *saecula* lasted exactly 100 years. Then the fifth period was 123 years, the sixth and seventh were each 119, and the seventh is conjectured also to have lasted 119 years. We learn from ancient authors that the eighth *saeculum* ended in 88 BCE, and the ninth in 44 BCE at the time of the appearance of the comet of Julius Caesar. Assembling these fragments of evidence and counting back from the known dates, we may conjecture the dates of the earliest *saeculum* and suggest a model of how the chronology may have run (Table II).

The schema is quite hypothetical, given that we do not know exactly how the hundred years (or more) would be counted, and whether a new generation would start in the last year of the old one, or in the next one, and given that we are not certain about the length of the eighth generation, or whether there were indeed eight or ten *saecula*. But the chart may at least give an *idea* of how the Etruscan belief about the *saecula* would apply. What is remarkable is that this, our best guess about the historico-religious chronology of the Etruscans, fits astonishingly well with what archaeologists and historians have deduced from other evidence about their presence in Italy: they appeared in the 10th century BCE and they were absorbed into the Roman Empire in the 1st century BCE.

Concerning the annual calendar of the Etruscans, various scraps of evidence indicate that they gave great importance to the cycle of the year and to the deities

Table II. The Ten Etruscan *Saecula*
Hypothetical Sequence

Saeculum	Number of years	Actual Dates
1	100	968-868 BCE
2	100	868-768 BCE
3	100	768-668 BCE
4	100	668-568 BCE
5	123	568-445 BCE
6	119	445-326 BCE
7	119	326-207 BCE
8	119?	207-88 BCE
9	44	88-44 BCE
10	?	44 BCE-?

and omens that might be connected with particular days.[6] It is known that their year normally began in the month equivalent to March and that their calculation of a particular day started at noon. There was some variation from city to city, as to be expected, and thus each surviving calendar must be evaluated on its own terms. The Zagreb mummy wrappings preserve the text of a calendar used in the area of Perugia and Cortona in the 3rd-2nd centuries BCE, which gives considerable detail concerning feast days and the rituals to be performed. The legible pages give information for the months of June (*acale*), August (*Θucte*) and September (*celi*, named for the earth goddess Cel), and mention offerings to Tinia, Culsu, Nethuns, and Usil (all of whom are known in representations in art). An inscribed baked clay tile from Capua, near the Bay of Naples, dated to the 5th century BCE, mentions Tinun (perhaps =Tinia), but also a number of deities that are not well known and for which we have no mythological information; these include Lethams, Natinusnai, and Sethumsai.

Another kind of calendar is the Brontoscopic Calendar recorded by the Roman antiquarian Nigidius Figulus (1st century BCE), apparently in a Latin translation from the Etruscan, which was in turn translated into Greek in a manuscript of John the Lydian in the 6th century CE.[7] The whole calendar, which relates to divination from the presence of thunder on a particular day, was said to go back to the prophet Tages. While it mentions no deities, it conveys vividly the context of the action of thunder and lightning initiated by the gods. It begins in June, a month from which come the following observations:

> June 2. If in any way it should thunder, women in labor will have an easy delivery, but there will be abortion of cattle, yet there will be an abundance of fish.
> June 16. If in any way it should thunder, it threatens not only dearth of the necessities of life but also war, while a prosperous man shall disappear from public life.

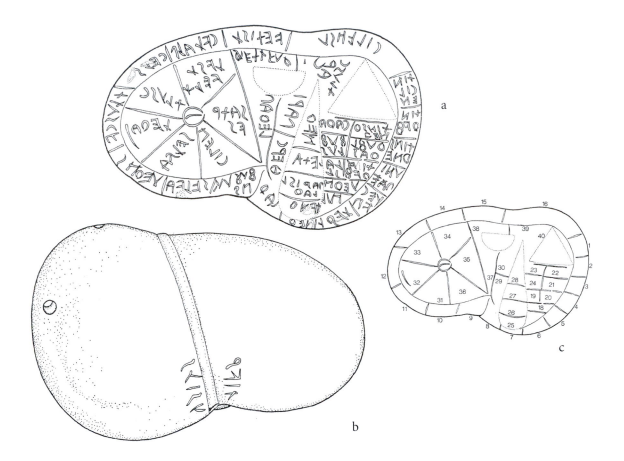

III.1 a, b, and c. Diagram of bronze model of a sheep's liver from Piacenza. Piacenza, Museo Civico. After Torelli 1986:211. 3rd-2nd century BCE. (a) Drawing of upper side of the liver with its 40 cells;(b) drawing of the underside, with two additional inscriptions (41 and 42) mentioning Usil (left) and Tivr (right); (c) drawing with numbering of the cells according to Maggiani 1982:fig. 1. Maggiani's readings of the cells, accepted with very few exceptions by Rix (ET Pa.4.2), are as follows: 1—tin/cil/en; 2—tin/_vf; 3—tins/śne;4—uni/mae;5—tec/vm;6—lvsl;7—neś;8—caś;9—fuflu/ns;10—selva;11—leśns;12—tluscv;13—cels;14—cvlalp;15—vetisl;16—cilensl;17—pul (ET tut);18—leśn;19—la/sl;20—tins/śvf;21—śvfl/śas;22—tinsś/ne_;23—caśa;24—fuf/lus;25—tvnś;26—marisl/la_;27—leta;28—neś;29—herc;30—mar (ET mari);31—selva;32—leśa;33—tlusc;34—lvsl/velś;35—satr/es;36—cilen;37—leśam;38—metlvmś (ET meślumś);39—mar;40—tlusc;41—tivs;42—usils.

In summary the calendar reveals that the gods would send warnings pertaining to weather, diseases, reproduction, fertility of animals and crops, warfare, and political activities.

The Universe

A good bit is known about the Etruscan concept of the structure of heaven and the location of the gods in the universe. It is certain that the Etruscans regarded the universe as divided into sixteen regions,[8] whereas the Romans normally divided the sky in quarters and the Greeks in eighths. Scholars have been able to figure out the relationship of the gods to the compass directions, and we know that Tinia normally sat in the northern part of the sky, looking south.[9] Thus his left hand was toward the East and the rising sun, and this side of the sky was regarded as generally auspicious. In fact the Romans called it the *pars familiaris*, the "Friendly Part." The West and the setting sun were unlucky, and were referred to as the *pars hostilis*, the "Hostile Part." (For the Greeks, exactly the opposite held true: the right hand was lucky and the left was unfavorable.) The part in front of Jupiter, in the South, was called the *pars antica* ("part in front") by the Romans, and the part behind, in the North, was the *pars postica* ("part behind"). It was important to know where the gods were sitting in the sky, because when lightning and thunder occurred, the priests had to decide which god was creating the celestial phenomenon. The Etruscans believed that there were nine gods who could throw the lightning bolt, in contrast to the Greeks and Romans, who generally reserved the power for the chief god alone. Roman writers[10] tell us the names of six of the gods who might throw lightning, using Latin designations: Jupiter, Juno, Minerva, Vulcan, Mars, and Saturn (their Etruscan names were Tinia, Uni, Menrva, and Sethlans, as well as, probably, Laran and Satre).[11] We do not know who the other three were.

A Roman text by the late writer Martianus Capella (5th century CE) preserves a description of where all the gods resided, thought to be based on an Etruscan account.[12] The passage comes near the beginning of a long allegorical novel known in modern scholarship as *On the Marriage of Mercury and Philology*. Mercury is getting married to a goddess, Philology, who personifies the love of learning, and messengers are going around the heavens to give out invitations to the gods. In contrast with our usual problems in studying the Etruscans, here we have an abundance of detail. But the text has baffled scholars and is seldom studied by anyone but specialists. In reading the passage, one may note the great number of different names of gods, some of whom are quite unknown elsewhere, and some of whom are mentioned only once or twice in other ancient texts. Their very rarity is of course consistent with the idea that they originate from an Etruscan source. It is interesting that we find the names of gods who are recognizably equated with the Greek and Roman chief gods, such as Jupiter, Juno and Mars, along with personifications such as Health, Fortune, Discord and Dissension. As is typical of the Etruscans, a number of gods occur in groups, only vaguely defined and remaining mysterious to us.

The text may be translated as follows:

> For in sixteen regions, it is said, the whole sky is divided, in the first of which, it is recorded, after Jupiter himself, the Consenting Gods (Dii Consentes) and the Penates, Good Health (Salus) and the Lares, Janus, the Secret Gods of Favor (Favores Opertanei) and the God of the Night (Nocturnus) have an abode.

> In the second, in like manner there dwelled—besides the house of Jupiter, which there, too, is very lofty, as he is well endowed in all things—Quirinus, Mars, Military Lar (Lars Militaris). Juno also had a house there, Fountain (Fons) also, the Fresh-water Goddesses (Lymphae) and the Ninefold Gods (Dii Novensiles).

But from the third region it was decided to invite one god. For the houses of Jupiter Secundanus and Jupiter's Wealth (Jovis Opulentia) and of Minerva were established there. But all had been present around Jupiter himself. Who would invite Discord (Discordia) and Dissension (Seditio) to the sacred marriage, especially since they were always enemies to Philology? Therefore from the same region only Pluto was summoned, because he was the uncle of the groom.

Then Lynsa Silvestris, Mulciber [=Vulcan], Heavenly Lar (Lar Caelestis) and likewise Military Lar (Lar Militaris) and Favor came from the fourth region.

From the next, as the homes of the royal spouses were traversed, Ceres, Tellurus and Earth's Father (Terrae Pater), Vulcan, and Genius were invited.

You, too, Jupiter's Sons, Pales and Favor, with Celeritas, Sun's Daughter (Solis Filia), are requested from the sixth region. For Mars, Quirinus, and Genius were asked above.

Thus also Liber and Secundanus Pales are called from the seventh region. From the same after long deliberation it was decided to include Deceit (Fraus), because she had frequently complied with [Mercury] the Cyllenian himself.

The eighth is passed through, because from it all had already been invited, and only Fruit of Spring (Veris Fructus) is included from this region.

The Genius of Juno Hospita is summoned from the ninth.

But Neptune, Lar of All and Everything (Lar Omnium Cunctalis), and Neverita, and you, too, Consus, were called from the tenth.

From the next come Fortune (Fortuna)and Wellness (Valetudo)and the Shepherd Favor, with the Shades (Manes) turned away, because indeed they were not able to come into the sight of Jupiter.

From the twelfth only Sancus is called.

From the next the Fates(Fata)are requested; but others, the Divine Shades (Dii Manes), tarry there.

From the twice-seven region Saturn and his Heavenly Juno (Juno Caelestis) are consequently summoned.

Veiovis and the Public Gods (Dii Publici)are called from the thrice-five boundary.

From the last region the God of the Night (Noctunus) and the Doorkeepers of the Earth (Janitores Terrestres)similarly are summoned.

Therefore when all the gods had been summoned from the regions of the sky, those whom they called the Zoneless (Azoni)were invited at the urging of [Mercury] the Cyllenian himself.[13]

We can lay out a chart of the regions of sky listing the deities mentioned by Martianus (Table III). It is important to note that sometimes he has not listed all the gods who dwelled in a particular region, because they had been invited from an earlier region, or indeed, were not to be invited at all. So it is very difficult to get an idea of how the heavens may have been balanced. But to a certain extent we can see how the houses of the gods fit with the scheme of the "Friendly Part" and the "Hostile Part." It has been noted that the celestial and favorable gods tend to reside on the East and the gods of earth and nature on the South, while the gods of darkness and those associated with the Underworld appear in the West, especially in the northern quadrant. There are certainly exceptions to this statement, however;

III.2 Bronze model of sheep's liver found near Piacenza, 3rd–2nd century BCE. Piacenza, Museo Civico. See discussion of Fig. III.1.

for example, Pluto, god of the Underworld, and Discord and Dissension appear in the "favorable" Region 3, and Caelestis Juno (Heavenly Juno) appears in Region 14. An important principle is that a god may have more than one abode. Jupiter, for example, dwells in the Regions 1, 2 and 3; Juno has 2 or 3 houses, Vulcan has 2, and so on.

We can compare this amazing passage in Martianus Capella with an even more surprising document about Etruscan gods, the artifact known as the Piacenza Liver (Fig. III.1-2). This is a bronze model of the liver of a sheep, of the actual size, marked out with cells or houses for the various Etruscan deities.[14] It was found outside of Etruria proper, near Piacenza, and may date to the 3rd or 2nd century BCE. We have already seen how part of the *Etrusca disciplina* taught by Tages related to studying the entrails of animals and in particular the liver (Fig. II.2). This model of a liver must have been used by priests who were trying to understand the messages from the gods, and the markings of the divisions indicate which god was sending the message. We may imagine that the real liver may have shown signs of disease in one area, or enlargement, or discoloration, and it would be the job of the priest to interpret the irregularities in the liver according to which god resided in the affected region. The margin of the upper side of the liver is divided into 16 cells,[15] which probably correspond to the 16 zones of the heavens.

There are several striking similarities between the Piacenza Liver and the passage in Martianus, which can be studied using Table III as a guide, and also looking at a schematic pie-like diagram that shows the 16 regions, with the gods of Martianus on the outer part of the wheel and the gods of the margin of the liver on the inner part (Fig. III.3). In the first three regions occurs the name of the chief god, Tin(ia), and, as in the heavens of Martianus, sometimes more than one god resides in a particular house. If we compare the macrocosmic statement of the residences

TABLE III. THE SIXTEEN DIVISIONS OF THE ETRUSCAN UNIVERSE

NORTHEAST QUARTER
GREAT CELESTIAL DEITIES

REGION ONE

⚡ **Jupiter**	**Tin**
God of the Night	**Cilen**
(16 and 36. Cilens)	
Secret Gods of Favor (2. 20. and 21 Thuf...?)	
Janus (14.Cvl)	
Consenting Gods	
Penates	
Health	
Lares	

REGION TWO

⚡ **Jupiter**	**Tin**
	Thuf (1. Secret Gods of Favor? 4. 6. and 11. Favor?)
⚡ *Juno (4. Uni)*	
Military Lars (26. Marisl Lar?)	
⚡ Mars	
Quirinus	
Fountain	
Freshwater Goddesses	
Ninefold Gods	

REGION THREE

⚡ **Jupiter Secundanus**	**Tins**
	Thne
Jupiter's Wealth	
⚡ Minerva	
Discord	
Dissension	
Pluto	

REGION FOUR

	Uni (2.Juno)
	Mae
Lynsa Silvestris (6.and 34. Lvsl?)	
Favor (2. 20. 21. Thuf...?)	
Military Lar (26. Marisl Lar?)	
⚡ Mulciber (Vulcan)	
Heavenly Lar	

SOUTHEAST QUARTER
TERRESTRIAL GODS AND GODS OF NATURE

REGION FIVE

	Tec
	Vm
Ceres	
Tellurus	
Earth's Father	
⚡ Vulcan	
Genius (26., 30. and 39. Marisl, Mar)	

REGION SIX

	Lvsl (4. Lynsa Sylvestris?)
Favor (2., 20. and 21. Thuf...?)	
⚡ Mars	
Quirinus	
Jupiter's Sons	
Pales and Favor	
Celeritas (13. Cels?)	
Sun's Daughter (8. Cath?)	
Genius (26., 30. and 39. Marisl, Mar)	

REGION 7

Liber (9.Fufluns)	*Neth (10.Neptune)*
Secundanus Pales	
Fraud	

REGION 8

	Cath
Fruit of Spring	

SOUTHWEST QUARTER	NORTHWEST QUARTER
TERRESTRIAL GODS AND GODS OF NATURE	GODS OF FATE AND THE INFERNAL REGIONS

SOUTHWEST QUARTER
TERRESTRIAL GODS AND GODS OF NATURE

REGION NINE
_____
Fufluns (7. Liber)
Genius of ⚡Juno Hospita

REGION TEN
_____
Selva
Neptune (7. 22. and 28. Neth)
Lar of All and Everything
Neverita
Consus

REGION ELEVEN
_____
Lethns
Shepherd Favor (2.20. and 21. Thuf...?)
Fortune
Wellness
Shades

REGION TWELVE
_____
Tluscv
Sancus

NORTHWEST QUARTER
GODS OF FATE AND THE INFERNAL REGIONS

REGION THIRTEEN
_____
Cels
Fates
Divine Shades

REGION FOURTEEN
_____
Cvl (1.Janus)
Alp
⚡*Saturn (35. Satres)*
⚡*Heavenly*   Juno

REGION FIFTEEN
_____
Veiovis   **Vetisl**
Public Gods

REGION SIXTEEN
_____
God of the Night   **Cilensl**
(1 and 36. Cilen)
Doorkeepers of the Earth

OUTSIDE THE REGIONS: The Zoneless

The chart lists the gods inhabiting the various regions of the sky, according to the two key documents, the Latin text of Martianus Capella (p. 45-46), and the Etruscan inscriptions on the Piacenza Liver (Figs. III.1-2). Martianus has a total of 16 regions, while the liver has 16 houses on its perimeter. All gods in these regions/houses are listed in the chart.

There are an additional 24 houses (nos. 17-40) on the interior of the Liver and it is not certain exactly how these relate to the 16 regions. They are not, therefore, listed in entirety here, but are only included when they correspond to a Latin name (e.g. Lar Militaris=26. Marisl Lar)

Boldface type indicates an exact correspondence, in an equivalent region, between two deities in the two documents (e.g., in Region One, Jupiter=Tin). The use of *italics* for the name of the deity, with a number and name of a deity afterward, indicates that the corresponding deity appears in the other document, but in a different region (e.g., in Region 7 of Martianus is the god *Liber,* who appears in the Liver, 9, *Fufluns*). A question mark indicates that the correspondence is not yet universally accepted. For convenience, the deities who correspond are listed first in each region. Then others in that region are listed according to the order in the documents.

A sign for lightning, ⚡, has been included next to the names of the gods who are known to have been capable of throwing lightning.

For the purposes of this table, I have taken the liberty of translating into English a good many of the names found in Martianus. On the cosmic wheel in Fig. III.3, the names may be found as they are given in Latin, but for this outline I wanted readers to have a quick perception of the spheres of these deities.

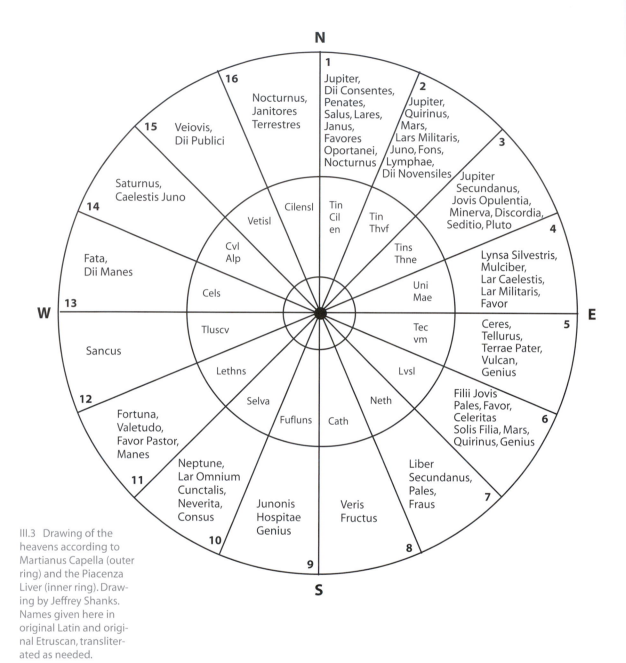

N

1
Jupiter,
Dii Consentes,
Penates,
Salus, Lares,
Janus,
Favores
Oportanei,
Nocturnus

2
Jupiter,
Quirinus,
Mars,
Lars Militaris,
Juno, Fons,
Lymphae,
Dii Novensiles

16
Nocturnus,
Janitores
Terrestres

15 Veiovis,
Dii Publici

14
Saturnus,
Caelestis Juno

3
Jupiter
Secundanus,
Jovis Opulentia,
Minerva, Discordia,
Seditio, Pluto

4
Lynsa Silvestris,
Mulciber,
Lar Caelestis,
Lar Militaris,
Favor

13
Fata,
Dii Manes

W   **E**

Sancus

5
Ceres,
Tellurus,
Terrae Pater,
Vulcan,
Genius

12
Fortuna,
Valetudo,
Favor Pastor,
Manes

6
Filii Jovis
Pales, Favor,
Celeritas
Solis Filia, Mars,
Quirinus, Genius

11
Neptune,
Lar Omnium
Cunctalis,
Neverita,
Consus

7
Liber
Secundanus,
Pales,
Fraus

10
Junonis
Hospitae
Genius

Veris
Fructus

8

9

S

Inner ring (Piacenza Liver) labels: Cilensl, Tin Cilen, Tin Thvf, Vetisl, Tins Thne, Cvl Alp, Uni Mae, Cels, Tlscv (Tluscv), Tecvm, Lethns, Lvsl, Selva, Neth, Fufluns, Cath

III.3 Drawing of the heavens according to Martianus Capella (outer ring) and the Piacenza Liver (inner ring). Drawing by Jeffrey Shanks. Names given here in original Latin and original Etruscan, transliterated as needed.

of the gods with the microcosm seen in the Liver, we can see this pattern clearly. It is interesting that Region 1 and Region 16 of Martianus both have a God of the Night, probably to help make the transition between the gods in the sunset area of the world and the gods on the sunrise side. The equivalent on the Liver is surely Cilens, who occurs in both 1 and 16. We can see many more correspondences between the gods of Martianus and those of the Liver (Table III), though sometimes they are in differing regions. Uni (Juno) is not in the second house of the Liver, but the fourth. Etruscan Nethuns is in the seventh of the Liver, while Roman Neptune is in the tenth of the heavens. And so on. It has been frustrating for scholars to try to make the two fascinating documents coincide with one another.

Another factor that must be considered is that the Piacenza Liver has a number of gods in inner houses of the Liver, and thus they do not carry out the idea of the 16 cells. Added in, they bring the total number of houses on the upper surface of the Liver up to 40. (There are two additional houses on the underside of the liver, labeled with the Etruscan words for sun—Usil, and moon—Tiv.) It is nevertheless true that the favorable and celestial gods tend to cluster around Tinia on what ought to be the "East" of the Liver, and gods of darkness may be recognized on the "West." It is also interesting that both documents omit a string of deities we might expect to be present: Venus/Turan, Apollo/Aplu, Artemis/Artumes and Persephone/Phersipnei. Of course Mercury is not listed among the gods invited to his own wedding in Martianus, but it is interesting that he is also missing from the Liver, for there is no Etruscan Turms present.

We shall have occasion to refer frequently to the various individual gods named on the Liver and in Martianus, and to try to understand their roles in Etruscan religion and myth. In particular, we shall return to the pantheon of Etruscan gods of the heavens in the following four chapters.

"The Principal God of Etruria"

IV

truscan inscriptions and representations in art confirm that Tinia (also written as Tin, Tina) is at the head of the Etruscan pantheon.[1] He is a sky god, referred to as "father" (*apa*),[2] often equated, as noted in Table I, with the Greek Zeus and the Roman Jupiter (whose name includes the Latin word for father, *pater*). A close association between Tinia of the Etruscans and Jupiter of the Romans is confirmed by the fact that the greatest temple of Rome, to Jupiter Optimus Maximus, was built during the period when Etruscan kings, the Tarquins, ruled Rome in the 6th century BCE.

The deity type is familiar in Indo-European mythology, and it is tempting to compare Tinia also with Odin, the "Allfather" and "Ruler of Weather" of the Norse pantheon,[3] especially when we consider that Odin stood at the head of a group of gods known as the Aesir, a name that is surprisingly similar to the Etruscan word for the gods as a group, *aiser*.[4] Of course each of these father-weather gods has his own particular nature; in this chapter we shall focus on the characteristics that make Tinia distinctive.

The Etruscan word *tin* occurs with the meaning of "day," indicating that the god was associated with daylight. The lightning bolt is his principal attribute, and especially appropriate is an image on an Etruscan mirror that shows him with a thunderbolt in each hand (Fig. IV.1). According to Etruscan lore preserved by the Romans, their lightning god was in fact in control of three main types of bolts, and he often used his power in close consultation with group gods, such as the ones in the heavens of Martianus, called the Consenting Gods (Dii Consentes), and the Secret Gods of Favor (Favores Opertanei).

The three types of bolts he might throw are as follows[5]: (1) A benign bolt that served only to give warning; the god could decide on his own whether to send it. (2) A bolt that did both good and harm, for which he needed the approval of the Twelve Gods (probably the same as the Consenting Gods). (3) A completely destructive bolt, for which he had to have permission from a group called the Shrouded Gods (Dii Involuti), probably identical with the Secret Gods of Favor of Martianus.

The Etruscan belief in a wide variety of lightning bolts is reflected in the many different sizes and shapes of such bolts depicted with Tinia in art. In Fig. IV.1, he clutches at least two types, and seems to contemplate which one to hurl. With him in the scene are two goddesses from Greek myth, Thethis (=Thetis, the mother of Achilles) and Thesan (=Eos, the mother of Memnon), probably entreating him to affect the destiny of their sons in their battle against each other. The undulating bolts in his proper left hand, held in a bundle, vibrate with power, while the single

53

IV.1 Bronze mirror, ca.
470 BCE. Vatican Muse-
ums, Museo Gregoriano
Etrusco. After ES:4.396.
Tinia, with lightning, en-
treated by Thethis (right,
=Thetis) and Thesan (left,
=Eos) to spare their sons,
Achilles and Memnon;
Menrva on far left.

IV.2 Bronze statu-
ette from Ferenzuola
(Florence), ca. 500
BCE. Cortona, Museo
dell'Accademia Etrusca.
Photo: Scala/Art
Resource, New York. A
beardless deity with
lightning, perhaps Tinia.

bolt in his right hand has a vegetal quality, and hints at its force through the arrow-like points on its end. A different bolt again is the one held by the youthful Tinia depicted in a bronze statuette of the Archaic period found near Florence (Fig. IV.2); the element has been described as having a pear-shaped knob at the bottom and at the top a thick point surrounded by four leaves.[6] Still other examples occur in the images in IV.6-14; each bolt is different from the others, making it impossible to construct a typology, quite unlike the situation in representations of the Hellenic Zeus, whose bolt is regularly symmetrical, usually with a flourish on each end.[7] Thus the Etruscan cultic understanding of lightning as having a rich and widely varying repertory is quite consistent with the representations in art.

While this attribute of Tinia is often shown in scenes lacking action as he stands or sits within a group carrying on a conversation, it may also appear in action scenes. Some scenes from Greek mythology may have been appealing in Etruria precisely because they featured the throwing of the lightning bolt. An

ETRUSCAN MYTH, SACRED HISTORY, AND LEGEND

IV.3 Painted terracotta sculpture, relief plaque from the *columen* (ridge beam) of Temple A, Pyrgi, ca. 470–460 BCE. Rome, Museo Nazionale Etrusco di Villa Giulia. Photo: Università di Roma La Sapienza, Pyrgi Excavations. Tinia (center), hurls lightning toward Capne (=Capaneus, far right); below, Tute (=Tydeus) devours the brains of his adversary (=Melanippus); Menrva (left) looks on in horror.

especially good example is the terracotta sculpture representation of the Seven Against Thebes that decorated one end of Temple A at Pyrgi, the port of Caere, dated to ca. 465 BCE (Fig. IV.3). It shows Tinia/Zeus in position to heave lightning (the sculpture is damaged and the bolt is now missing) at the impious Capaneus, who boasted that the god could not stop him from breaking into Thebes. Below, Tydeus, equally despicable, indulges in cannibalism on the head of his foe Melanippus, as Athena/Menrva comes from the left and registers her dismay.

We have also learned that Tinia was a god of boundaries. In the prophecy of Vegoia, he is involved with organizing the cosmos and administering justice within it, especially as regards the use of land. These lands clearly relate to agriculture, and the god could show his control over stolen fields by causing whirlwinds, hail, rain and mildew that would ruin the crops. In this connection, Tinia takes on the characteristics not only of a weather god, but one who controls fertility and productivity. Perhaps an Etruscan connection may be seen in the fact that the temple of Jupiter Optimus Maximus at Rome included an unroofed space sacred to the god Terminus (Ovid, *Fasti* 2.669). That Tinia continued to protect boundaries down to the end of Etruscan civilization may be seen in the three boundary stones sacred "to Tin" found at an Etruscan colony of the 2nd-1st century BCE in Tunisia.[8]

It is remarkable that Tinia also has Underworld connections. These were recognized in the city where there is important archaeological evidence of a center for his cult, modern Orvieto, believed to be identical with ancient Volsinii. There we find an inscription referring to Tinia as Calusna (*ET* Vs 4.7), i.e., associated

IV.4 Bronze statuette found near Florence, Museo Arcaeologico Nazionale. 3rd century BCE. Photo: Soprintendenza per i Beni Archeologici della Toscana. Votive statuette of a dog with inscription ś. *caluśtla* (*ET* Co 4,10) suggests that the offering was made to the Underworld figure Calu.

with Calu, a god connected with wolves and the Underworld, a further reference to whom appears in an inscription on a small bronze sculpture of a wolf or dog found at Cortona (Fig.IV.4).[9]

There are also representations of Tinia as an Underworld figure along with Turms (Hermes/Mercury), in which he is shown with unruly serpent-like locks of hair, normally reserved for Etruscan gods of the afterlife (cf. Chapter X below). On the bronze handles of a vessel thought to have originated in Orvieto (but found in a tomb at Spina, on the Adriatic Sea), we see two pairs of Turms and Tinia (Fig. IV.5).[10] In one pair, the bearded, long-haired Tinia is shown with lightning bolt, while Turms carries a hammer, normally the attribute of the Underworld demon Charu. In the other pair, Turms carries the traditional attribute of Greek Hermes, the caduceus, but his partner has seemingly turned into an Underworld deity. The

IV.5 Bronze handles of a vessel from Spina, ca. 400 BCE. Ferrara, Museo Archeologico. After Hostetter 1986:pl. 6d. Relief sculptures show pairs of Tinia with Turms of the Underworld (with hammer) and Tinia of the Underworld (with snaky hair) with Turms.

bearded male, resembling the Tinia of the other pair, now has snaky locks of hair to link him with Charu, Persephone and other deities of the dead. As a god of the dead he is accordingly associated with concepts of rebirth, fertility, and wealth. Possibly it is because the chief deity has such a connection with the Underworld that his brother Pluto (the word *ploutos* means "wealth" in Greek) is allowed into the third region of Martianus, one of the three regions of Jupiter.

Tinia is also represented with Turms on a mirror scene along with Apulu, which probably does not relate, however, to the Underworld (Fig. IV.6). The three handsome deities seem to converse, and it has been suggested that the topic may be the dispute between the sons of the god concerning the theft of cattle by the younger, Hermes. There are instances in both Etruscan and Greek art in which Tinia seems to throw the thunderbolt as a sign of a decision or judgment and thus becomes a peacemaker.[11] But Turms is not represented as a baby here, and Tinia himself is not shown as a father, but rather as a beardless young man, wearing a wreath of ivy—a rare, if not unknown, attribute for this god in Greece or Rome. Again the theme of fertility comes up, this time with a Dionysiac twist. Relevant

IV.6 Bronze mirror, ca. 330 BCE. Formerly Munich, Antikensammlung, now lost. After *ES*:1.74. Tinia (center), flanked by Aplu (left) and Turms (right).

here is the report of Pliny (*NH* 14.1) that at the old Etruscan city of Populonia there stood in his time an ancient cult image of Jupiter, i.e., Tinia, carved from a single huge vine stock, and thus also manifesting a Dionysiac connection.

Even more remarkable is the scene on a mirror that seems to show Tinia being treated by Aplu for an injury to his foot (Fig. IV.7).[12] The bearded god holds his lightning in one hand and looks back over his shoulder to see what the younger god is doing. A bird flies above, carrying an adornment (necklace, diadem?) and weaponry appears on the right side (a bow and possibly a spear). The story is otherwise unknown in the ancient world, but a possible reading is that Aplu treats a wound for Tinia, who, although injured, was victorious in battle.

Tinia is frequently shown with his consort, Uni,[13] sometimes in scenes that are quite intimate, with Uni naked and Tinia as a beardless and eager youth (Figs.

IV.7 Bronze mirror, ca. 400 BCE. Formerly Stuttgart, private collection. After *ES*:5. p. 222. Aplu tends a wound in Tinia's foot.

IV.8-9). The god with the lightning is also shown in an erotic scene on an Etruscan mirror; we are not sure who the mate is, but it may well be Uni (Fig. IV.10; the wings would be unusual for Uni). Some have suggested, however, that the female here is from the Greek myth of Zeus's affair with Semele (Etruscan Semla, also normally wingless), who asked him to appear to her in his most characteristic form, and the god thereupon turned into a lightning bolt. He literally burned his lover up, but from the ashes he rescued her offspring Dionysos (Etruscan Fufluns), and installed the child in his thigh until the baby came to term.

Scenes of a philandering Tinia are actually quite rare in Etruscan art—nowhere nearly as common as in Greek art and literature. What is interesting is that far more popular, at least on Etruscan mirrors, were scenes of the god with a baby, especially when Tinia was himself giving birth! The birth of Fufluns is known from one mirror (Fig. IV.11): the god calmly holds his lightning bolt and scepter as the baby emerges beside his thigh, to be taken up by the Etruscan birth goddess Thalna[14] as Aplu stands by. Behind Tinia is the winged female Mean, who elsewhere

IV.8 Bronze mirror, 350–300 BCE. Berlin, Staatliche Museen, Antikensammlung. After *CSE* Bundesrepublik Deutschland:4.20a. Tinia embraces Uni as an attendant with perfume bottle and dipper stands right. The chief god and his consort are shown as youthful and nude.

IV.9 Bronze mirror, 300–275 BCE. Copenhagen, Danish National Museum. After *CSE* Denmark:1.13a. From left to right, Tinia, Uni, Turms, and Menrva, in council.

appears as a goddess of victory; here her celebration involves applying fragrant oils with a dipper (to the new baby rather than the father?), a ritual act quite literally resembling christening ("anointing") and imparting immortality.[15] Tinia also appears giving birth from his head to Athena/Menrva—the child is winged—as he throws his lightning (Fig. IV.12), with different birth goddesses to help, Thanr (left) and Ethausva (right). Yet another mirror shows the theme of the birth of Menrva (Fig. IV.13) this time with Thalna (left) and Thanr (right), and Sethlans, the Etruscan counterpart of Hephaestos, holding in his left hand the axe he has used to help open up a birth canal for the child.

Another myth of Tinia with a baby shows the presentation of the child Epiur (Fig. IV.14; here spelled Epeur). The story represented in the upper register of this large and ambitiously decorated mirror[16] has never been successfully linked with any Greek myth and we do not know exactly what the meaning of this scene may be. Hercle, a nude, handsome youth carrying his club, seems to present the winged baby to Tinia, as Turan (left) and Thalna (right) look on approvingly.

The theme of Epiur has been identified so far on a total of six mirrors and also on an Etruscan red-figured vase, all but one dated to the 4th century BCE, and several closely associated with the Etruscan city of Vulci.[17] Two of the mirrors are

IV.10 Bronze mirror, 4th century BCE. London, British Museum. After *ES*:1.81.2. Tinia, holding his attribute of the thunderbolt, makes love with a winged partner, perhaps his wife Uni or his lover Semla. An attendant youthful satyr holds the two pipes but does not play them.

especially useful for further details of his life. On the first (Fig. IV.15) is a scene of Hercle carrying an unnamed baby, most likely Epiur, as Menrva holds the child's arm and Turan appears on the left, again seeming to regard the child tenderly. The baby, balding and looking rather like an old man, holds a flower in his hand, probably an unopened poppy (the child in Fig. IV.14 also holds something small and rounded, perhaps also a poppy or an egg). The scene is closed on the right by the Etruscan goddess Munthu(ch),[18] who here assumes the role of crowning Hercle for his apparent success. Elsewhere (Fig. IV.16) Epiur is shown as an older child, being lifted up (or set down?) by Hercle, in the presence of Menrva. In all of these Hercle is shown as nude and beardless, indicating that this was an adventure of his youth. The baby, divine and looking old and wise, recalls the myth of Tages, but the story itself does not match at all with what we know of that theme.

So how should we interpret the myth? It has been suggested that Hercle and Menrva are the divine protectors and foster parents of Epiur, and it is the task of Hercle to deliver the child to the appropriate place. Perhaps he first receives the

IV.11 Bronze mirror, 4th century BCE. Naples, Museo Archeologico Nazionale. After *ES*:1,82. Tinia, holding his lightning bolt in his left hand and a scepter topped by a bird with extended wings in his right, looks down at a child emerging from behind his thigh (unlabeled, but most likely Fufluns). The child is received by the birth goddess Thalna as Aplu looks on from left. At far right Mean raises a dipper to apply ointment. In upper exergue, a prophetic head.

child (rather than presenting him) at the throne of Tinia, then takes Epiur to be received by Menrva. The interaction with Tinia may relate to the role of the great god in promoting fertility, reproduction and rearing of children. The scene of Hercle and Menrva with the older Epiur may refer to the conclusion of the rearing and education of the youth, and indicate that Hercle must return him to society.

Most scholars today believe that Tinia was known to the Romans by a completely different name. Varro, writing in the first century BCE (*De Lingua Latina* 5.46), in making reference to the *deus princeps Etruriae*, "principal god of Etruria," uses the name Vortumnus. Scholars agree that this is an alternate Roman spelling for the name of the god who appears normally in Latin as Vertumnus (and this is the name we shall use) but also as Voltumna, a feminine name. It is possible also that this is the same god who is labeled in Etruscan as Veltune on the famous Tages

IV.12 Bronze mirror from Praeneste, ca. 400–350 BCE. London, British Museum. After *CSE* Great Britain:1.1.24d. Birth of Menrva from the head of Tinia. The winged child springs from the head of Tinia fully armed with shield, spear, and helmet. The birth goddesses, winged and beautifully dressed, are Thanr (left), who wraps a band or bandage around the head of Tinia, and Ethaus-va (right), who soothes his head with her right hand and braces his shoulder with her left.

mirror (Fig. II.2). As we have noted, Veltune may be equivalent to Jupiter, i.e., the grandfather of Tages. In fact, the figure of Veltune generally resembles the many images of Tinia as a mature, bearded god. The argument for the equivalence of Vertumnus and Tinia is strengthened by the fact that Vertumnus is said to have had his principal cult at Volsinii (Orvieto), and as noted there is abundant evidence there for the worship of Tinia.

A lot is at stake in this debate, because Roman writers tell us that the shrine of Voltumna (called the *Fanum Voltumnae*) was the most important religious center for the Etruscans and was the periodical meeting place of the 12 major Etruscan peoples.[19] Allusions to these meetings indicate that their purpose was political and recreational as well as religious. There is good reason to believe (though not conclusive proof) that the sanctuary of Voltumna was located at or near Volsinii. If this is so, activities there may have been suspended after the Romans sacked Volsinii in 264 BCE and resettled its inhabitants elsewhere. Currently investigations are underway on the plain outside Orvieto in a site that may well turn out to be the original great federal Etruscan sanctuary.[20]

IV.13 Bronze mirror from Arezzo, ca. 330–320 BCE. Bologna, Museo Civico Archeologico. After *CSE* Italia:1.1.13a. Tinia, seemingly exhausted by the birth of Menrva from his head, holds his scepter with his left hand while a lance-shaped lightning bolt dangles limply from his right. Birth goddesses tend him—Thalna (left), embracing his abdomen as if it were the source of the birth, and Thanr (right), reaches up to receive the baby. The beardless Sethlans, at the far right with axe, raises his hand in a gesture indicating that he has sighted the new divinity.

What do we know about Vertumnus? In fact we have some quite vivid depictions of the god in Latin poetry, including a long poem by Propertius (4.2) written in the 1st century BCE that describes a statue of him that had been set up in Rome. The statue, standing near the Forum on a busy street called the Vicus Tuscus ("Etruscan Row"), talks and describes the nature of the god Vertumnus, presumably reflecting a general and traditional Roman view of his identity. It is most interesting that the deity stresses his changeability—that he can be like Bacchus or Apollo, like a warrior or a farmer or a bird catcher. He also points out that he can pass for female, if properly dressed for the part. The poet plays with the Latin verb *vertere*, "to turn," to indicate the etymology of the name of the god:

Why do you marvel that my one body should have so many shapes? Learn about the signs of the descent of Vertumnus. I am Etruscan, from Etruscans sprung, nor am I sorry that I deserted the hearths of Volsinii amid the battles. This crowd around me pleases me, even though I don't enjoy an ivory temple;

IV.14 Bronze mirror from Vulci, ca. 325 BCE. Paris, Bibliothèque Nationale, Cabinet des Médailles. After ES:2.181. This unusual mirror shows decoration in two registers, perhaps with the heavens above and the Underworld below. Upper register: Hercle stands with the child Epiur before Tinia (center), as Turan (left) and Thalna (right) look on. Lower register: Elinai (center) shakes hands with Achmemrun as Menle stands by; Mean crowns Elchsentre (=Paris), as Aevas (=Ajax; far left) gazes toward the center scene (far left); Lasa Thimrae, with perfume (far right); lower exergue, Lasa Racuneta, with perfume, sits in flower.

IV.15 Bronze mirror, ca. 350 BCE. Berlin, Staatliche Museen. After *ES*:2, pl. 165. Menrva and Hercle tend the infant Epiur in the presence of Turan (left) and Munthuch (right), who crowns Hercle for his success. The pretty lady Menrva is dressed in a flowing gown and is adorned with diadem and jewelry; only a few serpents allude to her usual protective aegis.

it is enough that I can see the Roman Forum. . . . My nature is suitable for all forms. Turn me [*verte*] into whatever you like, I'll still be handsome. Dress me in Coan silk, I'll become a girl, and not rough. When I wear the toga, who will deny that I am a man? Give me a sickle and bind my brow with twisted hay, and you'll swear that the grasses were cut by my hand. Once I bore weapons, and as I recall, was praised for them. . . . Wrap my head with a turban, and I'll steal the appearance of Iacchus [Bacchus]; I'll steal that of Phoebus [Apollo] if you'll just give me the lyre pick. With nets on my shoulders I go hunting; with the bird twig in my hand I'm Favor, the god of feathery fowling. Vertumnus is also the image of the charioteer and of the one who lightly throws his weight from horse to horse. . . As a shepherd I can bend over my staff, or carry the rose in a rush-basket in the dusty summer. Now why should I add that the choicest gifts from the garden are in my hands, since for that I am best known? The dark green cucumber and the gourd with the swell-

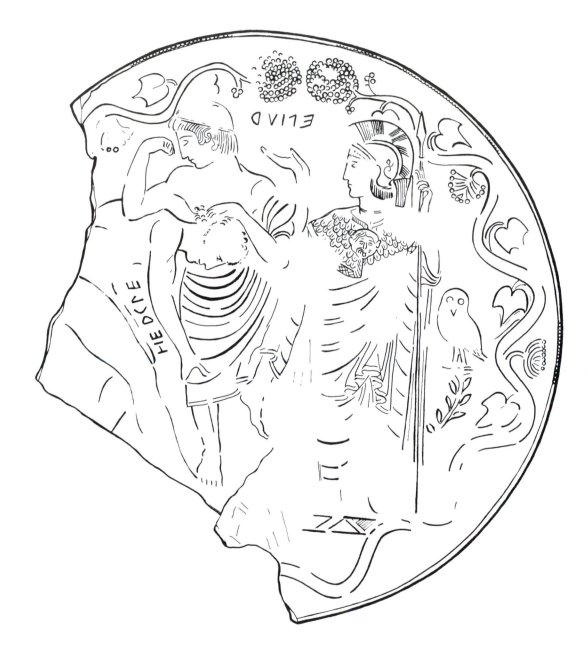

IV.16 Bronze mirror from Vulci, ca. 425–400 BCE. Berlin, Staatliche Museen, Antikensammlung. After CSE Bundesrepublik Deutschland:4.14a. A nude beardless Hercle, lacking his usual attributes of lion skin and club, manages the
burden of the child Epiur, with attention from Menrva, who raises her right hand in a gesture that could indicate
farewell or perhaps simply affection.

ing belly mark me out and the cabbage tied on with a light reed. There is no flower that opens in the fields that is not appropriate to place hanging on my forehead. Well, because I am one who was turned [*vertebar*] into all forms, my own language has given me my name.[21]

So the concept in Rome in the 1st century BCE of the chief god of the Etruscans was of a versatile deity who could be depicted as a warrior or a woman, a farmer, a shepherd or a fisherman, a Bacchus, Apollo, or Favor.[22] Is this image consistent with that of Tinia? The sexual ambiguity and the general versatility of the divinity certainly have an Etruscan aura. But unfortunately even though there are numerous Etruscan gods who may appear as now male, now female, Tinia has not been recognized among them. He does appear as sometimes young, sometimes mature, but in fact this variation is not included in the poem of Propertius. Most important of all, the poet never mentions lightning, the foremost attribute of Tinia.

But the reference to Vertumnus converting himself into Apollo or Bacchus fits especially well with the Etruscan mirror scene of Tinia with Turms and Apulu, where the god actually wears the ivy wreath of Bacchus. And it is his identity as a fertility god that has encouraged researchers to think of Vertumnus as being identical to Tinia. We have seen how the latter, through his protection and power over the fields, his Underworld connections, and perhaps also through his involvement with birth and babies, may qualify as a fertility deity.

There is one more important source for studying Vertumnus, also verses of the later 1st century BCE, written by Ovid as part of his long poem, the *Metamorphoses* (14.623-771). Here we have a true mythical narrative, concerning the love of Vertumnus for a beautiful nymph named Pomona, a spirit of fruits and orchards. As she avoided all sexual involvements and failed to return his love, the god found a way to enter her garden by disguising himself as a laborer who might help her: he came with a hook to prune the vines, with a ladder to pick the apples. Or he appeared as a visitor who would carry a rod and pretend to be a fisherman, or came as a soldier with a sword. His ultimate disguise involved change of sex and age, as he pretended to be an old woman who came to admire the garden. Praising the gardener along with her fruits, Vertumna/us drew her into intimate conversation and began to kiss her and advise her affectionately. Pointing to the union of the elm and the vine, of course (s)he told Pomona that she should seek a mate to make her life meaningful, and who better than Vertumnus? The god tells her the story of a rejected suitor who committed suicide, bringing sorrow to the girl he loved and causing her to turn to stone. After various attempts at persuasion, (s)he finally revealed himself:

Then he resumed his own
young shape and shed the trappings of old age,
and stood revealed to her as when the sun
triumphs in glory through the clouds and rain
and bright with beams untrammeled shines again.
No need of force, his beauty wins the day,
as she with answering love is borne away.
(*Meta.* 14.765-71[23])

The Roman poet has undoubtedly embroidered the story in observance of his own literary aims, in particular the need to address his theme of metamorphosis. But the changeability of Vertumnus is a natural subject for his poem. Further, he has added in Pomona, an old Italic, but probably not Etruscan, divinity,[24] as a consort of Vertumnus; for this nymph we find no parallel in Etruscan evidence about Tinia. The principal Etruscan remnant in the story is the bisexuality of the god. We remember that the great shrine was said to belong to Voltumna, a female name, and can point to all the other evidence that the Etruscans conceived of their gods as spirits without a fixed gender. But given that Tinia himself was never represented as female, in the end, we must say that if indeed Tinia and Vertumnus were originally equivalent, the Roman writers of the 1st century BCE have moved a long way from the Etruscan concept of the myth.

Great Goddesses

Scholars of ancient religion and myth have argued that in prehistoric times there was a concept of a great mother goddess who related especially to fertility and the earth and who was generally versatile in regard to the things her devotees might pray for.[1] She was the most important deity, and could be helpful in regard to war or weather, crops or crafts. In Greece, the vestige of this idea is seen in the myth of Gaia, "Earth," who is described as bringing order out of Chaos in the beginning, and who was for a while in the history of the universe the only goddess and the most powerful force. But the Greek story tells how the competing force of the sky, her husband Ouranos, started a conflict with her that echoed down the generations until Zeus emerged from the turmoil as ruler of gods, men and the universe. At the same time the concept of female deity became fragmented into various goddesses who were in charge of various spheres: Hera was concerned with marriage, while Aphrodite oversaw love and sex, Artemis protected virginity, and Athena was goddess of war and crafts. Demeter took agriculture as her special interest, and myths about her also show her as the archetypical mother.

This model is given in a highly simplified form here, but it helps to provide a basis for discussion of the major Etruscan goddesses. For they fit with neither scheme. We do not have any evidence of a single great earth mother goddess;[2] neither do we find that the Etruscan deities were associated with one particular sphere. Rather we see considerable fluidity in their identities.

Menrva

We may begin with Menrva (also spelled Menerva, Merva, and Mera) as perhaps the best example of this versatility. Her name is indigenous to Italy (many, though not all, scholars think that it is originally Etruscan, and then was adopted by the Romans and other Italic cultures[3]) and her cult was widespread among the Etruscans. She was a powerful weather god, known to the Romans as one of the nine Etruscan gods who controlled lightning, and was placed by Martianus in Region 3 in the favorable northeast sky. She does not have a cell on the Piacenza Liver, but she is represented in art with the lightning bolt (Fig.V.1) and with the wings appropriate for a deity who frequently takes to the air. These attributes distinguish her from the Greek Athena, with whom she is often compared, and it is clear that she does not originate in Greece. But the Etruscans considered Athena her parallel and in art often represented her with attributes of Athena. Menrva is a goddess of war, and may appear in military panoply, sometimes as elaborate as helmet, shield, spear and *aegis*, the special breastplate adorned with the powerful

V.1 Bronze mirror, 3rd
century BCE. Berlin,
Staatliche Museen,
Antikensammlung. After
CSE Bundesrepublik
Deutschland:4.24a. A
winged Menrva flies to
the left, carrying a thunderbolt as a weapon.

protective device of the head of the Gorgon Medusa. Menrva is represented as formidable in battle, with spear raised on high for attack (Fig. V.2). At other times she does not look military at all, but wears a pretty dress, a diadem, or earrings, with a single attribute such as a spear or helmet to identify her as a war goddess (Figs. V.3-4).

Menrva may have been associated with prophecy, as seen from the mirror in which she consults with Lasa Vecu (Fig. II.7). Even more important, she was a goddess of health, and her sanctuaries have yielded votive offerings of terracotta sculptures in the shape of parts of the body, indicating that her followers believed she could heal.[4] The Romans also worshipped the deity with an epiclesis (by-name) indicating this function: Minerva Medica. In Etruria she was especially regarded as a nurse of children, and we have already seen that she played a role in the Etruscan story of the child Epiur (Figs. IV.15-16).

One of the most remarkable myths of Menrva in Etruria has to do with the group of babies named Mariś (Figs. V.5-6), shown on two mirrors. In one scene,

V.2   Bronze statuette,
ca. 500 BCE. Modena,
Galleria Estense. Photo:
Soprintendenza per
il Patrimonio Storico,
Artistico ed Etnoantropo-
logico, Modena e Reggio
Emilia. Menrva hurls a
spear (or lightning?).

V.3 Bronze mirror from Chiusi, ca. 300 BCE. Present location unknown. After *ES*:5.67. Pherse (=Perseus) starts to behead Metus (=Medusa) as Menrva (left) looks on. The goddess wears no armor, perhaps as part of the narrative, since she has not yet received the head of the Gorgon to place on her breast.

from Bolsena, there are three babies, labeled Mariś Halna, Mariś Husrnana, and Mariś Isminthians. On the second mirror, from Chiusi, Mariś Isminthians is not depicted, but the other two are shown. In both renderings, the babies seem to be going into or coming out of a large amphora or krater with the guidance of Menrva. Standing next to this action on both is the goddess Turan. The rest of the cast varies, but Turms appears on the first (Fig. V.5), holding one of the babies, along with the nude youth Laran, who leans upon a spear, and a female figure otherwise unknown, Amatutunia, who likewise holds a child. On the second (Fig. V.6) we have two nude youths with spear, the one on the left labeled Leinth, and the other unlabeled (perhaps Laran). The scene has been much discussed by specialists, without conclusion, since we have no narrative text for this totally Etruscan myth.[5] My own belief is that the babies are probably newborn spirits, who are to be protected and nurtured by the goddess and her entourage. On the mirror from Chiusi, Menrva bares one breast (a unique detail for the goddess), indicating that she will nurse them. It is hard to say why she wears an animal skin but it is clear

V.4 Bronze mirror, 475–450 BCE. Paris, Bibliothèque Nationale, Cabinet des Médailles. After *ES*:2.146. Menrva leads a young woman (identity unknown), holding her by the wrist.

that the scene depicts a ritual, perhaps providing a paradigm for the initiation of boy babies.[6]

It has been pointed out that Athena also may protect infants, as in the case of Erichthonius, the child born from the Earth (Gaia) when Hephaistos, making an attempt on Athena, spilled his seed upon the ground. Athena received the child from Gaia and handed him over in a box to the daughters of Kekrops.[7] Thus Menrva's difference with Athena in this case could be one of degree. But while there seems to be no doubt about the virginity of Athena, concerning Menrva, and this may come as a surprise, there is good evidence that she was involved in romance. Some think she may even be the mother of Epiur. Even more surprising is that her consort may be none other than the great hero/god Hercle.[8] They appear on a mirror in Brussels in quite an affectionate attitude (Fig. V.7), and on another mirror, Menrva is ardently embraced by a handsome youth who seems to have a bow underfoot, perhaps intended to signify that this, too, is Hercle (Fig. V.8). Other examples could be adduced.

V.5 Bronze mirror from Bolsena, ca. 325–300 BCE. London, British Museum. After ES:3.257b. Menrva helps Mariś babies in large vessel, probably an amphora; from left to right, Turms with Mariś Isminthians, Menrva with Mariś Husrnana, Turan, Laran, Amatutunia with Mariś Halna; upper exergue, goddess of the dawn with chariot. Lower exergue, the boy Hercle, carrying his club and kneeling on a raft. A continuity of theme can be noted in that the raft is supported by amphoras tied together. With his left hand, Hercle adjusts a hanging of cloth, with a mantle wrapped around his waist and his lion skin tied around his neck.

Menrva is represented in Etruscan art in various adventures that closely parallel those of Athena in Greek art, for example, the scene of the Seven Against Thebes in which she comes forward with the jug of liquid with which she had planned to make Tydeus immortal (Fig. IV.3). She is commonly the protector of heroes, especially Hercle and Pherse (=Perseus; Fig. V.3) to be discussed in subsequent chapters. One of the most popular Greek myths in Etruria was the story of the Judgment of Paris, the beauty contest of Aphrodite, Hera and Athena. In order to acknowledge the Etruscanization of the myth, we shall here refer to the mythologem as the Judgment of Elcsntre, the name given to Paris in Etruria, based on his alternate Greek name of Alexander.

The three goddesses are depicted in quite various ways. An early, interesting version occurs on two painted plaques from Cerveteri, the "Boccanera" slabs (Plate

V.6 Bronze mirror from Chiusi, ca. 325–300 BCE. Berlin, Staatliche Museen, Antikensammlung. After CSE Bundesrepublik Deutschland:4.28a. Menrva with babies in vessel; from left to right, Leinth with Mariś Halna, Turan, Menrva with Mariś Husrnana, unidentified youth (Laran?); lower exergue, the goddess Recial, perhaps connected with rejuvenation.

V.7 Bronze mirror, ca. 325–300 BCE. Morlanwelz, Musée Royal de Mariemont. After *CSE* Belgique:1.25a. In center Hercle and Menrva form an intimate pair, flanked by a spirit of anointment on the left labeled as Eris, and on the right, Thethis. The story is unknown, but may represent a union of Menrva and Hercle.

I).[9] Here, as Elcsntre awaits on the left, Turms (Hermes) leads the way, carrying a staff with a bull on the top instead of his caduceus, followed by Menrva, bearing in one hand a spear as her identification and in the other a wreath, presumably her offering to the judge. She is followed by the other two goddesses, Uni carrying a pomegranate branch with three pieces of fruit, and Turan, bearing a branch with what appears to be two mature pomegranates and five flowers. In addition, Turan reveals her identity by lifting her skirt and displaying her shapely legs.

Uni

We may use this image of the Judgment of Elcsntre (Plate I) to initiate discussion of Uni, inasmuch as the goddess shows here her Etruscan character by being associated with the fruits of fertility, unlike Hera, whose display at the Judgment is normally limited to tugging at her veil to remind the viewer of her marriage (a motif also appearing in Etruria). That Uni had richer associations in Etruria is suggested by the remarkable bilingual sacred gold tablets from her sanctuary at Pyrgi, where the name of Uni is rendered in Phoenician by that of the great fertility goddess Astarte. There is also evidence at Pyrgi that suggests the practice

V.8 Bronze mirror, ca. 300 BCE. Berlin, Staatliche Museen, Antikensammlung. After *ES*:2.161. Menrva walks to the right, aided and embraced by a naked youth. Three other figures (unidentified) look on.

of sacred prostitution in connection with her cult.[10] We have already noted how the image of Uni with her husband Tinia may be youthful and nude in Etruria, referring to her as sexually active (Figs. IV.8-9). In fact her name in Etruscan may come from an Indo-European root *iuni*, meaning "young."[11]

A quite astonishing representation of Uni with Tinia has recently been explained by E. Simon (Fig. V.9).[12] The scene is dominated by the central standing figure of the god—nude, beardless, curly-haired, leaning on a spear. At his feet on the left is a large thunderbolt, standing upright as if it has been thrown. Further on the left is Uni, a seminude female with arms behind her back, while on the right approaches Turms, wearing his characteristic hat, the *petasos*. The scene has been convincingly linked with a passage in Homer's *Iliad* 15. 12-22. Hera is upbraided by Zeus for harassing the Trojans:

> Hopeless one, it was your evil design, your treachery, Hera, that stayed brilliant Hektor from battle, terrified his people. I do not know, perhaps for this

V.9 Bronze mirror, late 4th century BCE. Schloss Fasanerie (bei Fulda). After *CSE* Bundesrepublik Deutschland:1.38c. In center a large figure of a youthful Tinia, with a thunderbolt by his side. The smaller figure of a female, enchained, on left, is probably Uni being punished by Tinia. Turms, also a smaller figure, on right.

contrivance of evil you will win first reward when I lash you with whip strokes. Do you not remember that time you hung from on high and on your feet I slung two anvils, and about your hands drove a golden chain, unbreakable? You among the clouds and the bright sky hung, nor could the gods about tall Olympos endure it and stood about, but could not set you free. If I caught one I would seize and throw him from the threshold.[13]

In this Etruscan scene the anvils have been omitted, but it is easy to believe that Uni has her hands enchained, and most likely Turms "stands about" wishing he could free the goddess. This is the only known representation in ancient art of the punishment of the goddess.

But in Etruria, Uni and Tinia normally tend to demonstrate better accord than in Homer or Greek myth in general. The various children he fathered by other goddesses are frequently treated with acceptance by Uni, and she even acts

V.10 Bronze mirror, ca. 300 BCE. London, British Museum. After Bonfante 1990:fig. 19. Tinia gives birth to Menrva. From left to right: Laran, Thalna, Menrva and Tinia, Uni, and Maristinsta. Uni attends her consort Tinia, without jealousy, perhaps because of her role as a goddess of childbirth.

as midwife for the delivery of Menrva (Fig. V.10), partnering Thalna in vigilance as the child springs forth from her father's head. In fact, Uni seems to have been a goddess of childbirth in Etruria, just as at Rome, Juno Lucina played this role.

Uni appears on the Piacenza Liver in House 4, and as Juno in the heavens of Martianus in Region 2, demonstrating clearly her affinity with Tinia. Also, rather strangely, she dwells in the unfavorable Region 14 of Martianus as Juno Caelestis or Heavenly Juno, along with Saturn. There does not seem to be any representation in Etruscan art that reflects this designation. Further, though Roman authors tell us she threw the lightning bolt, she has not been identified in Etruscan art with this attribute. She does appear with weapons, however; like Astarte, Uni had a warlike aspect. She was sometimes represented armed, and instead of a helmet and breastplate, she wore the skin of a horned goat, occurring elsewhere in Italy in the Latin cult of Juno Sospita at Lanuvium.[14] A story unknown in Greece is the

V.11 Detail of painted black-figure amphora, ca. 550–535 BCE. London, British Museum. Photo: © Copyright Trustees of The British Museum. Hercle, supported by Menerva (far right), fights against Uni, wearing goatskin armor (like that of Juno Sospita). Tinia stands on the far right, brandishing a thunderbolt and attempting to deter Uni.

myth represented on a painted Etruscan amphora in the British Museum (Fig. V.11), where Uni appears in this garb, brandishing a sword, seemingly under attack by Hercle. Nearby are two large cauldrons adorned with serpents' heads, evidently the object of the dispute between the two adversaries. The reason for the quarrel and the outcome of the attack are unknown, but it is likely that Tinia (far right) requires them to make peace and that they end up becoming friends, collaborating in other adventures.[15]

The enmity between Hera and Herakles is, of course, notorious, and Etruscan art includes the standard Greek theme of the story of Hera sending the serpents to strangle the twins Herakles and Iphikles (Fig. V.12).[16] There are several details, however, that are surprising and original in the Etruscan version. Instead of Iphikles, we have Iolaus (labeled *Vile* in Etruscan), nephew of Herakles in Greece, who is frequently shown in Etruria as the twin of Hercle. The large serpents resemble sea monsters. In addition, the scene is unique in showing Uni and Tinia overlooking the scene as if through a window. The pair looks confrontational, as Tinia brandishes his thunderbolt, and Uni, raising her veil with the characteristic bride's gesture, holds up her scepter topped with a pomegranate.

But in other representations Uni and Hercle are often shown as friends, for example in a scene in which Uni is attacked by satyrs, the part-human, part-equine followers of Bacchus, and she is attended and defended by Hercle (Fig. V.13).[17] Details of this interesting collaboration are otherwise unknown. The most intriguing statement of their reconciliation lies in the series of representations of Hercle being adopted by Uni, in a most unusual ritual: the hero nurses at the breast of the

V.12 Painted red-figure vessel (stamnos) from Orvieto, Settecamini, ca. 350 BCE. Florence, Museo Archeologico Nazionale. Photo: Soprintendenza per i Beni Archeologici della Toscana. The infant Hercle strangles snakes sent by Uni (above, with Tinia) as his twin Vile runs away.

goddess (Figs. V.14-17). A beautiful rendering on a mirror from Volterra (Fig. V.14) shows Hercle bearded, leaning on his club, as the goddess sits enthroned. Tinia stands by and indicates a tablet that announces the import of the scene, one of the rare examples of a legible text about an Etruscan mythological theme. *Eca: sren: tva: iχnac: hercle: unial: clan: θras: ce* (ET Vt S.2), most likely meaning: "This shows how Hercle, the son of Uni, was adopted." Other divinities are present, but they are not inscribed. In the other representations, the hero is represented as youthful, even adolescent, rather than as the fully mature adult of the Volterra mirror. The cast of characters varies considerably from scene to scene, showing a situation that is common in the myth of Etruria. The Etruscans never had canonical texts dictating the way a scene was to be represented, and thus they rarely showed a standardized predictable theme. (There are a few important exceptions, as will be noted later.) Several Greek texts relate to the myth here,[18] but they only reinforce this point. They tell of how Hera was tricked into nursing the infant Herakles, and how the baby pulled so hard on her breast that she jerked him away, and her milk spilled out all over the sky, creating the Milky Way.

Obviously the story here has a radically different content. In one mirror, as Hercle is nursed, his Etruscan twin Vile eagerly watches the proceedings (Fig. V.15); in another version (Fig. V.16), the adoption takes place in a large, cheerful group of divinities that includes Tinia, Menrva and Turan, along with the victory goddess Mean, who tenders vegetation for the crowning of the triumphant youth. Finally, in a newly excavated, strange rendering of the theme (Fig. V. 17),[19] the youth nurses, as a winged goddess prepares to celebrate him (with a wreath? using

V.13 Bronze statuettes from a tripod, ca. 500–480 BCE. Copenhagen, Ny Carlsberg Glyptotek. Photo: Museum. Hercle and Uni as friends and opponents against the Satyrs, who appear on another part of the tripod (not shown).

V.14 Bronze mirror from Volterra, ca. 325 BCE. Florence, Museo Archeologico Nazionale. After ES:5.60. Hercle nurses at the breast of Uni and is thereby adopted and made immortal. Other participants, from left to right: Aplu (?), unknown figure, Hebe (?), and Tinia. In upper exergue a satyr drinks from and gazes into a patera probably seeking a prophecy from it. Winged child in lower exergue holds eggs.

a patera for a libation?) and a bird flies in carrying a shield for him. The female hovering behind Uni parallels the figure standing behind the goddess on the Volterra mirror who extends her mantle around Uni. She has not been specifically identified. Considering, however, that the story represented is the adoption of Hercle, and that he will now become a god worthy of the family of Tinia and Uni, this female figure may well represent the bride he takes upon arrival at Olympus in the Greek story of his deification: Hebe, the daughter of Hera.[20] The myth thus thematizes not only the adoption and apotheosis of Hercle, but possibly also the ceremony of marriage, of which Hera/Uni was patroness.

V.15 Bronze mirror, ca. 400–375 BCE. Bologna, Museo Civico Archaeologico. After CSE Italia: 1.1.15a. The youth Hercle nurses at the breast of Uni as his Etruscan twin Vile looks on.

Turan

The third goddess of the Judgment of Elcsntre, Turan, is normally assumed to be the victor, and thus she is shown in a very fine Etruscan mirror in the Indiana University Art Museum (Fig. V.18). In Etruria, as in Greece and Rome, she is the goddess *par excellence* of beauty, love, and sex, and the great majority of the representations in Etruscan art bear out these themes. As in Greece, her familiar creatures are the fertile egg-laying birds such as the dove, goose, and swan. She may be shown riding upon her swan (Fig. V.19), although she is also sometimes represented with her own wings.

Turan is also known in Etruria as caring for babies, as in Fig. IV.14, where the goddess, enthroned and holding a scepter with pomegranate, looks admiringly at Epiur (see also Fig. IV.15), and in Figs. V.5 and V.6, where she stands next to Menrva in the ritual myth of the Mariś babies. In fact, in Etruscan she may even be referred to with the word for "mother," *ati*. Only rarely, however, is she shown with her own son from Greek mythology, Eros (Fig. V.29; see the discussion below).[21]

V.16   Bronze mirror from
Vulci, ca. 400–350 BCE.
Berlin, Staatliche Museen.
After ES:5.59. Hercle
nurses at the breast of
Uni. Other figures, from
left to right: Mean, Turan,
Tinia, and Menrva. Uni
holds in her left hand an
object that resembles a
drinking horn (perhaps
for another ritual drink?).

The name Turan may be quite ancient, coming from the eastern Mediterranean, from a pre-Greek root meaning "Mistress" or "Lady."[22] The goddess seems to have received cult in Etruria, as is witnessed by inscriptions with dedications to her, but she is not on the Liver and was not set in the heavens by Martianus. Nor is she on the list of deities known to throw lightning. It is a sign of her importance in the calendar, however, that the Etruscan month of July, recorded in Latin as Traneus, was named after her.[23] An interesting clue to the reason for the exclusion of Turan from various aspects of cult comes from the Roman architectural writer Vitruvius (1.7.1-2), who notes that in a town planned in the Etruscan manner, the temple of "Venus" must be outside the city limits, "so that Venereal pleasure may not be customary to young men and matrons in the city."

V.17 Bronze mirror from Tarquinia, Fondo Scataglini, ca. 350–300 BCE. Tarquinia, Museo Archeologico Nazionale. After Serra Ridgway 1996: pl. 140. Hercle nurses at the breast of Uni in the presence of two unidentified goddesses. The unusual drawing style leaves some details unclear (for example, the relationship between the nursing Uni—seated?— and figure standing behind her).

In the Indiana mirror (Fig. V.18) the goddesses of the Judgment show a quite different comportment from that normally depicted in Greek art. Here they behave as cordial, even affectionate friends: Turan the victor holds her mirror, as Uni solicitously tilts her chin and adjusts her diadem, as if wishing to help the goddess to perfect her toilette. Menrva, recognizable by her helmet and a vestigial Medusa head on her breast, leans in from the left, holding a floral bud in her right hand, perhaps a gift for the winner. Behind her is the boyish figure of Elcsntre. The figure on the far right is unique, never occurring in the Greek version of the myth, and her presence is not fully understood. She is labeled *Alθaia*, Althaia, with a name that does occur in Greek myth but that seems unrelated to this story. She holds a bough of vegetation, perhaps a laurel of victory.[24]

The theme of the Judgment of Elcsentre is represented over and over on Etruscan mirrors, an obvious selection for this instrument of beauty. The basic elements of the mythologem are the three females, in poses that display their charms, and the single male figure, often seated and in some way indicating his role as

V.18 Bronze mirror, ca. 325–300 BCE. Bloomington, Indiana University Art Museum. After CSE U.S.A.:1.4a. Judgment of Elcsntre, with figures, from left to right: Elcsntre, Menrva, Uni, Turan, and Althaia. Chariot of the dawn in upper exergue. In lower exergue, Vile strangling serpents.

V.19 Bronze mirror, ca. 300–275 BCE. Paris, Louvre. After ES:4.321. Turan rides a swan, holding her mantle up with one hand and embracing the neck of the swan with the other.

judge, gazing, meditating (hand raised to his chin) or speaking his decision (hand extended in a pointing gesture). Much of this may be seen on a standardized specimen found at Tarquinia (Fig. V.20): Elcsntre looks over the three beauties, from left to right, nude Turan, equally-naked Uni, and Menrva.

The demand for mirrors with this subject led to it becoming logographic, a visual motto for the beauty of the user of the instrument, often with parts abbreviated. Indeed, it can be lamented that if there are no inscriptions, one cannot be sure whether the subject is the Judgment or some other theme that calls for a four-figure group. A mirror in Seattle belonging to the 3rd century BCE is a case in point, quite on the borderline (Fig. V.21).[25] The decoration is stylized with conventions typical in Late Etruscan art, including the box-like gowns and the triangular gable in the back to suggest a setting. There are three female figures in the foreground, and they may be (from left to right) Turan, Uni, and Menrva. Turan and Menrva wear a Phrygian-style head covering (that of Menrva seems to be a helmet), and a seated figure in the background wears a very similar hat. Is this Elcsntre? He fits the mythologem by being a male (judging by his mantle), by being seated and by

V.20 Bronze mirror from Tarquinia, 3rd century BCE. Oberlin, Allen Memorial Art Museum, Oberlin College. After CSE U.S.A.:1.28a. Judgment of Elcsntre, with participants, from left to right: Elcsntre, Turan, Uni, and Menrva.

raising his hand to his chin as if in thought. The gesture of the females is similar, though the fingers extend higher up on the face, and may well indicate that each goddess is gesturing toward herself, as if to say "Pick me!"[26]

There are still other surprises in this theme: on a mirror from Todi (Fig. V.22), the cast of characters includes, along with Turan, a *Snenaθ Turns*, "Handmaid of Turan," who carries her fan (far right) and on the left stands *Teurs*, i.e., Teukros, an early Trojan king, long before the time of Paris. But nothing can quite prepare us for the stunning variant in Paris (Fig. V.23) that shows the seated judge choosing among (left to right) Uni, Menrva, and a figure attended by a swan who has the breasts of a woman and the genitals of a man. Could Hermaphroditus have won the beauty contest in Etruria?[27]

V.21 Bronze mirror, 3rd century BCE. Seattle, Seattle Art Museum. After Nagy 1996:fig. 6. The Judgment of Elcsntre is stripped to its essentials, the three goddesses standing and the judge seated.

The depiction may well be meant as a jest, for yet another bizarre treatment of the "Judgment of Elcsntre," known on at least three mirrors, has been convincingly characterized as "an obscene parody."[28] A version in Brussels (Fig. V. 24) shows a wreathed male figure with three females in a composition which, even if it is not actually a Judgment, would certainly recall the popular theme to whoever looked at the mirror. The female figures, easily equated with the three goddesses though not individually identifiable, are grandly dressed and raise their hands in the typical gesture of deliberation. The "judge" no longer raises his hand to his chin, for both his hands are quite occupied with lifting his skirt, and thus exposing himself to the goddesses. The mirror is worn away in a critical area and we cannot see clearly what the goddesses saw, but we can still understand and share the humor of the reversal of roles. Instead of the goddesses displaying themselves, they become

V.22   Bronze mirror from Todi, ca. 300 BCE. Rome, Museo Nazionale Etrusco di Villa Giulia. After *Monumenti Antichi*:23, pl. 3. Judgment of Elcsntre, with participants from left to right: Teurs, Elcsntre, Uni, Menrva, Turan, and Snenath Turns. In upper exergue, chariot of the dawn. In lower exergue, youthful Hercle, seated despondently over flames.

V.23 Bronze relief mirror, ca. 300 BCE (doubted by some as a forgery). Paris, Petit Palais, Musées des Beaux-Arts de la Ville de Paris. Photo: Photothèque des Musées de la Ville de Paris. Judgment of Elcsntre, with participants, left to right: Elcsntre, Uni, Menrva, and hermaphrodite with swan.

the judges of Elcsntre as he shows his charms! This kind of obscenity is not common in Etruscan mythological art, and it is impossible to be sure about the overall intent of the artist or the owner who commissioned or chose the decoration of the mirror.[29]

Closely related to the Judgment series are the many representations of Turan as the protector and advocate of Elcsntre and his bride Elinai (=Helen). She tenderly introduces the couple in one scene (Fig. V.25), and in another oversees the birth of their child Ermania (=Hermione; Fig. V.26). Elinai remains her protegée, as for example, when the Greeks sack Troy (Fig. V.27), and Menle (=Menelaus) threatens his wife. As Elinai seizes the statue of Menrva (the Palladion) for protection, Turan and Thethis attempt to restrain the angry warrior, while Aivas (Ajax) and a nude, spear-bearing female labeled Phulsphna watch the action. (The name Phulphsna has been compared with that of Polyxena, daughter of Priam; in that case we have the novelty of Polyxena as a warrior.) Turan may also protect Elcsntre from danger, as seen on Etruscan ash urns, where the hero kneels upon an altar and a naked, winged Turan bars the way of a menacing soldier.[30] The story seems

V.24 Bronze mirror from Praeneste, 3rd century BCE. Brussels, Musées Royaux d'Art et d'Histoire. After Lambrechts 1978:p. 33. The theme of the Judgment of Elcsntre receives a surprising twist, perhaps as a joke. The judge exposes himself to the three goddesses by lifting high his tunic. Since all three are depicted alike, it is not possible to know which is Uni, Turan, or Menrva.

to be that of the Recognition of Paris, in which the exiled Paris returns to Troy to compete in games, and is attacked by the other contestants, including his brother Deiphobos, because of his success.

By far the most frequent appearance of Turan in Etruscan art is in the romantic myth of Turan and Atunis (=Adonis). The goddess is regularly represented as mature, and her lover as younger, even a boy. In one scene (Fig. V.28), Atunis, as if in an inversion of the theme of the young girl in the embrace of her husband-to-be, pulls out his mantle in a display gesture. Much of the central medallion of this mirror is taken up by the huge bird of Turan, here labeled as *Tusna*. All around the rim of the mirror are the various spirits who tend to the love of Turan, spirits who will be discussed at length in Chapter VII. In another similar representation (Fig. V.29) the boy Atunis swoons backwards for a passionate kiss, as Aplu watches, and the son of Turan, labled *Turnu*, sits and plays with a lovers' toy named *iynx* in Latin, the same word as used for the bird called a wryneck in English. The instrument is often associated with magical spells and oracles. It is significant that Turan

V.25 Bronze mirror from Perugia, 4th century BCE. New York, Metropolitan Museum of Art. After CSE U.S.A. 3.9a. Turan stands between Elcsntre and Elinai, her left hand extended to touch the chin of Elinai as if to direct her attention toward Elcsentre.

also holds an *iynx*, but it dangles limply from her right hand (perhaps to indicate that she has used it, but no longer needs it). The child Turnu fits in every way with the identifiable image of Eros or Cupid, as a naked winged boy. As he handles the *iynx*, he raises his left leg up onto a rock, assuming a prophetic stance. An actual wryneck sits in the middle of the ground on which all are standing, possibly as a bird of omen that may help Turnu in making a prophecy about the couple.[31]

An especially serious rendering of the Turan-Atunis theme occurs on a large mirror dating ca. 320 BCE (Fig. V.30).[32] Here Fate is personified in a grand, beautiful winged, wreathed lady who holds a hammer in one hand while with the other she inserts a nail into a boar's head. She affixes the head to the wall with an air of finality appropriate for the dire message that is communicated. On the left are Turan and Atunis, in whose romance the boar played a critical part, wounding Atunis to death and thus separating the lovers. On the right are Atalanta and Meleager, whose success in the Calydonian boar hunt unfortunately led to the downfall and death of Meleager. The two couples were not connected in mythological

V.26 Bronze mirror, early 5th century BCE. Paris, Bibliothèque Nationale, Cabinet des Médailles. Turan attends the birth of Ermania (=Hermione) to Elinai. A sphinx flies in from the upper right (to announce the birth?), and there is also a footstool with sphinx protomes upon it, underneath the bed. Elcsntre sits beside the bed. The pair of pointed-toe shoes hanging in the circular field logically belongs to the new mother.

narrative, but are brought together here as part of the mythologem of the death of the hero and separation from his beloved as a result of the highly dangerous boar hunt. They are united in the composition as well by the goddess of Fate in the center, who is here labeled Athrpa. The name obviously comes from Greek, reflecting one of the three Fates, Atropos, whose role was to decide where to cut the thread spun out for each mortal and thus end life.

Instead of scissors, Athrpa uses the hammer and nail, well known as having sacred significance in Etruria. We know, for example, that a periodic ceremony at the temple of the goddess Nortia at Volsinii featured the driving of a nail into the wall of the temple (Livy 7.3.7). The reason is not certain, though Livy stated that it served to mark the passing of time.[33] Since the Romans equated the Etruscan Nortia with Fortuna or Necessitas, it seems likely that the driving of her nail may have reflected the action of fate or destiny. The Athrpa mirror probably has a similar import.

V.27   Bronze mirror from Cerveteri, 4th century BCE. London, British Museum. After ES:4. 398. Elinai takes refuge at the Palladion as Menle attacks her. From left to right: Thethis, Menle, Turan, Elinai, Aivas, and Phulphsna (=Polyxena?). In upper exergue, chariot of the dawn. In lower exergue, the boy Hercle on an amphora raft. His lion skin seems to be incorporated into the sail on the raft.

V.28 Bronze mirror, ca. 325 BCE. St. Petersburg, State Hermitage Museum. After ES:4.322. The embrace of Atunis and Turan, attended by swan or goose, labeled Tusna (left), and Zipna (right), with perfume bottle and applicator. Around the border, attendant spirits, clockwise from bottom: Hathna (a satyr), Alpan, Achvizr, Munthuch, Mean, and two unnamed spirits.

V.29 Bronze mirror from Castel Viscardo, near Orvieto, ca. 375–350 BCE. Orvieto, Museo Archeologico Nazionale. After Feruglio 1998, fig. 2. Turan and Atunis embrace as Aplu looks on, left, and Turnu, son of Turan, plays with the love-toy, the *iynx*.

Artumes

We must also include here the Etruscan Artemis, whose name occurs as *Artumes* or as *Aritimi*, and who probably does not in fact qualify for the title of "great goddess" in Etruria. Her claim depends on the identity of a female figure shown frequently in the very earliest Etruscan representations, who is depicted as controlling a pair of animals such as lions, birds, sphinxes, deer, horses, or even wolves (Fig. V.31).[34] A powerful nature goddess is known in Greece from the Bronze Age, and is often referred to as *Potnia Theron*, "Mistress of Animals." She has been equated with Artemis in Greece, and there are those who support this designation

V.30 Bronze mirror, ca. 325–300 BCE. Berlin, Staatliche Museen. After Zimmer 1987:fig. 19. Athrpa, goddess of fate, affixes a boar's head with hammer and nail; Turan and Atunis (left), Atlenta and Meliacr (right).

in Etruria as well. But there are no known representations of the Mistress of Animals with an Etruscan inscription labeling her as Artemis, and it is probably best to reserve judgment and await new evidence on this subject.

For there is little evidence of Artemis being an important deity in Etruria. She is not on the Liver, not in the heavens of Martianus, and is not known for throwing lightning. Inscriptions with dedications to her are relatively few, and no temple or altar is certainly dedicated to her.[35] She provides an interesting case of a Greek Olympian deity who appears as either male or female in Etruria, perhaps a result of the fact that she was little known and her image remained ambiguous to the Etruscans.

There are three possible instances of a male Artumes in Etruria. There can be no doubt about the gender of the deity in a conversation group on a mirror from Tarquinia (Fig. V.32), where the two figures on the left, clearly marked as males

V.31 Bronze silvered belt buckle plaque, ca. 600 BCE. Vatican Museums, Museo Etrusco Gregoriano. Photo: Museum. The design, repeated, shows a lady of the beasts attended by leaping wolf puppies and two male figures. This may be one of the earliest Etruscan representations of Artumes.

V.32 Bronze mirror from Tarquinia, 3rd century BCE. Copenhagen, Danish National Museum. After CSE Denmark:1.21a. Assembly of deities with, from left to right: Aplu, a nude male figure labeled as Artumes, Malavis, and Hercle. The combination of these mythological figures is unique.

V.33   Bronze mirror, ca. 350 BCE. Tübingen, Sammlung des Archäologischen Instituts der Eberhard-Karls Universität. After CSE Bundesrepublik Deutschland:3.17a. Menrva confronts the dragon guarding the Golden Fleece, as Artumes (male) looks on. Jason is not visible and perhaps has been devoured by the dragon.

by their genitals, are labeled Aplu and Artumes. Completing the scene are the figures of Malavis, a bride in Etruscan myth (see Chapter VII), and Hercle. On a mirror with the theme of the Golden Fleece (Fig. V.33), rather strange because it shows the dragon and the fleece but no image of Jason, Athena seems to interrogate the dragon, and she is attended by a seated figure labeled Artumes. The latter is represented as wearing a mantle that leaves one shoulder bare, a fashion that is masculine, and seems to have short hair.

Finally, and most spectacularly, a bronze votive figure in Paris, showing a handsome young male, is dedicated to Aritimi, and very likely again shows the deity as masculine (Fig. V.34). The statuette was given by a lady named Fasti Rufriś as an offering on behalf of her son: *mi:flereś:spulare:aritimi fasti rufriś:trce:clen: ceχa* (*ET* OB 3.2). It is frequently named as her brother Aplu, but he is nowhere mentioned in the inscription, and given the other masculine representations of Artemis, there is no reason to resort to this identification.[36]

V.34 Bronze votive statue, Second half of 4th century BCE. Paris, Bibliothèque Nationale. After Pfiffig 1975:fig. 110. The statue bears an inscription to Artumes (spelled Aritimi here) but has frequently been identified as Aplu.

There are several other notable scenes of Aplu and Artumes together, e.g., a mirror from Vulci (Fig. V.35) that shows the pair facing each other. The gender is in accord with Greek myth, but it is surprising to find that Artumes, rather than her twin, is playing the lyre. On another mirror, Aplu has the lyre, but Artumes remains musical, for she is holding a pair of pipes. Here, the goddess known for her virginity in Greece appears as almost completely nude. She is attended by her familiar animal, the deer. Artumes rarely appears in action myths in Etruria, but occasionally she and her brother use their bows and arrows against their adversaries. A quite charming scene apparently shows the twins as children (Fig. V.36), attacking a great serpent, the Python of Delphi, a deed normally attributed to Apollo alone. Judging from the male parts depicted on the second child, Artumes is leading the way in the attack. The adult female with them must be their mother (Leto, called Letun in Etruria).

One of the most eloquent myths of Artemis in Etruria is the story of Esia, known from its representation on two very similar mirrors (Fig. V.37 shows one in Brussels, the better preserved of the two). Artumes is depicted carrying a small female figure labeled Esia, wrapped snugly in a mantle, as the goddess clutches her bow and arrows in one hand. The wrapping and carrying of the body is a common motif in Etruria for the transport of the soul and the implication that Esia is the soul of someone slain is consistent with the Greek idea that Artemis in Greece is the one responsible for taking away the life of maidens who die young. Here the goddess seems to discuss the fate of the maiden with a winged Menrva and the god of wine, Fufluns, both of whom gesture in a lively manner. Out of the ground below comes a head, a motif that appears regularly in Etruscan art to indicate that a prophecy is being announced. We do not know how the story ends, though some have suggested that this may be a rendering of a rare Greek myth according to which Artemis killed Ariadne, and then presented her to Dionysos to be revived and made immortal.

Catha, Cel Ati, and Thesan

There are three other deities of Etruria who qualify as goddesses of significance, but evidence is scant. Recent excavations at the great sanctuary of Pyrgi have shown that the goddess Catha or Cavtha, who appears on the Liver, House

V.35 Bronze mirror from Vulci, ca. 470 BCE. Berlin, Staatliche Museen, Antikensammlung. After CSE Bundesrepublik Deutschland:4.7a. Aplu and Artumes face each other as Artumes plays the lyre.

V.36 Bronze mirror from Cerveteri, 450–400 BCE. Rome, Museo Nazionale Etrusco di Villa Giulia. After ES:4.291A. The twin children Artumes and Aplu attack a great serpent as their mother encourages them and a satyr and maenad look over the hill in evident surprise.

23, was probably a very important goddess of cult. Inscriptions refer to her as śeχ, "Daughter," and some have suggested that she is the same as the Daughter of the Sun in Region 6 of Martianus.[37] Being the daughter of the sun may well mean that her significance was lunar.[38] She is believed to be the consort of another major deity at Pyrgi, Śuri, and the pair is thought to have Underworld connections. Unfortunately we have no clues as to her appearance or her mythology.

The goddess Cel, appearing on the Liver, House 13, is referenced in a group of votive figures found near Lake Trasimeno dedicated to *Cel Ati*, i.e., "Mother Cel,"[39] and it is clear from other evidence that she is in fact "Mother Earth," for a mirror showing the battle of gods and Giants has the label, *Celsclan*, son of Cel, beside one of the Giants, who is being attacked by Laran (Fig. V.38). Celsclan is a fairly literal translation of the name Giant, which means "born from Gaia," or Earth. Here the Giant is shown fighting in typical gigantesque style, lifting a boulder up over his head—a makeshift weapon beloved of the sons of Earth. Yet another representation of Giants shows them with snake-legs, in an Etruscan tradition that goes back

V.37 Bronze mirror,
late 5th century BCE.
Brussels, Musées Royaux
d'Art et d'Histoire. After
Lambrechts 1978: 71.
Artumes brings the
wrapped figure of Esia
and presents her to Men-
rva and Fufluns. Below, a
prophetic Silenus head.

to Archaic times (Fig. X. 25). In this case, they are accompanied by a goddess
with lower body made up of vegetation. It has been argued convincingly that this
depiction in fact shows Mother Earth, a precious image indeed.[40]

Cel very likely is the namesake of the Etruscan month of Celi (September;
TLE 824). In spite of various indications of cult, there is not nearly as much evidence of the popularity of this deity as there is for Uni, Turan, or Menrva; she thus
does not emerge as the great mother goddess of the Etruscans.

Finally, we may turn to Thesan,[41] goddess of the dawn, who is shown in a radiant close-up on a bronze mirror of the 4th century BCE (Fig. V. 39). She wears a
winged cap and a necklace with the bubble ornament, the *bulla*; her head is surrounded by an aureole with rays of the sun. Although Thesan does not occur on
the Piacenza Liver, nor is there a reference to a goddess of the dawn in the heavens

V.38 Bronze mirror from Populonia, ca. 400 BCE. Florence, Museo Archeologico Nazionale. Photo: Soprintendenza per i Beni Archeologici della Toscana. A warrior, Laran, attacks a Giant labeled Celsclan. Radiating lines above the upraised hands and the head of the giant indicate the boulder he throws at his opponent.

of Martianus, this deity did receive cult in Etruria, as is indicated by references to offerings for her on the Zagreb mummy wrapping and by a tablet with a dedication to her found near Temple A at the important international sanctuary at the Etruscan port of Pyrgi.[42] There is a likelihood that she was in fact one of the principal deities worshipped there. Although Thesan is often compared with the Greek Eos and the Roman Aurora, Greek texts suggest that they understood her cult persona at Pyrgi to be rather a counterpart of Leukothea, the "White Goddess," who had a special connection with the sea, and who in turn was assimilated to the Roman Mater Matuta, a goddess of the morning and of childbirth.[43]

The associations are complex, and the evidence from Pyrgi continues to be surprising and elusive. One of the buildings there (probably the 20-celled structure) was decorated with a series of antefixes of unique iconography, having astral and marine references that would be consistent with the worship of Thesan (Fig. V.40). The types include a goddess carrying two stars, perhaps Thesan herself, and

V.39 Bronze mirror, ca. 325–300 BCE. Essen, Museum Folkwang. After CSE Bundesrepublik Deutschland:1.13a. The head of the goddess of the dawn, Thesan, is shown; her name is inscribed beside her.

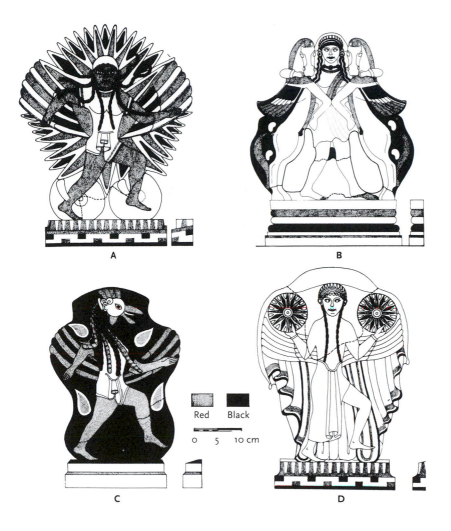

V.40 Terracotta antefixes from Pyrgi, late 6th century BCE. Pyrgi, Antiquarium and Rome, Museo Nazionale Etrusco di Villa Giulia. After Haynes 2000: fig. 153. Images show a running or flying youth, perhaps Usil (A); a goddess with two horses (B); a rooster-headed god, running or flying (C); and an astral goddess, perhaps Thesan (D).

A · B · C · D

Red · Black

0   5   10 cm

a running youth with a sunburst behind him (probably the sun-god Usil), a goddess who tames two horses, and a rooster-headed deity surrounded by drops of water; he is otherwise quite unknown, but a good candidate for morning iconography.[44]

Thesan appears elsewhere as a more recognizable parallel for Eos and Aurora. In particular, she may be seen represented frequently in Etruscan art as winged and flying through the air carrying a male youth (Fig. V.41), in some cases evidently her own son in Greek myth, Memnon, judging by the limpness of his dead body and by the armor he wears (though sometimes the body is stripped of its armor).[45] At times the youth appears alert and nude and in such cases it may be argued that she is carrying off one of her lovers, such as Tithonos or the hunter Kephalos.[46] But it should be remembered that in antiquity there was a widespread belief that the soul of a deceased person left the body at dawn,[47] and thus these scenes may represent an allegorical theme.

V.41 Bronze mirror, ca. 470–460 BCE. Cleveland, Museum of Art. After CSE U.S.A.:1.15a. A winged goddess, Thesan, moves to the left, tenderly carrying the armored body of a youth, probably her son, Memnun. His bare head falls backward (his helmet lies on the ground), and his limbs dangle lifelessly.

Thesan is almost certainly the deity represented in the upper zone of many mirrors (e.g., Figs. V.18, V.27), driving the four-horse chariot of the dawn to indicate the beginning (and continuation) of a particular day on which a particular event did or should take place. That is, Thesan has a calendrical role, and it may be conjectured that many scenes with the motif of the chariot of daybreak actually commemorate a feast day of a certain deity or ritual.

Thesan is frequently shown as astral and glowing, with an aureole or halo around her head, or appears with other deities with such an attribute. She takes her place in a handsome group of cosmic figures on a mirror from Tuscania (Fig. VI. 36), where the sun god, Usil, bears a halo of light, as he is flanked on the left by the god of the sea, Nethuns, and on the right by the goddess of the dawn.

To close this chapter, we turn to one of the most famous Etruscan representations of a goddess, a true cult statue, found in the sanctuary at Orvieto called the Cannicella (Fig. V.42) and dating to the Archaic period.[48] There are many things about this statue that are quite unusual. To begin with the sculpture is of marble, a rare material in Etruscan art and architecture, but even more surprising is the fact that two different kinds of marble were used, evidently to piece the statue together. The breasts were attached separately, and one of these was never found in the excavations. The figure, under life size but still monumental in aspect, is a unique example of a goddess appearing in the nude in the Archaic period in Etruria. Finally, it is worth noting that the sanctuary in which the statue was found is a cemetery, and thus the cult of the deity played a very particular role.

Who is the goddess? She is conventionally referred to as "The Cannicella Venus," actually an unfortunate habit, because it blocks our ability to interpret the statue on its own terms. It is true that her sexuality is emphasized, but the attribute of nudity need not be confined to Turan. (Uni, for example, is shown nude in

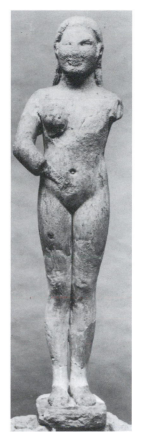

V.42 Marble statuette from the Cannicella sanctuary, Orvieto, late 6th century BCE. Orvieto, Museo Faina. Photo: DAI. The identity of the nude goddess is not certain, but she may be Vei, a deity named in an inscription from the sanctuary.

V.43 Relief sculpture in nenfro (tufa) from Tarquinia, ca. 550 BCE. Tarquinia, Museo Archeologico Nazionale. Photo: Soprintendenza per i Beni Archeologici del Lazio. In lower zone, a figure identified as female, naked with legs spread wide and arms raised. She has been interpreted as a goddess giving birth, but no context of narrative for this depiction is known. The type of relief, featuring rectangular frames flanked by a stair-like pattern, is known only at Tarquinia; the provenance, when known, is funerary. Above the crouching figure, a winged goddess flies left.

Etruria.) Is she perhaps identical with the unusual naked female figure, also unidentified, depicted in Archaic art with her legs spread wide as if to give birth, also from a funerary context (Fig. V.43)?[49] The images of this goddess figure occur on stone plaques from Tarquinia (only); they have been found exclusively in tombs.

A focus on sexuality and the concomitant fertility makes very good sense in the funerary sanctuary where the Cannicella goddess was found, and the primary point to establish is that she is a goddess of the dead.[50] There is a very good chance that her name has actually been preserved, for a votive bronze plaque from the Cannicella records a dedication to a deity named Vei, thought by many to be the counterpart of the Greek Demeter. She is little known, but a growing number of inscriptions give evidence of her cult among the Etruscans. Vei, too, may be among the great goddesses of the Etruscans.[51]

More Gods VI

After Tinia, it is difficult to say which Etruscan gods are next in importance. Various criteria may be used to evaluate their significance. Is the deity named on the Piacenza Liver, i.e., was he the recipient of cult connected with revelation? Does he appear in the heavens of Martianus Capella? What evidence for the power of the deity is provided by archaeology, in the form of inscriptions, votives, temples? What other clues exist about the status of the god (e.g., family relationships, sheer frequency of references, etymology of name)? Most important for the purpose of this book, what evidence is there for true mythical narratives about the deity within an Etruscan context?

At this point we encounter a very Hellenized stratum of Etruscan myth and religion, for we find that almost all of the candidates for the next places in the hierarchy (if indeed we should speak of a hierarchy) are brothers or sons of Zeus/ Tinia. This chapter is devoted to Fufluns, Turms, Sethlans and Aplu (all sons of Tinia), along with Laran (probably also son of Tinia) and Mariś.[1] In fact several sons of Tinia who will not be considered in this chapter are really more important than the figures treated here: Hercle and the twins Kastur and Pultuce (=the Dioskouroi), who in Greece were the sons of mortal women and thus are technically heroes, rather than gods. (As will be discussed, in Etruria this distinction may not be relevant). They have been allotted sections in the chapter on Heroes (VIII), and will be discussed there at some length. This chapter closes with Nethuns, brother of Tinia. Their other brother Aita (Hades), will be discussed in the chapter on the Underworld.

Fufluns

Fufluns, god of wine, and very similar to the Greek Dionysos, may well be the second most potent Etruscan male deity after Tinia. He is named twice on the Liver (Houses 9 and 24) and appears as the god Liber (=Roman Bacchus) in Region 7 of Martianus. He was already present in central Italy by the 7th century BCE, and inscriptions record a number of dedications to him, especially in the city of Vulci, where he was referred to as Fufluns Pachies.[2] His charming Etruscan name of Fufluns is thought to be related to an Etruscan word meaning "bud" or "sprout," referring to him as a vegetation god. The designation Pachies is quite obviously the equivalent of the name Bacchus (the Etruscans did not use the letter *b*, but instead devoiced it as *p*) and there is evidence that Bacchic cult became strong, even rampant, in Etruria in the Hellenistic period. As a result of Greek influence, the cult became so notorious and violent in Etruria, spreading to and infecting Rome,

VI.1 Bronze mirror from near Viterbo, 470 BCE. Brussels, Musées Royaux d'Art et d'Histoire. After Lambrechts 1978, p. 129. A maenad and a satyr dance merrily; they are labeled as Munthuch (left), who is dressed as a fine lady or goddess and Chelphun (right), who sports an animal skin cape and has pointed ears, a horse's tail, and a hairy chest—all typical satyr characteristics.

that it had to be suppressed by the Roman Senate, with the famous decree *On the Bacchanals*, of 186 BCE. The event was described by the historian Livy (39.8):

> The trouble had started with the arrival in Etruria of a Greek of humble origin . . . . he dealt in sacrifices and soothsaying. But his method of infecting people's minds with error was not by the open practice of his rites and the public advertisement of his trade and his system; he was the hierophant of secret ceremonies performed at night. There were initiations which at first were imparted to only a few; but they soon began to be widespread among men and women. The pleasures of drinking and feasting were added to the religious rites. . . . When wine had inflamed their feelings, and night and the mingling of the sexes and of different ages had extinguished all power of moral judgment, all sorts of corruption began to be practiced. . . . The corruption was not confined to one kind of evil, the promiscuous violation of free men and women; the cult was also a source of false witnesses, forged documents and wills, and perjured evidence, dealing also in poisons and in wholesale murders among the devotees . . . the violence was concealed because no cries

VI.2 Bronze mirror cover with relief sculpture, 3rd century BCE. London, British Museum. Photo: © Copyright Trustees of The British Museum. The bronze piece served as a cover or lid for a disc mirror, rather like a modern lady's compact. The scene represented is the popular theme of the drunken Fufluns, supported by a winged boy and with a musician to lead his way.

for help could be heard against the shriekings, the banging of drums and the clashing of cymbals in the scene of debauchery and bloodshed.[3]

It is not known when Dionysiac frenzies among the Etruscans may have begun. From an early date in art there are numerous examples of the cavorting rustic spirits who followed the god—maenads (nymphs) and the half-animal creatures known as satyrs. Munthuch dances with the satyr Chelphun–the names are both unknown in Greece[4]—on a mirror of the 5th century from Viterbo (Fig. VI.1), testifying to the local adaptation of these mythical cult devotees. Other familiar figures of the Bacchic routs occur, in particular Silenus, the balding old satyr who gets hopelessly drunk, but who is also very wise and has great prophetic powers. In Etruria, he may appear as a head emerging from the ground or the sky to deliver his prophecy (Figs. II.13 and V.37). Fufluns himself is often shown lurching along in a drunken stupor, carrying his characteristic wand, the thyrsos, attended by his revelers (Fig. VI.2).

Other themes from the life of Fufluns were popular in Etruscan art. We have already noted the birth of the god from the thigh of Tinia (Fig. IV.11), attended by Etruscan spirits Thalna and Mean; Aplu stands to the left and a prophesying head of Silenus, hair wild from the *afflatus* of the god, appears above. The sense is

VI.3 Bronze mirror, 350–325 BCE. Vatican Museums, Museo Gregoriano Etrusco. After ES:4, 298. Turms carries the baby Fufluns away from his father. Tinia waves his right hand, while his left hand loosely holds a bird-topped scepter.

VI.4 Bronze mirror from Vulci, late 4th century BCE. Philadelphia, University of Pennsylvania Museum of Archaeology and Anthropology. After Turfa 2005:235. Fufluns, holding a thyrsos, embraces an older woman thought to be his mother Semla. The figure standing by is Turms, holding his characteristic hat in his right hand. He raises his left hand in a gesture often used to show that a divinity has been sighted.

that the newborn child is destined to accomplish special things. The sequel to the scene is shown on an Etruscan mirror from Vulci (Fig. VI.3), where Turms seems to carry the baby away from his father, presumably to be raised by nymphs, as in the Greek story.

There are several mirrors that show Fufluns in the company of his mother Semla (Figs.VI.4-5). In a scene on a mirror in Philadelphia, he stands with her, holding his thyrsos. The theme of the two together is a little unexpected, given that Semele was supposedly burned up by the lightning bolt of Zeus before her baby was born. But it has been pointed out that there are passages in ancient literature referring to Dionysos going to the Underworld to bring her back.[5] Not so easily explained is the explicitly romantic connection between the two (Fig. VI.5), showing them in the same erotically passionate embrace used for the representation of Turan and Atunis (Fig. V.29). Aplu looks on, but Turnu has been replaced by a piping child satyr. The ardent couple recurs elsewhere, and cannot but raise some questions about an unusual relationship between mother and son in Etruria.

ETRUSCAN MYTH, SACRED HISTORY, AND LEGEND

VI.5 Bronze mirror from Vulci, 400–350 BCE. Berlin, Staatliche Museen, Antikensammlung. After CSE Deutsche Demokratische Republik:1.5b. Fufluns embraces an older woman, here labeled Semla. Left is Aplu with a laurel branch and a seated satyr boy making music.

As a youth Fufluns has a romance with Areatha, the Etruscan Ariadne (Fig. VI.6), attended by his mother and a satyr named Sime. The pair also occurs on a problematic mirror, from Bolsena (near Orvieto), showing a story so far without parallel in Greece or Italy (Fig. VI.7). Fufluns and Areatha stand in the center, flanked on the left by Castur and with a groveling youth below on the right, pulling on the leg of Fufluns in a gesture that seems to entreat. Fufluns raises his right arm in a threatening gesture (not easy to interpret, but he may have a weapon such as a rock in his right hand). The youth is labeled Eiasun, which ought to equal Jason, but no such story of the Greek Jason and Dionysos and Ariadne is known. The presence of Castur implies that the tale comes from the Argonaut cycle.[6]

Yet another elusive matter is the figure of the small winged boy, who stands with a pitcher in one hand and a tilted patera in the other, raised over the head of Eiasun in a gesture that normally means the individual is being consecrated and that a sacrifice is under way. He is labeled Aminth, and through a specious etymo-

VI.6 Bronze mirror from Chiusi, 350–325 BCE. London, British Museum. After ES:4. 299. Fufluns and Areatha embrace as the satyr Sime (left) watches; right is seated Semla. Fufluns holds a lyre.

VI.6 Bronze mirror from Chiusi, 350–325 BCE. London, British Museum. After ES:4. 299. Fufluns and Areatha embrace as the satyr Sime (left) watches; right is seated Semla. Fufluns holds a lyre.

logical connection has been identified with Amor, i.e., Eros.[7] We have seen that Eros/Amor is identified convincingly by the inscription *Turnu* (V.29), and without further evidence it is best not to posit a second Etruscan name for the Greco-Roman deity. The ending in *-th* , in any case, refers to an agent in Etruscan, and this little spirit is probably, "One who . . .," i.e., some kind of personification (cf. the discussion of personifications in Chapter VII). Until further evidence appears we can go no further with this interesting mythological narrative.

Fufluns also appears on another puzzling mirror from the Orvieto area (Castelgiorgio; Fig. VI.8) with a tall, lovely goddess inscribed with the Italic name of Vesuna,[8] perhaps meant to be understood as a maenad in ecstasy, since she is dressed in an animal skin and seems to hold a thyrsos in her proper right hand (behind the back of Fufluns). She wears a crown with a crescent upon it. The scene relates to prophecy, as we may deduce from the way in which the patera is used here, in a Dionysiac ritual that differs from the one seen in the Aminth mirror. Fufluns holds up the saucer in his proper left hand, to be filled with wine from

VI.7 Bronze mirror from Bolsena, 300–275 BCE. Florence, Museo Archeologico Nazionale. After ES:5.88.2. The unusual scene shows Eiasun (=Jason?) embracing the leg of Fufluns, evidently in entreaty. From left to right: Castur, Areatha, Fufluns, and Eiasun, and the little winged figure of Aminth, who seems to hold a sacrificial patera over the head of Eiasun.

the pitcher in his right hand, so that the shining surface may be used as a mirror for obtaining a vision. This practice, known as *lekanomanteia*, is well attested in Greece and Italy[9] and is clearly displayed on a red-figured kylix (drinking cup) from Chiusi, where a bearded Fufluns and a female attendant (again, probably a maenad) gaze at the patera she holds and seek a message (Fig. VI.9).

On the Castelgiorgio mirror an attendant labeled Svutaf gently turns the head of Vesuna so that she will look into the patera and see the revelation. This is the only occurrence of Svutaf in Etruscan art, a vaguely hermaphroditic figure with elongated body and a pony-tail hairstyle that looks feminine. Predictably some scholars have suggested *he* is Eros, but again convincing evidence is lacking.[10] It is quite possible that he may be a personification of some other quality associated with sex and love, such as Desire. Hercle sits on the left with his club between his knees, awaiting the outcome of the consultation. His connection with Vesuna and the ritual proceedings is brought out by the fact that he, too, has a crescent moon on his head. This mirror has frequently been interpreted as showing Fufluns and Vesuna as a couple, but in fact their association may be no closer than that of Dionysos with one of his maenads. Vesuna could be seeking a prophecy in regard to

VI.8 Bronze mirror from Castelgiorgio, near Orvieto, ca. 325–300 BCE. Baltimore, MD, Walters Art Museum. Drawing by Elizabeth Wahle. Fufluns, wearing a crown, holds a patera in his left hand and a pitcher in his right. He assists Vesuna, in maenad's costume, in reading a prophecy. Svutaf (right) turns her head toward the patera. Hercle, seated on the left, awaits the outcome. Cf. commentary on Fig. VI.9.

VI.9 Painted red-figure drinking cup (kylix), ca. 350–300 BCE. Berlin, Staatliche Museen. Photo: Bildarchiv Preussischer Kulturbesitz. A bearded Fufluns holds his drinking tankard (kantharos) in his right hand and looks to his left to gaze into a patera held up by a female attendant, who holds a pitcher in her proper left hand. The pair is practicing *lekanomanteia*, the reading of a prophecy in a liquid.

Hercle, and her vision could have to do with a connection with him, rather than Fufluns. There is no need to propose, as is sometimes done,[11] that Vesuna is the consort of Fufluns, a kind of "Etruscan Ariadne" (as noted above, Ariadne's name in Etruria is Areatha); the myth told here should be allowed to make its own statement, that is, that this is a story about an individual named Vesuna.

A similar methodological problem arises in regard to the scene of the presentation of Esia by Artemis (Fig. V.37), which shows a bearded, mature Fufluns. His role in the scene is by no means clear; he and Menrva throw up their hands in a type of gesture that suggests reception of some significant revelation, presumably the prophecy uttered by the Silenus head coming up from the ground. Again, scholars have rushed to call her the "Etruscan version of Ariadne," but there is nothing to indicate that he will marry Esia and make her immortal, as he did with Ariadne. We should reserve judgment until further support for that idea appears and simply call this the myth of a maiden named Esia.

We may close our discussion of Fufluns with reference to a myth well known in Greece, since it was told at length in the Homeric *Hymn* to Dionysos, the kidnapping of Dionysos by Tyrrhenian (Etruscan) pirates. The famous representation

VI.10 Greek black-figure vessel painted by Exekias, ca. 550–540 BCE. Munich, Antikensammlungen und Glyptothek. Photo: Museum. Dionysos sails in the ship in which he was taken prisoner, having turned his captives, the Tyrrhenian pirates, into leaping dolphins and caused his grape vine to sprout from the ship.

in Greek art by Exekias, dated ca. 540 BCE. (Fig. VI.10), shows the god after he took control of the ship and turned the pirates into leaping dolphins. An Etruscan black-figure vase of about thirty years later does not show Fufluns, only the Etruscan pirates who are being turned into dolphins (Fig. VI.11). We can follow quite literally the transformation of their bodies as they leap over the waves.

Turms

The origin of the name Turms (also spelled Turm, Turmus, and Turamus) is quite unknown, but this figure provides a fairly close parallel for the messenger god called Hermes in Greece and Mercury in Rome. We should not expect to find him placed in the heavens of Martianus, since that tour of the skies is to extend invitations to his own wedding. But he also is not listed on the Liver of Piacenza. Attempts to find inscriptions with dedications to him have thus far been unconvincing. It is likely, however, that he did receive cult recognition in relation to his Underworld duties. In sheer numbers of representations,[12] Turms outranks the other gods presented in this chapter, because of the fact that he is often an atten-

ETRUSCAN MYTH, SACRED HISTORY, AND LEGEND

VI.11 Painted black-figure amphora, ca.520–500 BCE. Toledo, Museum of Art. Photo: Museum. The Etruscan vessel shows Tyrrhenian pirates in various stages of turning into dolphins. A grape vine sprouts on the left side of the scene, but Fufluns does not appear on the vessel. On the shoulder, a Triton, and on the neck, two athletes.

dant or assistant in various myths. In this chapter we shall review his adventures above ground, and then say more about his role in the Underworld in Chapter X, below.

Turms is usually quite recognizable in Etruscan mythological representations. In a conversation group with Tinia, Uni and Menrva (Fig. IV.9), he is instantly identified by his beardless face, his traveler's hat, and his characteristic staff, the caduceus. He sometimes has wings upon his shoulders, as in a scene where he

VI.12 Bronze mirror from Tarquinia, ca. 325–300 BCE. Tarquinia, Museo Archeologico Nazionale. Turms, winged and wearing a winged hat, converses with a naked, winged goddess.

confers with a nude winged goddess (Fig. VI.12), and as we have noted he may be twinned, perhaps indicating that he has two major spheres of influence (i.e., above and below the earth; Fig. VI.13). His winged brimmed hat may serve as the diagnostic identifying feature, as in a terracotta sculpture found at the temple site of Portonaccio at Veii (Fig. VI.14); the sculpture of the body is missing and his identity must be guessed from the head only. In that scene, he seems to have been an onlooker at the fight between Aplu and Hercle over the deer sacred to Artumes (discussed below in conection with Aplu). In Etruria he seems to have kept up his messenger role, for example in the popular story of the Judgment of Paris. The early representation on the Boccanera slabs (Plate I) is a little unusual, since he is shown as bearded and with a strange spike on top of his hat, as well as carrying a staff with bull finial rather than a standard caduceus. The myth also appears, sometimes with local variations, in Etruscan vase painting as on a well-known amphora from Vulci (Fig. VI.15), where Turms leads, in order from left to right, Uni, Menrva, and Turan, and is preceded by an elderly noble figure (also carrying

VI.13 Bronze mirror from Vulci, ca. 300 BCE. Rome, Torlonia Collection. After ES:5.8.1. Twin figures of Turms, one holding a staff (with lotus?).

the caduceus!), perhaps again Teukros, as on the mirror from Todi (Fig. V.22). It is surprising, but Turms rarely appears in the numerous scenes of the Judgment on Etruscan mirrors; perhaps it is because in these images, more emphasis is placed on the actual beauty contest than on the procession of the goddesses.

Turms is interested in the protection and nurturing of children, and as noted, is charged with carrying the newborn Fufluns to be educated (Fig. VI.3). He attends Menrva's ceremony with the Mariś babies (Fig. V.5), and the birth of Menrva. It is within this role that he appears in one of his most interesting Etruscan adventures, the delivery of the egg of Helen (Elinai). That Helen of Troy was born from an egg was a story told in two different versions in Greece—either that she was one of the four children born from the mating of Leda with Zeus in the form of a swan, or that the egg came from the union of Nemesis and Zeus, and was given to Leda and her husband Tyndareus for hatching.[13] In Greek art, Tyndareus and Leda discover the egg, sometimes on an altar, and stand and look at it. In Etruria Turms delivers it and often seems to discuss it with the recipients.

On an exceptionally fine relief mirror in Boston (Fig. VI.16),[14] the god extends the egg to Tuntle (=Tyndareus) as Latva (=Leda) looks on, and on another

VI.14 Terracotta sculpture from the Portonaccio sanctuary, Veii, ca. 535–500 BCE. Rome, Museo Nazionale Etrusco di Villa Giulia. Photo: Soprintendenza per i Beni Archeologici del Lazio. The beardless god Turms wears a winged hat. It is not certain where he was placed among the sculptures from the temple at the Portonaccio sanctuary (cf. Figs. VI.21-24).

example, Tuntle, this time alone, is already holding the egg (Fig. VI.17). Turms appears here in the pose of a prophet or soothsayer, his left leg lifted and his right arm raised with one finger extended in instruction. Certainly the egg of Helen could be read as having prophetic significance, a portent of dire events to come. An ambitious composition with six figures from Porano, near Orvieto (Fig. VI.18) excludes Turms this time, but shows the whole family gathered round to discuss the egg: Tuntle on the left, Latva on the right, and in between Castur and Pultuce, the twin brothers of Elinai. Turan stands near Tuntle, perhaps making plans for the future of the child in the egg. Latva holds her hand up to her mouth in a meditation pose well known in prophetic scenes, and others echo her gesture.

Yet another, and quite extraordinary, scene of Turms with an egg shows him presenting it to a lady labeled Urphea, rather than Latva, in the presence of These (Fig. VI.19), a scene that should not be attributed to the ignorance of the artist, as some have done,[15] but to the great variation of mythology possible in Italy. In particular, it has been noted that even in Greek art, in southern Italy, the egg of Helen was associated with the cult of Orpheus and had Underworld connections.[16] We are reminded that the Etruscans often utilized eggs in a funerary context, as real food served at the feast of the dead or as imitations in terracotta or stone placed

VI.15 Painted black-figure ("Pontic") amphora, ca. 550–540 BCE. Munich, Antikensammlungen un Glyptothek. Photo: Museum. Turms, led by a white-bearded gentleman, escorts the three goddesses to Judgment of Elcsntre: Uni, Menrva, and Turan. Elcnstre (=Paris) is on the other side of the vessel.

ETRUSCAN MYTH, SACRED HISTORY, AND LEGEND

VI.16 Bronze mirror, ca.
400–350 BCE. Boston,
Museum of Fine Arts.
After CSE U.S.A.:2.28a.
Turms presents the egg
of Elinai to Tuntle and
Latva.

VI.17 Bronze mirror from Vulci, late 4th century BCE. Berlin, Staatliche Museen, Antikensammlung. After CSE Deutsche Demokratische Republik: 1.32b. Turms presents the egg of Elinai to Tuntle.

in the tomb,[17] no doubt meant to aid in rebirth and immortality. So Urphea in this Etruscan version, unknown elsewhere in classical myth, must be taken seriously as a meaningful personage in the story; clearly she should be identified as someone with Orphic capabilities. In fact, the various Orphic associations may help to explain why Turms takes on such a prominent role in the Etruscan myth. Since emphasis is being placed on the afterlife connotations of the egg rather than the role of Helen in the Trojan War, it is entirely appropriate that this god of double spheres of the upper and lower world be its deliverer. The character labeled "These" on this mirror certainly has a connection with the themes proposed here. In Greek myth, Theseus was the abductor of Helen, along with his close friend Peirithous and accordingly would take an interest in the future implied by the egg. Also relevant is their subsequent adventure visiting the Underworld, when they attempted to kidnap Persephone as the bride of Peirithous. The two sat down at the invitation of Hades and were unable to rise from their seats (cf. Fig. X.14). It is possible that the fourth figure in this scene may be Peirithous, the alter ego of These; they probably are not yet in the Underworld, however, and the principal theme rather has to do with fertility and marriage in the upper world.[18]

VI.18 Bronze mirror from Porano, ca. 350–325 BCE. Orvieto, Museo Archeologico Nazionale. After ES:5.77. Castur presents the egg of Elinai to Tuntle. Left to right: Tuntle, Turan, unknown female figure, Pultuce, Castur, and Latva.

Aplu

Apollo was a Greek god respected in Italy for his prophetic abilities, to the extent that the Etruscans and Romans would seek out his oracle at Delphi; the Etruscan cities of Caere and Spina even built treasuries there, presumably because their visits and offerings were numerous. The most Hellenic of the deities found in Etruscan myth, he came into Etruria in Archaic times as Apulu (Aplu in later inscriptions) with very little adaptation.[19] This phenomenon seems related to the fact that he was not a popular god of cult: he is absent from the Piacenza Liver, is never mentioned in the heavens of Martianus and Etruscan inscriptions relevant for his worship are quite rare. On the other hand, there are Greek dedications to Apollo at both Gravisca and Spina, where Greeks no doubt lived among Etruscans.[20] Further, there is evidence that Śuri, the principal male deity at Pyrgi, was regarded by the Greeks as equivalent to Apollo (discussed further below).[21]

VI.19 Bronze mirror, ca. 300–275 BCE. Berlin, Staatliche Museen, Antikensammlung. After CSE Deutsche Demokratische Republik:1.13b. Turms presents an egg to Urphea; These (=Theseus?) sits on the right. The story is unknown apart from this mirror.

His name remains Greek (only the letters omicron and omega in Greek turn into *u* in Etruscan) and his appearance is absolutely consistent with the way the god was represented in Greek art: a handsome, long-haired youth with bow and arrow, lyre, and/or laurel wreath (e.g., Figs. IV.6, IV.11). Sometimes he holds a branch of laurel in an upright position (Figs. V.14, V.29).

As a mythological figure in Etruria Aplu has relatively few adventures, but he occurs again and again as a supporting or attending figure, for example in scenes of Turan with Atunis and Semla with Fufluns (Figs. V.29, VI.5), of Uni suckling Hercle (Fig. V.15) and of the birth of Fufluns (Fig. IV.11). Sometimes in such scenes he mingles with purely Etruscan figures, for example as he watches over the prophetic activities of Umaele and Alpan (Fig. II.17). Aplu may stand around in a family conversation group with his father Tinia and his brother Turms (Fig. IV.6) or with his mother Letun and his twin sister Artumes (Fig. VI.20). He and his sister are depicted in twinning poses enjoying music together, with either deity holding the lyre (Figs. V.35).

VI.20 Bronze mirror from Chiusi, ca. 350 BCE. Palermo, Museo Archeologico Regionale. After ES.1.77. From left to right, seated half-naked Artumes, standing Aplu with his bow, their mother Letun, and the beneficent spirit Thalna.

The most famous representation of Aplu is the lifesize terracotta sculpture made for the Etruscan temple at Veii located in the sanctuary called the Portonaccio (Figs. VI. 21-22).[22] The prominence and beauty of this figure has misled some into calling this a temple of Apollo, but in fact, the dedications found at the sanctuary belong to female deities: Menrva, Turan, and Aplu's twin sister, here called Aritimi.[23]

The principal subject that has been identified involves the statue of Aplu and one of Hercle, identifiable by his lion skin, that seem to have stood opposite one another as akroteria on the ridge pole of the temple (Fig. VI.21). Between the legs of Hercle (Fig. VI.23) are the remains of the body of a deer,[24] tied up, leading scholars to conclude that the theme here was a fight between Apollo and Herakles over the hind from Mt. Cerynea that was sacred to Artemis. Normally in the Greek version, Artemis herself stops Herakles and rebukes him, but here, according to

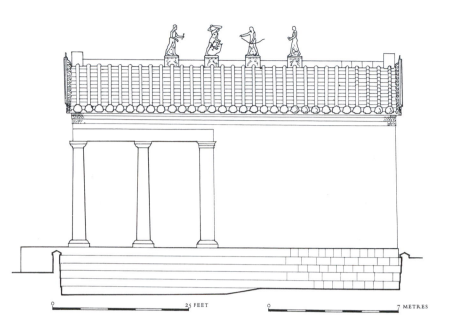

VI.21 Elevation drawing of the temple at the Portonaccio, Veii, ca. 525-500 BCE. After Boethius 1978:fig. 51. The drawing shows the sculptures on the roof skyline (akroteria) illustrated in Figs. VI.14 and 22–24, reconstructed as, from left to right: Turms, Hercle, Aplu, and Letun (?).

VI.22 Terracotta statue from the temple at the Portonaccio, Veii, ca. 525–500 BCE. Photo: Soprintendenza per i Beni Archeologici del Lazio. The god Aplu, dressed in a curved mantle, lunges forward; he probably was carrying a bow.

the way the evidence has been interpreted, Hercle is opposed by Aplu. (It is worth noting that in fact no attribute of Aplu was found at the site; the architectural element that stands between the legs of this figure has a decorative motif that suggests a lyre, but a similar design is used on the support of the statue of Hercle, suggesting that it is only an abstract decoration.) There are other lifesize figures from the Portonaccio that may have belonged on the ridgepole as well—the image of Turms already discussed (Fig. VI.14) and a striding female figure who carries a child (Fig. VI.24); the child wears a skirt and the gender is not certain, but it is often suggested that this is Leto holding the youthful Apollo shooting at Python, a theme we have noted on an Etruscan mirror (Fig. V.36). Given that Aritimi was honored in the sanctuary and that the story of the Cerynean hind was a tribute to her, we cannot discount the possibility that this theme of Delphi related to her as well.

A representation that certainly pertains to Delphi is found on a mirror in Philadelphia (Fig. VI.25) showing Urste (=Orestes) seeking purification from Aplu. The youth who murdered his mother embraces the sacred omphalos at Delphi as the god holds a pig over his head in preparation for a sacrifice. On the left is a figure labeled Vanth, evidently meant to be one of the Furies that pursued Orestes (but in Chapter X we shall see that Vanth has many more duties than a Greek Fury), and on the right a figure inscribed Metua (unknown).

Usil and Śuri

Aplu was assimilated to two deities with Etruscan names, Usil and Śuri. Usil's nature is clear: the word *usil*, meaning "sun" in Etruscan, occurs on the underside of the Piacenza Liver, suggesting a cult connection, and we know the appearance of this god from the mirror with the cosmic grouping of Nethuns, Usil and Thesan

(Fig. VI.36).[25] Quite obviously his iconography has been influenced by that of Apollo, for the radiant youth carries a bow. Very likely a deity represented on a mirror with a halo and juggling balls of fire as he rises from the waves is also Usil (Fig. I. 10; uninscribed).

As for Śuri, it is most unfortunate that we do not have any inscribed images of this deity nor do we know his appearance. His name allies him with the Latin deity Soranus, sometimes known as Apollo Soranus, worshipped on Mt. Soracte not far from Rome. He was a highly important deity at Pyrgi, the port of Caere, as shown by the excavation of inscriptions with his name and evidence of his cult,[26] and was surely the consort of Catha, whom we have noted in Chapter V. The excavations also revealed that like Apollo, Śuri was an oracular god who utilized leaf-shaped pieces of metal—*sortes*, or lots—to assist his worshippers in obtaining messages (Fig. VI.26). The *sors* from Pyrgi reproduced here is made of bronze and measures nearly 20 cm in length.

Tiv

The name of the Etruscan god of the moon is known: Tiv (also written Tiur or Tiu). The word Tiv occurs on the underside of the Piacenza Liver, in a zone adjacent to that of Usil (Fig. III.1), and various inscriptions give evidence that this is also the Etruscan word for "month."[27] It has been assumed that we do not have any images of this deity, but I would like to propose that at least one image does occur, and that after looking at this one it may be possible to identify other depictions of the god.

On a mirror from Perugia showing Elinai with her brothers Castur and Pultuce (Fig. VIII.21), the upper exergue is occupied by a team of horses and their driver, as on many Etruscan mirrors (Figs. II.2, V.5, V.18, V.22, V.27, VI.18, VI.34). I have suggested that such an adjunct to the main scene on the mirrors, generally thought to represent the chariot of the dawn goddess, Thesan, is meant to indicate a particular day or time of day when the event depicted took place. On the Perugia mirror, however, there are some important differences: there are two horses instead of four, the driver is male rather than female, and the horses seem to be sinking rather than rising. Proof that they have finished their job lies in the bridles that are hanging on a nail behind them. It has been argued that these are the horses of the Dioskouroi in their stable, being tended by a groom,[28] a tidy enough theory. It does not explain, however, the inscription above the youth's head, which is to be read as *auri*, a word that has been linked with Latin and Italic terms relating to dawn (*aurora*) and the sun, but may better be compared with the Latin word for charioteer, *auriga*. This youthful figure was, in fact, identified earlier by some as Usil, the male charioteer of the sun. But perhaps the number of horses, two instead of four, may indicate a lesser heavenly body, i.e., a lunar connection. Is it possible that instead of the more usual rising and shining of the sun in Etruscan art, we have here an indication of the setting of the moon? The hypothesis remains to be tested by reference to other representations of a youth driving two horses.[29]

Sethlans

We would like to know more about Sethlans, but as it stands he appears as a relatively minor member of the Etruscan pantheon. It is clear that he was a god

VI.23 Terracotta statue from the temple at the Portonaccio, Veii (former restoration; under revision in 2005), ca. 525–500 BCE. Photo: Soprintendenza per i Beni Archeologici del Lazio. Hercle stands astride a trussed deer, probably to be identified with the Cyrenean hind sacred to Artemis in Greek mythology.

VI.24 Terracotta statue from the temple at the Portonaccio, Veii. Ca. 525–500 BCE. Photo: Soprintendenza per i Beni Archeologici del Lazio. Possibly Letun, the goddess-mother of Aplu; she holds a child, perhaps Aplu at the age when he killed the python.

VI.25 Bronze mirror, late 4th century BCE. Philadelphia, University of Pennsylvania Museum of Archaeology and Anthropology. After Turfa 2005:231. Aplu sacrifices a pig over the head of Urste. Vanth on left, as a Fury; Metua (otherwise unknown) on right.

VI.26 Bronze sheet in shape of a leaf, 480–470 BCE. Prophetic Sors ("lot") from the south sanctuary at Pyrgi. After Colonna 2006:fig. VIII.8. Such lots, used in prophetic ritual, were probably associated with the cult of śuri.

VI.27 Bronze coin from Populonia, 4th–3rd centuries BCE. After Pfiffig 1975:fig. 124. Obverse: head of Sethlans; reverse: hammer and tongs of the blacksmith. Populonia, as a center of metal working, had reason to place the smith god on its coins.

of crafts, holding the place of Greek Hephaistos in several well-known myths, and if he is indeed equivalent to Roman Vulcan, he was a lightning god and dwelled in Region 4 of the heavens of Martianus under the name of Mulciber. But there is little to recommend the suggestion that he should be equated with *velχ* in House 34 of the Liver.[30] There is no evidence of his cult in Etruria, but he does seem to have been a patron deity of the metalworking coastal city of Populonia, since he was represented on coins of the city (Fig. VI.27). He appears on the obverse as beardless and wearing the *pilos*, a worker's peaked hat, while on the reverse are represented his tools, including tongs and hammer. As for his name, it is obscure, but the fact that it is so utterly different from Hephaistos and Vulcan suggests that the Etruscans had at an early date their own hammer god, who was then assimilated to the others.

Sethlans, beardless and evidently not crippled, appears as a beautiful youth in the Birth of Menrva (Fig. IV.13); he cradles a double-axe, which he must have utilized to help with the birth. He is shown throwing up his right arm in a gesture found in ancient art known by the Greek term of *aposkopein* ("to look steadily"), displaying awe at the sight of a god.[31] Several other narrative themes with Sethlans are known in Etruscan art. The story of the Return of Hephaistos to Olympus,[32] very popular on Greek vases imported into Etruria, was picked up and narrated with great charm by an early vase painter from Caere (Cerveteri) who decorated almost exclusively the type of vessel known as a hydria (water jar; Fig. VI.28).[33] The story seems to be that Hephaistos, unloved by his parents because of his deformity and thrown out of Olympos by Hera, decided to get revenge by sending his mother a beautifully crafted throne, which had a clever deceptive feature: whoever sat in it would be seized by magic chains and would not be able to stand up. Of course the goddess became ensnared and it was evident that only the maker of the throne would be able to extricate her. But Hephaistos refused all requests for his

VI.28 Painted black-figure water jar (hydria), from Cerveteri, ca. 525–500 BCE. Vienna, Kunsthistorisches Museum. Photo: Museum. The story of the return of Sethlans to Olympus is narrated. Fufluns leads the way, dressed in an animal skin covered with spots and holding up his great drinking cup, the kantharos. Sethlans sits astride a donkey, his crippled legs indicated by the twisting of his feet. Maenad and satyr follow.

VI.29 Bronze mirror from Chiusi, ca. 300–275 BCE. Berlin, Staatliche Museen, Antikensammlung. After CSE Bundesrepublik Deutschland:4.32. The return of Sethlans. The boyish drunken smith is supported on the shoulders of Fufluns. On left, Mariś; on right, Laran.

VI.30 Bronze mirror probably from Tarquinia, late 4th century BCE. Dresden, Staatliche Kunstsammlungen. After CSE Deutsche Demokratische Republik:2.8b. A youthful, healthy Sethlans frees Uni from the magic throne with a helper labeled Tretu (the name known only from this representation).

return, including the bullying of Ares, god of war. Finally Dionysos was sent to ply him with wine and cajole him into coming back. The Caeretan hydria shows a quite entertaining version of the tale, with the god of wine lifting high his great drinking cup as a lively mule romps forward bearing the crippled boy. The retinue of Dionysos joins in as a maenad waves a serpent and an excited satyr plays the pipes.

This scene follows fairly well the iconographic pattern established in Greek Archaic art, differing only in being a broader, more vivid rendition of the myth. Very different from the Greek models is a version that appears on a later Etruscan mirror from Chiusi (Fig. VI.29), which has been translated sufficiently to merit the title of the Return of Sethlans. The figures are all labeled with Etruscan inscriptions and we can identify the boy with the hammer and *pilos* easily. He leans drunkenly on the youthful Fufluns, in the presence of Laran (=Ares?) and Mariś (not in the Greek myth).

The sequel to this action is represented on another mirror (Fig. VI.30), a very rare scene of the freeing of Uni by Sethlans. He uses his hammer to knock away

VI.31 Bronze mirror, 3rd century BCE. Paris, Bibliothèque Nationale, Cabinet des Médailles. After ES:2.235.2. Sethlans and Etule labor over the horse Pecse. Written on the box or tablet on the right is the word *huins*.

the chains, aided by an assistant who employs a hammer also, but pounds it against a chisel or perhaps a nail. He is labeled Tretu, a name without parallel in Greek myth. As we have noted, the motif of hammer and nail was important to the Etruscans, in light of the fact that they used these items for ritual purposes.

The hammer appears again in one of the most remarkable narratives in Etruscan art (Fig. VI.31), the making of the horse Pecse. Again a beardless Sethlans is involved, but he does not wield the instrument himself. The horse, labeled Pecse, clearly takes its name from Pegasos, but nothing in the scene is connected with the Greek myth in which that horse appears (the slaying of the Chimera by Bellerophon). In addition, the horse is not winged (though in fact the horse of Bellerophon is sometimes represented without wings in Etruria). Further, the myth here seems to involve shaping the horse. It is kept chained up so that it will not get away, as Sethlans applies (or removes?) some kind of material around its neck, perhaps clay, used in creating the horse. An assistant, labeled Etule, hammers away at the head of the animal. Of course it is natural to suspect that the famous story of the building of the Trojan horse is behind this representation. The plaque

VI.32 Bronze mirror, 3rd century BCE. Present location unknown. After ES:3. 257c. Aplu (left) holds up his hand in an expository gesture, as Menrva listens; Laran, on right, holds his hand up in a gesture of listening. The naked Turan gazes at Laran.

on the right, with the inscription *huins* has been taken to refer to Hellenes, and to show that the horse comes from the Greeks.

But there are many problems with trying to cut and paste this representation to make it fit a Greek model. The name Etule does not appear in the Greek story. In the *Odyssey* (8.493) a craftsman named Epeios makes the horse, and furthermore he does it with the help of Athena, not Hephaistos. Finally, it is worth noting that Etule wears the long sleeves and cap of a Trojan, not a Greek. We may throw up our hands and say that the artist has hopelessly bungled two Greek myths about horses. Or we may say, more prudently, that myths may vary greatly depending on where, when, and for whom they were created, and without written texts we simply do not know what this story was.

Laran

We have encountered several times Laran, a figure with military attributes who has often been compared with Ares and Mars, and who is increasingly ac-

VI.33 Bronze mirror, late 4th century BCE. Hamburg, Museum für Kunst und Gewerbe. After CSE Bundesrepublik Deutschland:2.16a. Left to right: Mariś, Tinia, and Lasa in conference.

cepted by authorities as constituting a true equivalent for those gods of war.[34] As we shall see, Mariś is also a candidate for this equation, but his case is less convincing than that of Laran. This god is known almost exclusively from mirrors, upon which his name is inscribed a dozen times, but he may also be listed on the Piacenza Liver, House 26, as *marisl laθ*, i.e., the Lar(an) of Mariś.[35] In this case we might have an intriguing connection with the heavens of Martianus, in which the figure would be equivalent to the Latin Lars Militaris (Regions 2 and 4) rather than Mars (Regions 2 and 6).

He definitely is a companion for Mariś, as we have seen on the mirror with the Return of Sethlans (Fig. VI.29), where the two nude military youths, seemingly age mates, flank the main scene. His role here is unclear, as in fact it is in the scenes of the birth of Menrva, where he is a seated attendant (Fig. V.10); on the other side is his counterpart Mariś, with the byname of *Tinsta*, who now looks older than Laran. He is also a beardless youthful Laran in the scene with the three Mariś babies (Fig. V.5). His identity with Ares is bolstered by the mirrors in which

VI.34 Bronze mirror found near Orvieto, ca. 300 BCE. Present location unknown. After ES:5, p. 220. Hercle makes a sacrifice, perhaps to Artumes and Aplu, who stand left. On right Mariśhercles and Vile.

he appears with Turan (Fig. VI.32) and the one in which he attacks the Giant labeled Celsclan (Fig. V.38). There the bearded, fully armored god makes an appropriately Olympian appearance in the Battle of Gods and Giants.

Mariś

We come now to one of the most enigmatic deities of the Etruscan pantheon. The name of Mariś is frequently spelled with the ending in a four-bar sigma on its side, looking rather like a large M in Etruscan (transliterated with the conventional ś), less often with a standard sigma. Here we shall use the sign for the four-bar sigma unless it is specifically countered in an inscription. This name suggested to many that the god might be the equivalent of the Roman Mars and thus also of the Greek Ares, but the representations of him were by no means consistent with this identification, and few will now defend that position.[36] Here will be presented a new argument for the identity of Mariś, based on a review of the key indicators of myth and cult in Etruria.[37]

VI.35 Bronze mirror from Vulci, ca. 325–300 BCE. Vatican Museums, Museo Gregoriano Etrusco. After ES:4.381. A loving couple is flanked by Alpan (left), and Maristurns, right. In upper exergue a frowning figure carries a stick (?), perhaps a malevolent spirit. In lower exergue a winged goddess, labeled Mus, plays a stringed instrument, attended by a serpent and two birds.

The name of Mariś occurs three times on the Piacenza Liver, in Houses 30 and 39 by itself, and in House 26 in close association with Lar. In one case the house of Hercle is adjoining, a relevant relationship.

There are two images of Mariś in art that seem fairly straightforward and unproblematic. He appears on one mirror as a young nude beardless male with a spear, in conference with Tinia and the nymph-like figure labeled simply Lasa (Fig. VI.33). This figure is sufficiently consistent with the Mariś who attends the Return of Sethlans (Fig. VI.29). After that, confusion breaks out, because all other labeled images of Mariś include a byname. At the Birth of Menrva, he is Maristinsta, perhaps the Mariś of Tinia, toward whom he gazes intently (Fig. V.10). Mar(i)shercles, the Mariś of Hercle, attends Hercle as he pours a libation in the direction of Artumes and Aplu (Fig. VI.34). Here the stance of Hercle, with left

VI.36 Bronze mirror from Tuscania, ca. 350 BCE. Vatican Museums, Museo Gregoriano Etrusco. After ES:1.76. Left to right: Nethuns, Usil, and Thesan. In lower exergue is a winged anguiped demon who holds up a dolphin in each hand.

foot raised (it is braced on a dead boar) may imply that the subject is prophetic. The Mariś of Hercle is shown as carrying a spear and wearing a mantle, as he hovers just over the hero's proper left shoulder. Closing the scene on the right, in garb similar to that of the Mariś of Hercle is Vile, the Etruscan twin of Hercle. The scene seems sacred, and above, the chariot of Thesan suggests that a special day is referenced, probably one marked on the calendar for this particular ritual. More than that we cannot say.

Also interesting is the mirror that shows a figure perhaps labeled Maristurns (Fig. VI.35), probably the Mariś of Turan, standing nude, with a spear, and this time with wings, next to an embracing naked couple. Their names are illegible. On the far left is Alpan, known as a personification, probably meaning something like the Latin Libens, "Willing" (see Chapter VII).

This provides a background for further consideration of the two mirrors with Mariś babies (Figs. V.5-6).[38] In some of the preceding references, the name Mariś

ETRUSCAN MYTH, SACRED HISTORY, AND LEGEND

VI.37 Bronze mirror, late 4th century BCE. Vatican Museums, Museo Gregoriano Etrusco. After CSE Vaticano:1.5a. Nethuns seduces a maiden, probably the nymph Amymone. A satyr spies on them.

seems generic, rather like the nymph/spirit Lasa, who also often has a byname. The Mariś spirit may attend a birth scene, a love scene, or a sacrifice, and may appear as winged or not winged, nude or clothed, bearded or nor bearded, older or younger. If we add in the scenes with the babies, we may add that Mariś may be singular or plural, may be an infant or adult, and may be unarmed as well as armed. In short, we have as wide a range of iconographic possibilities as we have with Lasa (Chapter VII).

An interesting comparison of a generic god from the Martianus heavens is provided by Genius, who may occur with only that name (Regions 5 and 6), or with a byname ("Genius of Juno Hospita," Region 9). The name Genius belongs to a fertility spirit,[39] and means literally "the begetter," but it came to be used in classical Latin to refer to the attendant spirit of every man, a kind of guardian figure. It was honored on one's birthday or at the time of marriage. Each household had its Genius, usually the *paterfamilias*. By extension a place or even a god could have

VI.38 Carved carnelian scarab from Vulci, 4th century BCE. Paris, Bibliothèque Nationale, Cabinet des Médailles. Photo: Bibliothèque Nationale de France. Nethuns kicks a rock and creates a spring. Next to him, an inscription reads *Nethunus*.

its own Genius.

It is here suggested that the name Mariś is the equivalent of Genius in Latin, a general term for a spirit closely associated with some particular figure.[40] Thus Maristinsta, the Genius of Tinia, attends the birth of Menrva (and is bearded like Tinia), Maristurns, the Genius of Turan, assists with a love affair (and is winged like the usual assistants of Turan), and Mar(i)śhercles, the Genius of Hercle, attends a sacrifice. The Mariś babies may be, precisely, Genii of the individuals who are named: Halna, Husrnana and Isminthians. They come under the care of Menrva and Turan, the former even baring a breast to suckle the little spirits (Fig. V.6). Their emergence from the large krater or amphora may refer to the birth or rebirth of the Mariś Genii.

It remains to note that if Mariś is indeed Genius, we recover a precious link in Etruscan mythological material handed down by the Romans: Tages was the son of Genius, who was in turn the son of Jupiter (Chapter II). This might translate into Etruscan to say that Pava Tarchies was the son of Mariś, who was in turn the son of Tinia. Thus in Fig. VI.33, Mariś sits with his father.

Nethuns

The name of the god of the sea, Nethuns, it has been argued, derives from the Latin name, Neptunus.[41] The latter appears in the heavens of Martianus, Region

10, and the Etruscan god seems to appear on the Piacenza Liver as (N)eth, in House 7 and as Neth in 22 (along with Tin), and in 28. Thus he is very prominent on the Liver, and it has been pointed out that his name appears on the appendage to the organ identifiable as the gall bladder. This fact is significant because it fits with what the Roman writer Pliny the Elder tells us (*Natural History* 11.195) about the gall bladder of a bull being an appropriate offering for Neptune. The connection may lie in the fact that the gall bladder contains watery bile, which would be appropriate for this god of waters. Further evidence of cultic attention to Nethuns is provided by the Etruscan calendar written on the strips of the linen book found wrapped around a mummy (Zagreb, Museum), where he is mentioned eight times, and wine is prescribed as an offering for him.

Representations of Nethuns in Etruscan art are rather rare. He is shown in a consultation with two other nature deities, Usil, god of the sun, and Thesan, goddess of the dawn on the handsome Etruscan mirror from Tuscania (Fig. VI.36), fairly close in date to the well-known Pava Tarchies mirror from the same area. Here Nethuns appears as a mature Tinia-like figure, carrying an unorthodox trident that is double-ended. His name is not on the list of gods definitely known to throw lightning, but this instrument is highly evocative. He appears with standard trident in other representations, for example another mirror scene, showing the god in an embrace with a seminude female (Fig. VI.37). The scenario includes a spring with a lion's head spout and a satyr peering over the hillside, completing a fairly appropriate ensemble for the story of Amymone, daughter of Danaus, who went in search of water for her father because Poseidon had caused a shortage. She was assaulted by a satyr whom Poseidon drove away. Afterwards the god enjoyed her favors (the satyr just watches) and shared with her his knowledge about where to find springs. On the Etruscan mirror it may be that he has created the spring himself, a subject that appears on carved Etruscan gems, for example, one from Vulci that shows the god kicking a rock to make water gush forth (Fig. VI.38).[42] There he is shown as youthful and nude, with the inscription *Nethunus* running next to the figure. Thus in these scenes the god of the ocean also appears as a deity of fresh water.

This concludes our survey of the "major" male deities of the Etruscans. In the next chapter we shall consider both male and female deities that might be ranked as secondary, but it should be kept in mind that sheer lack of information may be conditioning our categorization.

Spirits **VII**

From the description of Martianus it is clear that the Etruscan pantheon was populated by a number of divine beings we might call secondary or intermediary, or at least not of the same category as the greater gods who ended up being equated with Greek Olympian deities. The Latin words for these spirits given in Martianus suggest various associations, and in most cases we shall begin with the Latin names and then relate them to evidence from Etruscan culture. In much of the discussion that follows, the table, diagrams and images that relate to the heavens of Martianus and the Piacenza Liver will be useful (Table III, Figs. III. 1-3).

Culśanś

In Martianus's Region 1 was Janus, the god whose name is related to the Latin word *ianua*, "door, portal," and who is regarded as a god of beginnings. His name was attached to the first month of the year in Rome as well as the first day of each month; he was often represented as a bifrontal god with two heads joined together, one face looking forward and the other backward (Fig. VII.1).[1] Etruscan mythographers find great satisfaction in the close correspondence of this known Roman god with an Etruscan deity also represented with two joined heads, for example on a bronze statuette found near a city gate at Cortona (Fig. VII.2). His name is Culśanś, judging from the inscription written on his leg: *v.cvinti.arntiaś.culśanśl alpan turce,* "V(elia) Cvinti, daughter of Arnt gave (this) gladly to Culśanś."[2] He is probably the god indicated on the Piacenza Liver in House 14 as *cvl*. The association of Culśanś with doors is confirmed by the fact that a goddess of the door to the Underworld, represented as standing beside a gate, is named by the inscription as Culśu (Fig. X.18; we shall return to her in Chapter X).

Culśanś appears as a nude, beardless male figure, wearing rustic boots and a strange flat hat that goes over both heads. (We probably should use the term "bifrontal" and not speak of "two heads" because the join between them is so close that they are really more like Siamese twins who have one head with two faces.) Culśanś also has a necklace, the twisted circlet open in the front called a torque. His fingers are in a peculiar position, and some have suggested that he may be making a special gesture that would fit well with a description of a statue of Janus once in Rome, which was said to show the god with his fingers in the shape of the number of days in the year (not extant; see Pliny, *NH* 34.33; various suggestions have been made about how the fingers could shape the Etruscan/Roman numerals). Thus Culśanś, like Janus, may have been a god of doors and calendars.

VII.1 Roman Bronze *as*, 225/217 BCE. Berlin, Staatliche Museen, Münzkabinett. Photo: Bildarchiv Preussischer Kulturbesitz. Obverse: bifrontal head of Janus, the Roman counterpart of the Etruscan door-god Culśanś.

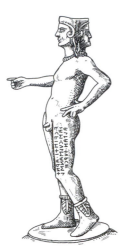

VII.2 Bronze statuette from Cortona, 300–250 BCE. Cortona, Museo dell'Accademia Etrusca. After Pfiffig 1975:fig. 108. Votive to Culśanś, thought to represent the god. Here he is a nude youth, wearing only rustic boots, a torque, and a flat cap. The positioning of his hands and fingers is very particular, though the meaning is uncertain.

Busts of a bifrontal god, both with and without beard, have been found at Tarquinia, Tuscania and Vulci, all within the same vicinity and from Tuscania also comes a stone sarcophagus (Fig. VII.3), that seems to show the deity in a narrative context.[3] Three pairs of warriors square off, their dress and weaponry varying greatly. The figure in question fights with a curved staff, which may lead to another point of comparison with Janus, who was known to carry a rustic staff.[4] But given the Etruscan context, there is no reason to identify the figure as Roman and even less as the Greek monster Argos being stoned by Hermes, as argued by one scholar.[5] Instead we probably have a genuine Etruscan mythological character. I propose that the theme is the battle of gods and Giants (Giants regularly use boulders in battle), a cosmic story set in Italy, with the defeated Giants being buried under Mt. Aetna in Sicily. This battle theme has a long history among the Etruscans, characterized by innovations and motifs unknown in Greece.[6] The inclusion of the bifrontal god, Culśanś, is quite consistent with that history.

Cilens

Also in Region 1 of Martianus dwelled the little-known God of the Night, Nocturnus, whose name also occurred in Region 16. As noted earlier, there is a deity on the Piacenza Liver placed in both House 1 and House 16, by the name of Cilens; the name also appears in an inner House, 36. It is logical to assume that these two deities are one and the same, thus providing another exciting link between the two documents.[7]

Further, we actually have a representation of Cilens (Plate II), a terracotta relief in which the figure is depicted in the company of *Mera* (i.e., Menerva). Unfortunately the head is missing, but it is almost certain that the dress is that of a female, and includes a heavy cloak, which would be appropriate for a deity of darkness. She also seems to have worn a large collar/necklace, now broken off. The sculpture is one of a group of antefixes used to decorate the ends of roof tiles

VII.3 Stone sarcophagus from Tuscania, ca. 300 BCE. Tuscania, Museo Archeologico. After Taylor 2000:fig. 13. Battle scene in which a bifrontal deity dressed in a short tunic, probably Culśanś, fights using a shepherd's crook against an adversary (perhaps a Giant) who heaves a stone.

of an Etruscan building, probably sacred, at Bolsena. The theme may have been the decapitation of the Gorgon Medusa by Perseus—key figures are missing, and the identification is tentative—in which case the goddess could have furnished a key item to Perseus, the Cap of Darkness by which he became invisible. The name Nocturnus is seemingly masculine and the deity is represented as feminine, but this poses no problem in Etruria, as we have seen with regard to Artumes, and will discuss further below. If indeed, Cilens does equal Nocturnus, we have knowledge of the appearance of quite a fine assemblage of deities in Martianus's Region 1: Tinia (cf. Fig. IV.1, etc.), Culśanś (Fig. VII.2), and Cilens (Plate II). The three go together well in the cosmos, with their spheres of Day (Tinia), Night (Cilens), and the liminal Door between the two (Culśanś).

Selvans

The Etruscan deity Selvans is frequently equated with the rustic Italic/Roman deity Silvanus,[8] but the latter does not appear in Martianus and it is preferable to start with the Etruscan documentation for this god. Selvans does appear on the Piacenza Liver, both in a border cell, no. 10, and in an interior one, no. 31, with his name given as the abbreviated *selva* (Fig. III.1). His cult was popular, for a significant number of dedicatory inscriptions (around nine) have been found, especially in the area of Cortona, Orvieto (Volsinii) and Bolsena. These inscriptions often include a byname for him,[9] but unfortunately, for most of them we are uncertain of their meaning. An exception is a bronze statuette of a nude youth that bears a dedication to Selvans Tularia,[10] i.e., Selvans of the boundaries. The association of his cult with boundaries has provided support for those who want to equate him with Silvanus, a deity who was called upon by the Romans to protect boundaries.[11] On a tufa marker from Bolsena (probably a boundary stone), he is called Selvans Sanchuneta, with an epithet that may relate to the Italic deity Sancus,[12] a figure by no means well understood but whose name does appear in Martianus (Region 12). Sancus was a god of sacred oaths, and thus could preside over the establishing of a boundary.

The role of Selvans as relating to boundaries and space comes up once again in the only recognized image of this god (Fig. VII.4). Found at Cortona near a city gate along with the statue of Culśanś (Fig. VII.2),[13] this bronze statuette is also inscribed with the name of Velia Cvinti (*ET* Co 3.3.) and bears a remarkable similarity to the door god Culśanś. He is a nude youth wearing rustic boots and a torque, as well as a strange animal-skin cap (identified as feline or that of a bear). His left hand was extended to hold a shaft of some kind, with his right hand on his hip, in a pose mirroring that of his partner Culśanś.

It is appropriate to discuss one other image of a youth in an animal skin cap, again a bronze statuette, found near Perugia, and close in date to the two statues from Cortona (Fig. VII.5). Without parallel and of uncertain identification is this image of a youth with his head facing backwards from his body.[14] He wears a headdress made of an animal skin (it has been described as canine or lupine, but also looks porcine) that comes down upon his shoulders. In one hand dangles what may be a branch of a tree, with a twig sticking out.

VII.4 Bronze statuette, 300–250 BCE. Cortona, Museo dell'Accademia Etrusca. After Cristofani 2000:pl. 105.   The youthful god Selvans is shown with nude body, wearing rustic boots, a torque necklace, and a head covering in the shape of a stylized feline's head; the cap comes down around his ears in a volute shape. His right hand rests on his hip and his left hand is extended as if to hold a staff or to present some object.

TABLE IV: A CHECKLIST OF ETRUSCAN SPIRITS ON MIRRORS

Spirit	Meaning of Name	Sphere(s)	Principal Companions
Achvizr	unknown	love, friendship	Turan, Thethis
Alpan	willing, with gladness	love, friendship	Turan, lovers
Evan	unknown	love, friendship, success	Alpan, Mean, Thethis
Hinthial	soul or shade	bridal adornment	Malavisch
Lasa	nymph	love, prophecy, adornment	Turan, Tinia, Menrva
Leinth	death, dying	infants, underwold	Mariś, Mean
Mean	victory	love, birth, success	heroes, Fufluns
Munthuch	adornment, elegance	love, bridal adornment	Turan, Malavisch
Thalna	growth, bloom	birth, infants, friendship, prophecy	Turan, Tinia, Menrva
Thanr	unknown	birth, friendship	Tinia, Menrva, Epiur
Zipna	unknown	love, friendship, adornment	Turan, Malavisch

VII.5 Bronze statuette, found near Perugia, 3rd–2nd centuries BCE. Perugia, Museo Archeologico Nazionale(?). After Minto 1929:pl. 72a. The figure, of unknown identity, stands with one hand on his hip and with the other loosely holds a club or branch. He wears an animal skin cap, and his head most remarkably faces in the opposite direction from his body.

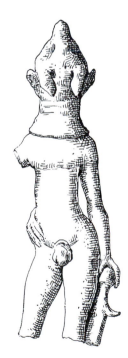

Thuf(ltha)

Part of the same company of small bronze statues of the Late Etruscan era is a work in the Vatican that may come from Vulci (Fig. VII.6). It shows again a rustic figure, wearing rough boots and also an animal skin, this time of a goat. His pose is a rare one in Etruscan art, but he probably is looking up at the sky with his arm extended to hold a twig to catch birds. The lunate shape on his head, only partially preserved, may well be a decoy bird or a real bird that has landed on him.

This striking figure carries an inscription with a reference to Thuf (perhaps the same name as Thufltha, which occurs elsewhere) and to Śuri, and may well be Thuf himself, a figure otherwise unknown in art. I have argued[15] that Thuf, who inhabits three cells of the Piacenza Liver (2, 20, and 21) and who must have been a prominent god of cult (with 10 additional inscriptions)[16] may be the counterpart of the divinity Favor in Martianus. The latter deity, a god of good will, appears in four regions (1, 4, 6, and 11) and is closely associated with Jupiter. Thuf on the liver shares a cell with Tinia twice, also indicating a close bond between the two. As for the birding motif, it may be found in a passage in Propertius written in the 1st century BCE that links Favor with the act of catching birds (4.2.34: *harundine sumpta Favor plumoso sum deus aucupio*; "With the bird-twig in my hand, I'm Favor, god of feathery fowling").

Personifications and Group Gods

Rather easy to comprehend are the deities of Martianus who personify various abstract qualities,[17] both desirable and undesirable (for their locations in the heavens see Table III and Fig. III.3): Health (*Salus*), Wellness (*Valetudo*), Favor (*Favor*), and Fortune (*Fortuna*), along with Deceit (*Fraus*), Discord (*Discordia*) and Dissension (*Seditio*). Similarly meaningful are Jupiter's Wealth (*Opulentia Jovis*) and Fruit of Spring (*Veris Fructus*). Then there are the spirits in groups, such as the Fates (*Fata*), and Divine Shades (*Dii Manes*), and—as we have already mentioned—those vague divine committees called the Consenting Gods (*Dii Consentes*) and the Secret Gods of Favor (*Favores Opertanei*). The Ninefold Gods (*Dii Novensiles*) and the Public Gods (*Dii Publici*) are likewise elusive. Finally we must call attention to the Lares, Penates, and Genius, all of whom appear in Region 1 of Martianus, and who are generally believed to have been important in Etruscan religion before they became well known for their roles in Roman private and public worship. We know that Lares appear elsewhere in the heavens, e.g., the Military Lar (*Lars Militaris*), the Heavenly Lar (*Lar Caelestis*), and the Lar of All and Everything (*Lar Omnium Cunctalis*).

But these and other deities named by Martianus remain vague for us. One would like to connect their names with spirits represented in Etruscan art, but so far little has been accomplished. This situation is especially disappointing in light of the fact that we do have representations of a number of spirits, especially on mirrors, and they are often labeled in Etruscan. Perhaps one reason the connections with Martianus are seldom made is that scholars have categorized the mirror spirits in terms of their roles in mythological scenes, and thus often lumped them together. They are seen as belonging to the Sphere of Turan, or to the Sphere of Fufluns, or are categorized as Birth Goddesses or Underworld spirits. In truth some of them hop about from one sphere to another, which would make more sense if they are in fact

VII.6 Bronze statuette perhaps from Vulci, ca. 250–200 BCE. Vatican Museums, Museo Gregoriano Etrusco. Photo: Museum. The rustic figure dressed in boots and an animal skin bears an inscription mentioning Thuf and śuri. He gazes toward the sky and extends one arm upward in a pose that may be reconstructed as holding up a twig to catch birds. He may be Thuf, here argued to be the counterpart of Roman Favor, a god associated with birding.

VII.7 Bronze mirror, ca. 325–300 BCE. New York, Metropolitan Museum of Art. After CSE U.S.A.:3.10a. Menrva, (center), presides over the cavorting of the satyr Sime (right) and the maenadic dancing figure of Thalna (left). Sime is nude, beardless, and snub-nosed; he carries a staff resembling a Bacchic thyrsos. Thalna wears slippers and a diadem; her mantle falls off her body in a Bacchic motif of stripping.

personifications. Table IV presents a checklist of these subsidiary spirits, in alphabetical order, as a guide to the reader in helping to distinguish their various names and spheres as we consider them in more detail in the rest of this chapter.

Thalna and Thanr

Our first case is Thalna,[18] a popular spirit who has been identified on some eighteen mirrors and whose name has been etymologized as having the verbal meaning of "sprout" or "bloom," and thus perhaps having to do with growth or youth. That this is a personification is strongly suggested by the fact that Thalna is represented on Etruscan mirrors as both male and female, indicating that the artists and most likely their patrons as well did not have a strong sense of the physical appearance of the god. We are reminded that the Romans would pray to a deity *si deo si deae* ("whether a god or a goddess"; Aulus Gellius, *Noctes Atticae* 2.28.2-3), without stipulating the gender.[19] We have already met a female Thalna, present at the birth of Menrva (Fig. IV.13) and the birth of Fufluns (Fig. IV.11) and

VII.8 Bronze mirror from Tarquinia, ca. 325–300 BCE. Tarquinia, Museo Archeologico Nazionale. After ES:5.25. The loving couple of Atunis and Turan is attended by Achvizr (left), who raises high an alabastron, no doubt containing perfumed oil, and a winged Thalna (right) who crowns Turan for her success.

she also oversees the cheerful scene of the presentation of Epiur (Fig. IV.14). But she changes spheres when she becomes a Bacchic maenad, flanking Menrva and dancing in symmetry with the satyr Sime (Fig. VII.7), and again changes as she joins Turan for a love scene with Atunis (Fig. VII.8), this time sporting wings and bestowing a wreath upon Turan. Then she changes sex, and becomes a beardless male conferring with Tinia and Turms (Fig. VII.9; sphere undefined). Finally, we may note that the male Thalna takes part in prophecy, in a scene with two other spirits who are not well understood (Fig. VII.10).[20] Prucnas, otherwise unknown in Etruria, seems to throw his head back in song, as Zipna listens intently. The husky youth Thalna assumes the stance of a soothsayer, with left leg raised and placed on a rock, and with right hand raised in a pointing gesture often used by someone explaining a prophecy.

So Thalna may play a supporting role in scenes of birth, romance, revelry, and prophecy. In addition, some have seen the deity as having a leading part in one scene, where she plays with the love-toy, the *iynx*, and is paired with the youth An-

VII.9 Bronze mirror from Vulci, 4th century BCE. Vatican Museums, Museo Gregoriano Etrusco. After ES:1, 75. Conference of three deities. A male Thalna (left) wears a mantle and a fillet. In the middle stands a beardless, lightning-wielding Tinia, and on the right is Turms, with winged hat and winged sandals. In lower exergue a satyr clambers over an ivy vine as two large birds peck at the berries.

chas, in the presence of a large bird, probably a swan (Fig. VII.11). There is really only one way to explain the amazing versatility of this spirit, who is represented as male or female and in a variety of contexts. She/he must be a personification of an abstract quality that can have an effect in all of these narratives. In fact it has been proposed that the deity is equivalent to Iuventas, "Youth," and perhaps that is indeed the appropriate identity. It may be better to choose a deity from Martianus (even though the name of Thalna is not attested on the Piacenza Liver). For example Salus, "Health," from Martianus Region 1, would actually fit as well, if not better, in the variety of scenes. We must leave the final answer open until there is further evidence.

As for Thalna's colleague Thanr,[21] she (female only) appears in several scenes with infants, and may indeed be a birth goddess (Figs. IV.12-13). Though she does not occur on the Liver, her list of inscriptions besides those on mirrors registers a respectable total of seven, and includes dedications that show cult, one of which

VII.10 Bronze mirror, ca. 350–300 BCE. New York, Metropolitan Museum of Art. After CSE U.S.A.:3.20a. Prucnas, a youth with neck-length locks, sits upon a rock in a tensed position with head thrown back and mouth open, as if singing. Zipna, depicted as a motherly figure with arm around him, listens carefully, while Thalna (here a muscular male) interprets. The scene is most likely prophetic. Zipna and Thalna wear pointed-toe shoes.

mentions her in company with Selvans. She appears on the Capua Tablet and on a lead disc from Magliano (ET AV 4.1), both of which show connections with the Underworld; Thanr could then be a goddess who affects both birth and death. I think it most likely that she, too, is a personification of an abstract concept (Valetudo, "Wellness," from Martianus would make a good companion for Salus), and we shall see shortly how she plays such a role in three mirrors with rich iconography (Figs. VII.17-19).

Mean and Other Spirits

A great bevy of these personifications, both male and female, appears mainly in scenes of romance and marriage, for example on the famous mirror in the Hermitage in St. Petersburg showing the embrace of Turan and Atunis (Fig. V.28). Fluttering around the border of the mirror, they create a festive, celebratory atmosphere as they bring items for the adornment or perfuming of the couple. Not all the names can be read, but beginning near the top, and moving from right to left,

VII.11 Bronze mirror, ca. 300 BCE. Paris, Musée du Louvre. After CSE France:1.3.3a. On the right Thalna (female; no wings; fully dressed) plays with the love-toy the iynx, probably trying to bewitch the half-draped youth Anchas (left). A large swan flutters behind his back.

we see Mean bringing a wreath, Munthuch with a perfume bottle, Achvizr with a ribbon, and Alpan with another wreath. Zipna, a splendid winged goddess, sits near the couple and offers perfume with her dipper (she elsewhere plies a mirror, as we shall see). At the base of the mirror we have a Bacchic note, with a funny plump satyr boy with horse's tail, pouring out the contents of a large amphora. His name is Hathna.

Mean[22] is often shown crowning a victor with a wreath, for example Elcsntre (Fig. IV.14) or Hercle (Fig.VII.12). She may occasionally pick up the perfume bottle and dipper to do another task, as in the Birth of Fufluns (Fig. IV.11). Scholars believe that she is very close in significance to the Roman goddess Victoria and the Greek personification Nike. Munthuch[23] may usurp her role, as on one of the Epiur mirrors, where the latter takes over the crowning of Hercle (Fig. IV.15), but

VII.12 Bronze mirror from Perugia, ca. 400–350 BCE. Perugia, Museo Archeologico Nazionale. After CSE Italia 2.1.1a. Hercle, with bow, club, and lion skin, is crowned by Mean. Cerberus, the three-headed dog of the Underworld, stands obediently at his feet. The goddess places one wreath upon his head with her right hand and holds another ready in her left. The fully clad female Leinth stands by but looks away and seems to point toward something outside the scene.

this goddess may cavort like a maenad as well, as in a dance scene with the older satyr, Chelphun (Fig. VI.1). Munthuch also plays a significant role in adornment, as we shall see.

Alpan, Achvizr, Leinth, and Evan

Alpan (also spelled Alpnu and Alpanu)[24] is evidently the deity listed on the Piacenza Liver as Alp, in House 14, with Cvl. The word *alpan* also occurs frequently in Etruscan votive inscriptions and seems to refer to willingness to give, or perhaps sometimes to a *thing* given willingly, i.e., a gift (cf. the inscription on the statue to Culśanś, above). The Latin word *libens*, "gladly, with pleasure," has been suggested as a translation of the verbal noun. Alpan's name is incised on seven mirrors and

VII.13 Bronze mirror, ca. 325–300 BCE. Providence, RI, Rhode Island School of Design. After ES:5.122. The Etruscan deity Achvizr (right) joins the Greek characters Thethis (=Thetis) and her son Achle (=Achilles) in a graceful, friendly dance. The context is intimate, with a basin for bathing behind the group.

she appears mainly in love scenes (see Fig. V.28), nude or dressed, winged or not. It is not surprising that this personification appears once as a male.

Achvizr (also spelled Achviztr, Achuveser, and Acaviser),[25] known from seven mirrors, also changes gender and also seems to be from the circle of Turan, but perhaps should not be too narrowly cast. *He* flies up with a ribbon or offers perfume (Fig. V.28) for Turan and Atunis, while *she* joins the merry dancing of Achule (=Achilles) and his mother Thethis (Fig. VII.13). Other scenes to be discussed below reveal the good will and kindness of this spirit.

Leinth,[26] appearing on only three mirrors, is a nude beardless male with a spear when attending the Mariś babies (Fig. V.6) and appears similarly in another scene that may show Epiur, but as a female attends Mean as she crowns Hercle for defeating the three-headed dog of the Underworld, known as Cerberus in Latin (Fig. VII.12). Philologists are convinced that the name Leinth relates to an Etrus-

VII.14 Bronze mirror from Tarquinia, ca. 300 BCE. Berlin, Staatliche Museen, Antikensammlung. After CSE Deutsche Demokratische Republik:1.31b. The youth Atunis stands in the center, holding a leafy branch and awaiting a wreath from Evan (left) and the application of perfume by Mean (right). A bird of good omen flies in from the left with a fine necklace.

can word for death or the act of dying, and have pointed out the appropriateness for the mirror with Cerberus; the mirrors with the babies might show an inversion of the sphere or duties of the deity, relating to birth and life.

Evan appears on four mirrors, once as male and the other times as female.[27] The masculine Evan appears conversing with a male Alpan in the presence of the goddess of love, Turan, while the female spirit is represented as a central figure in an affectionate embrace with a young man labeled Itinthni (a story otherwise unknown; even if Itinthni=the Greek character Tithonos, no light is shed). Evan may also offer a wreath to Atunis as Mean applies his perfume (Fig. VII.14).

Malavisch

An exceptional case is that of the figure labeled Malavisch[28] on six mirrors; we have already mentioned the conference of gods in which she appears with Aplu,

VII.15 Bronze mirror, ca. 350 BCE. London, British Museum. After Bonfante 1990:fig. 17. Adornment of the bride Malavisch (center); she is attended by a group of personification deities (left to right), Zipna, Hinthial, and Munthuch; Turan (right) looks on, with a bird perched upon her shoulder and a fragrant twig in her right hand. In exergue a hen and a rooster, beak to beak. Below this, a child wearing a necklace with bullae grasps an ivy vine.

male Artumes and Hercle (Fig. V.32). But in all other cases she has a characteristic role: she is always shown as the central figure in rich adornment scenes. All scholars agree that she is to be identified as a bride, though it is not decided whether Malavisch is a personal name or simply the Etruscan word for "bride."

The scheme may be fairly simple, with only two attendants, or more developed, as on a mirror that adds in the theme of prophecy for the marriage; a head (=voice) of Silenus emerges from the clouds above as Aplu, a prophetic god, oversees the adornment of the bride and preparation of her hair (Fig. II.13). On a fine mirror in the British Museum (Fig. VII.15) a crowd of attendants ministers to Malavisch.[29] Turan, on the far right, is supervising as Munthuch adjusts the lady's diadem; this spirit carries a pointed stick that may be multipurpose in adornment scenes (for applying perfumes, but perhaps also for arranging the hair). Her name has been equated with the Latin word *mundus*, one of the meanings of which is "adornment, elegance." Zipna is assigned to arrange the hair in back; she and Munthuch both wear a thin, sensual, see-through chiton. Meanwhile, another attendant, dressed in a body-concealing mantle, holds a mirror in the scene. It is interesting that she does not hold up the mirror for the bride to look into, but gazes intently at it herself. This depiction may relate to the idea, demonstrable in several other cases, that the mirror was an instrument of prophecy used at the time of marriage to foretell the future of the couple. Although it cannot be proven, most scholars accept the suggestion that the Etruscan mirror was in fact frequently used as a marriage gift.

VII.16 Greek painted red-figured water jar (hydria) by the Meidias Painter, found at Populonia, late 5th century BCE. Florence, Museo Archeologico Nazionale. After Becatti 1947:pl. 3. In center, Adonis in the lap of Aphrodite is surrounded by personification deities. Before the face of Adonis, Eros plies the iynx; behind him Eurynoe ("Breadth of Knowledge") converses with a small bird. On the right Paidia ("Games and Play") sits in the lap of Hygieia ("Good Health").

Hinthial

The figure with the mirror is very evocative, for she is labeled Hinthial, a word that is also used in Etruscan Underworld scenes to label shades of the dead. She must be, then, the Soul, who attends the bridal scene, just as Psyche, the personification of the soul in Greek and Roman myth, was often represented in such a context. When Pysche married Cupid, from the union came a child called Voluptas in Latin. That is, to speak in allegorical terms, the union of Love with the Soul generated Pleasure. Just possibly, we have a similar abstract language at work in this scene. The Bride is attended by Love (Turan) and the Soul (Hinthial), and she is groomed by Elegance. (The meaning of the name of Zipna is not known.)

Allegorical Scenes

Almost all of the Etruscan mirrors with personifications and allegorical tone belong to the 4th century BCE. A similar allegorical language may be seen in Greek art of a slightly earlier period (late 5th century BCE). On two fine hydriae (water jars) imported into Etruria and deposited in a tomb at Populonia,[30] we see depictions of Aphrodite and Adonis surrounded by playful figures inscribed as Himeros ("Desire"), Eutychia ("Good Fortune") and Pannychis ("All-night Festival"), while in another scene a loving couple, Phaon and Demonassa, are attended by Hygieia ("Health"), Eudaimonia ("Happiness"), and Herosora ("Springtime").

VII.17 Bronze mirror, 4th century BCE. Basel, Antikenmuseum und Sammlung Ludwig. After CSE Schweiz:1.17. A gathering of spirits of love and good will, all represented as female; left, Turan is seated with a swan in her lap and a fragrant twig in her right hand. Thanr and Thalna, standing center, kiss and embrace affectionately; right Achvizr, seated, holds out pomegranates in each hand.

In this atmosphere of good cheer and harmony the personifications are sometimes shown as warm and affectionate to one another (Fig. VII.16).[31]

This same kind of allegorical tone and vocabulary may be present in three Etruscan scenes that have always baffled scholars (Figs. VII.17-19). The three representations have an almost identical composition and the participants are almost the same in each case, though they alternate roles. The similarity of the ground line of the scene and of various details of clothing suggest that they came out of the same workshop, but unfortunately none of the find spots are known. In each, the center is occupied by two female figures who look into each other's eyes; in two of these, they kiss each other on the lips, a motif that is actually quite rare in Etruscan art. It has been suggested that the scenes are erotic and show lesbian love,[32] although the clothing is formal and matronly and not particularly suitable for such an interpretation.

In one of these scenes (Fig. VII.17), the loving pair is labeled as Thanr and Thalna, whom we have seen as goddesses who help out at the birth of Menrva; if the hypothetical interpretation of these colleagues as Health and Wellness may be

VII.18 Bronze mirror, 4th century BCE. Berlin, Staatliche Museen. After ES:4.324A. Personifications associated with love, good will, good health, and success left to right: Thalna holds up an egg; Thanr and Alpan embrace and kiss; Zipna looks into a mirror, probably to ascertain a prophecy.

used as a model (the precise Etruscan identification need not be thus, but these names help to demonstrate the idea), in fact their attraction to one another seems quite logical. They are attended by a seated Turan on the left and Achvizr on the right. On the second mirror (Fig. VII.18) Thanr embraces this time Alpan, goddess of gladness, as Thalna and Zipna sit near, again forming a group of figures who are likely candidates for the role of abstract personification. And on the third example (Fig. VII.19), Alpan now demonstrates her affection for Achvizr; Thanr is seated and opposite her is Zipna.

It is interesting that in two cases Zipna gazes into a mirror, again perhaps relating to the use of mirrors for prophecy.[33] If these goddesses are gathered to show their unified support of a forthcoming marriage, we can imagine that the message of prophecy is encouraging and harmonious. Further, the mirrors include many positive signs of fruitfulness and fertility. On Mirror 1 Achvizr carries two pomegranates while Turan has her swan and a twig flourishing with leaves, while

VII.19 Bronze mirror, ca. 300 BCE. Berlin, Staatliche Museen. After ES:4.324. Personifications as in Figs. VII.16–17: left, Zipna, seated, looks into a mirror; Alpan and Achvizr embrace, center; Thanr, right, has a small bird perched on her hand.

on mirror 2 Thalna holds an egg, and on mirror 3, Achvizr holds a bird (probably giving an omen). In short, the interpretation of these scenes as homosexual is probably quite inappropriate. Instead, we seem to have the use of personifications and an allegorical language to convey a message of good fortune and well-being, most probably to celebrate a new marriage.

I would like to view within this context a rather different mirror, long known but recently restudied, interpreted, and published with an excellent new drawing that reveals many new details about the subject matter (Fig. VII.20).[34] In this scene, Achvizr is once again shown as a protagonist, sweetly kissing a partner. This time, though, Achvizr is male, and the partner is none other than Turan, personification of love. I suggest that the subject is allegorical, as on the others, showing the concord of spirits. The two other figures on the mirror are more difficult to explain. Uslanes, on the right, unknown apart from this representation, has a name that connects him with the sun god Usil; so perhaps we have a figure joining in, rising

VII.20 Bronze mirror from Corchiano, ca. 350–300 BCE. Civita Castellana, Museo dell'Agro Falisco. After Ambrosini 1995:fig. 2. Turan, personification of love, embraces and kisses the kindly spirit Achvizr (spelled Acaviser), frequently female but here represented as masculine. A nude deity named Uslanes, whose name connects him with Usil, the Etruscan god of the sun, gazes at them from right. Sethlans (left) turns his back as he tends a great wheel divided into approximately 16 segments.

up behind Turan, making a reference to the sun itself, or a day or a time of day as often on Etruscan mirrors (cf. Figs. I.10, II.2, V.5, V.39). The figure on the left, labeled Sethlans, turns his back to the viewer as he stands within (supporting?) a great wheel that, judging from the surviving segmentation, had four divisions in one-quarter of the wheel; that is, all in all it had 16 parts, like the universe of the Etruscans. The overtones are cosmic, but I am as yet unable to explain why the smith god would be in charge of this cyclical element.

In contrast, Ambrosini[35] has made an ingenious explanation of the subject on the basis of Greek mythology as follows: Achvizr is taking the place of Ares in the Homeric tale of the adulterous love affair of Ares and Aphrodite (Homer, *Odyssey*, 8.267-366), and Uslanes, the sun is spying upon them (not in the Homeric tale, but Helios was known for his spying proclivities); Sethlans, as the spouse of Turan, waits to punish them for their crime, not, as in Homer, with a magic net thrown around the lovers, but with a wheel like the one he used to punish Ixion, who made an attempt on the virtue of Hera. In this argument the result is a coherent interpretation of every detail of the scene, though of course we must admit that we are

VII.21 Bronze mirror, from Montefiascone, ca. 325–300 BCE. Naples, Museo Nazional Archeologico. After ES:1.115. Seated left, Atunis, half-draped in an elegant mantle, holds a rustic stick; Turan (center) holds out a leafy twig to him; an attendant (right) labeled Lasa Sitmica, a male winged figure in a fine mantle. A cosmetic basket hangs in field (upper left).

falling back on the old methodology of cutting and pasting from several Greek accounts. The biggest problem, however, is that nothing we know about the Etruscan divinity Achvizr qualifies him for this kind of adulterous, punishable role. He/she is unequivocally a kindly, helpful, gentle spirit, in no way like the Greek god of war. Another problem lies in the fact that in Etruria, there is no evidence that Sethlans was consort of Turan.[36] Thus neither explanation of this mirror scene is perfectly convincing, but they are both included here to give an example of the lively debate possible when two different methodologies are used to interpret Etruscan myth, either beginning from inside Etruria or else invoking Greek influence.

Are there any spirits of ill will in Etruscan art? We know that the Etruscan heavens of Martianus supported dwellings for Deceit, Discord, and Dissension. In the Underworld scenes in Etruscan art, there were certainly demons, and the goddess Vanth is sometimes dressed rather like a Greek Fury (Fig. X.19). But she and her colleagues belong in another part of the universe and will be discussed in Chapter X. For the normally more favorable parts of the sky, we are almost com-

VII.22 Bronze mirror from Perugia, ca. 300 BCE. Florence, Museo Archeologico Nazionale. Photo: Soprintendenza per Beni Archeologici della Toscana. Atunis dances with a winged female labeled Lasa Achununa. Her mantle flies off her body as they whirl. Left, a swan hovers over the shoulder of Atunis.

VII.23 Bronze mirror, ca. 350 BCE. London, British Museum. After CSE Great Britain:1.1.28b. A solemn winged female figure, evidently Lasa, holds up a scroll before the warriors Hamphiare (=Amphiaraus, left) and Aivas (=Ajax, right). The names on her scroll are Lasa, Aivas, and Hamphiare.

pletely without any information. The one really good candidate for this category is a figure whose name is not given, but who certainly seems to have a malevolent nature. On the mirror with Maristuran (Fig. VI.35), in the upper zone of the mirror appears a quite hideous figure (thought to be female; does she wear earrings?) who seems to be brandishing a weapon. It is most unfortunate that not all the inscriptions on the mirror can be read, and we do not know who the couple in the middle is. But with what we do have, we can say that the lovers are attended by the Genius of Turan on the right and Alpan, the goddess of giving with gladness on the left, but that the happiness of the pair is threatened by a dangerous spirit from above (Discord?).

Lasa

There remains one very important deity to discuss, perhaps the most significant of all the secondary spirits, the figure of Lasa.[37] The inscribed name occurs

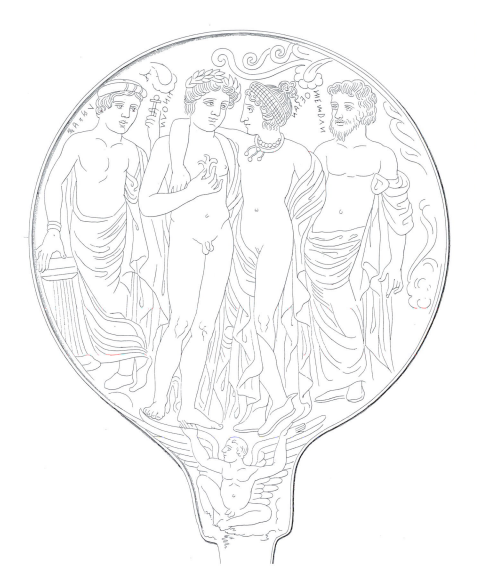

VII.24 Bronze mirror from Chiusi, ca. 300 BCE. Florence, Museo Archeologico Nazionale. After ES:4.290. The amorous couple of Tinthun (=Tithonos) and Thesan (=Eos) is flanked by Lasa (left) and Memrun (=Memnon, son of Eos)(right). Lasa may be holding a perfume dipper. In lower exergue, a winged child.

14 times next to figures on mirrors, one time on a gem, and once on the Piacenza Liver in House 19, near the Houses of Tinia. There has been endless discussion about the nature of Lasa, whether the name is generic, and means something like "nymph," or whether it refers to one particular deity who demonstrates great variation in appearance and is active in a number of different contexts. The heavens of Martianus do not have Nymphae, though they do harbor Lymphae in Region 2, and these deities have been said to be deities of *lympha*, i.e., water, and thus to qualify as Nymphae. There is little evidence, however, that Lasa is connected with water. What is worth noting is that Lasa does seem to have a parallel in Mariś, as they appear together flanking Tinia (Fig. VI.33), where we might "translate" the group into Latin and say that Jupiter is attended by a Genius and a Nymph.

VII.25 Bronze mirror, ca. 300–275 BCE. Columbia, MO, Museum of Art and Archaeology, University of Missouri. After CSE U.S.A.:1.18a. A naked winged spirit, probably Lasa, flits delicately to the left, carrying an alabastron and a perfume dipper. She wears a diadem, necklace, earrings, and bracelet on her upper arm, and slippers on her feet.

VII.26 Terracotta relief sculpture, akroterion from a shrine at I Fucoli, Chianciano Terme, 2nd century BCE. Chianciano Terme, Museo delle Acque. After Haynes 2000:Fig. 270. The lovely airborne spirit (identity unknown) flies to her right and looks back over her shoulder, her right arm raised to shade her eyes as if she has caught sight of a divinity. She is nude except for her slippers, body jewelry, arm bracelet, earrings, and diadem with tiny wings upon it. She carries her mantle loosely over her left arm.

Lasa is normally represented as female (but once as male), winged or without wings, dressed or clothed, in scenes of love and of prophecy. We have seen that the deity may have a byname, as in Lasa Vecu (or Lasa Vecuvia), who is surely equivalent to the Latin designation Nympha Vegoia (Figs. II.7-8) and was a spirit of prophecy. The male example, Lasa Sitmica, attends Turan and Atunis (Fig. VII.21), while another Lasa with a byname, Lasa Achununa, is depicted alone with Atunis in a swirling atmosphere of embrace (Fig. VII.22). The two other Lasas with bynames both appear on the grand Epiur mirror (Fig. IV.14). Lasa Thimrae plies her perfume dipper and bottle next to the enthronement of Elinai, and Lasa Racuneta, with the same equipment, is ensconced in the flower of a morning glory in the lowest zone of the mirror. There is no telling what these various bynames may mean. Not very convincing or helpful is the suggestion that they may associate the Lasas with particular families, as a special spirit of that household.

The single name Lasa also occurs in an intriguing scene (Fig. VII.23) of two dispirited warriors, Hamphiare (=Amphiaraus) and Aivas (=Ajax). In Greek myth the two heroes do not interact or appear together, and the combination here is unique. The goddess holds up a scroll with three names written upon it (Lasa, Hamphiare, Aivas), a device which some think is meant to announce their fate. (Elsewhere Lasa Vecuvia shows clearly that the goddess may serve in a prophetic role, and that theme may in fact be the unifying element.) Both were destined to die, and the death of Amphiaraus at Thebes and of Ajax at Troy may be the subject of the prophecy.

For the rest, Lasa seems to serve mainly at love scenes, as an attendant for Turan and Atunis, Elinai and Elchsntre, and Thesan and her beloved Tinthun (=Tithonos; Fig. VII.24). From these and the Epiur mirror Lasas have earned the reputation of being spirits of love and adornment, within the circle of Turan. This designation is quite accurate, but always with the reservation that Lasa may go to other spheres and take care of other duties. There may be many more, even dozens, of representations of Lasa in Etruscan art, and scholars have a tendency to use the label for any goddess without an inscription who has equipment for adornment, especially if she is winged (Fig. VII.25). Some also wish to include Mean, Thalna, and many other spirits under the generic name of Lasa, but given our ignorance of details about Etruscan spirits it is safer to restrict the name to the images that are specifically labeled with an inscription Lasa.

A Water Spirit?

We may conclude this chapter with reference to a stunning terra cotta sculpture of a goddess (Fig. VII.26), newly discovered along with a number of other sculptures at a place of cult near Chianciano Terme (Chiusi area).[38] These are assumed to have decorated a shrine or temple, perhaps focused on a cult connected with a nearby thermal spring.

From the various sculptures unearthed it is not possible to state what the overall theme of the decoration was, nor is it possible to identify the deity under discussion, the best preserved of the figures. More than half life-size, she served as an akroterion on the right hand side of the gable of the building. The spirit is dressed in a mode similar to that of the Lasas we have discussed, winged and nude except for her shoes and jewelry; she also carries her mantle across her left arm, and in her hand, what has been identified as a kantharos, a large cup normally used for drinking wine. The gesture of her arm, raised up as if to protect her against something (the sighting of a deity?), creates a narrative touch. An unusual detail is that her diadem is decorated with miniature wings. On the basis of her kantharos and a terracotta wreathed krater (mixing bowl for wine) found among the sculptures the figure has been said to be Dionysiac. Another possibility is that she is a water spirit, one of the Lymphae of Martianus (Region 2). Without inscriptions we cannot know for sure who she is; perhaps further study of the context will help to clarify her identity.

Heroes and Heroines VIII

Etruscan art does have representations of Etruscan heroes who are readily recognizable, in particular, the Vipinas brothers, already mentioned as appearing in the story of the prophecy of Cacu (Figs. II.5-6).[1] But due to the paucity of sources, it is not possible to tell if they follow the literal definition of a hero as one who is born from the union of a god and a mortal, nor can we tell if they qualify as heroes through the structural pattern of their lives,[2] which is often used as a diagnostic measure. The hero in myths told worldwide is usually distinguished by having something unusual about his birth, as well as threats to his life in infancy. Next often comes a period of exile and a challenge of great trials at the hands of an adversary, and he accomplishes great deeds. Sometimes the hero has a twin or close comrade, a kind of alter ego, who helps him with his deeds. The hero marries well, usually to a woman of high status in some locality where he is a visitor. Finally, the hero often dies a cruel death and has a cult established in connection with his tomb. All of these elements may be found in the life of Herakles in Greek myth; we have abundant literary sources that help us to identify these characteristics. But for the Vipinas brothers, our best evidence is representations in Etruscan art, and after that, there are a few Roman texts that may give clues about them. But we do not know their parents or anything about their birth, nor anything about their marriage or death.

Apart from their legendary deeds, the one characteristic of a hero we may point to here, and in several other Etruscan heroes, is the presence of the alter ego. Accordingly a few words may be said about this mythologem in the hero tradition.[3] Many heroes have an attendant or a double who can make up for the weaknesses of the hero. Given that the hero has human characteristics and is not fully divine, he often has need of someone who can play his role before he goes into action or when he is incapacitated or can simply help him to finish a job. The alter ego may also take on a balancing role, helping to keep the hero steady, or on the other hand may act as a foil to the hero, by being his subordinate or his opposite, bringing into relief just how good and strong he is. A very good example of all these aspects of the alter ego theme is provided by the Near Eastern myth of Gilgamesh and his close friend, Enkidu. Other hero stories contain some or all of these characteristics of the companion: Aeneas with Achates, Romulus with his twin Remus, Jesus with John the Baptist, the Norse Baldr and his twin Hodr (the former symbolizing light and the latter darkness).[4] An especially interesting case is that of Herakles, who has two alter ego figures, his twin brother Iphikles, and his nephew Iolaus (one shows inferiority and the other acts as an assistant). We shall see how the alter ego theme recurs in Etruria, beginning with Avle and Caile Vipinas.

VIII.1 Alabaster ash urn from Sarteano, 2nd century BCE. Siena, Museo Archeologico. After Brunn-Körte:pl. 119.1. The seer Cacu (center) holds his lyre and makes a gesture of explanation with his right hand. He is under attack by twin bearded soldiers, the Vipinas brothers, with drawn swords; his assistant Artile, sitting at his feet, clutches a scroll and laments. Other warriors participate, nude (left and right below, defeated?) and dressed (left and right, above). Horse's head in field, upper right.

The Vipinas Brothers and Cacu

In the Cacu myth, we may deduce from the various representations (which in themselves show some significant variation; Figs. II.5-6, Figs. VIII.1-2) some of the action, as described above in Chapter II. The Vipinas brothers are often depicted in twinning positions as warrior captors, who have come to seize the prophet. The same theme of catching the prophet occurs in Roman poetry (e.g., Virgil, *Eclogue* 6) when shepherds seize Silenus and make him tell the secrets of the universe and in Greek mythology when Menelaus seizes Proteus to learn what fate awaits him and how to deal with his future (Homer, *Odyssey* 4.370ff.).

Looking further at the Etruscan burial urns with the story of Cacu (there is a series of eight of them, from the area of Chiusi), we see that the conflict with the prophet may involve other participants and we may be able to deduce a bit more about the Vipinas brothers. Cacu's assistant Artile (himself perhaps an alter ego figure) is regularly present and there are also other soldiers who participate— seemingly defeated (Figs.VIII.1-2), shown as nude and fallen down on the ground as the ambush takes place. In addition, the Vipinas brothers seem to have their own assistants—standing, dressed, in attacking positions. On one urn a tree suggests the outdoor setting for the attack, similar to the landscape on the mirror. An interesting but unexplained recurring motif is the head of a horse that protrudes into the scene. Sometimes the horse seems to be rearing or jerking its head around as one of the Vipinas warriors or an assistant tries to bring it under control. The horse's head also occurs on a variant of the scene that seems to show the actual capture of Cacu (Fig. VIII.3).

There at sword point the naked seer is led away in bonds as Artile sits in dejection, joined by an equally despondent female figure, whom we have suggested earlier may be the sister of Cacu mentioned in Latin texts as a hearth goddess,

VIII.2 Alabaster ash urn from Cittá della Pieve, 2nd century BCE. Florence, Museo Archeologico Nazionale. Photo: DAI. Cacu and the Vipinas brothers, in a scene similar to Fig. VIII.1. Cacu throws his right arm over his head in a pose of transport. One of the Vipinas warriors embraces and restrains the horse on right. Artile holds up one hand in a pleading gesture. By his side is a yoke with two vessels attached.

Caca. She is nude and thus qualifies as a goddess, and carries a tablet or scroll in her hand, perhaps once again a prophetic motif. A further detail, particularly Etruscan, is the inclusion of two female figures with swords, dressed in the short tunic and cross-straps on the breast that are typical of the Underworld goddess Vanth. Their presence is ominous, for when these death spirits appear in Etruscan funerary art, they frequently indicate that bloodshed is to take place.

How may we summarize the story of the Vipinas brothers and Cacu? There are many gaps in our narrative. The best we can say is that Cacu, in the act of prophesying or teaching the youth Artile in a grove, and under the protection of soldiers, is suddenly seized by the Vipinas brothers and their followers in a rough encounter. They lead him away in captivity, and he may even perish, bringing great sorrow to his youthful follower and to his female ally, perhaps his sister and a goddess.

The Vipinas Brothers and Rome

The interaction between the Vipinas brothers and other figures that are clearly mythological establishes them as mythological as well. This is an important point, because if we go by other scraps of evidence about them, we find there is good reason to believe they were real historical characters. But as happened with other heroic figures in Greece or other cultures, stories and legends grew up around them and they were thus mythologized. One of the most famous stories about them was narrated by the Roman emperor Claudius (ruled 41-54 CE),[5] in a speech he gave concerning Roman citizenship. In making the point that non-Romans could be accepted in the city, he referred to Caele Vipinas, whom he called Caelius Vivenna, and said that he was an Etruscan general who was a close associate of Servius Tullius, king of Rome in the 6th century BCE, often listed as ruling in between the two Etruscan kings of Rome, Tarquinius Priscus and Tarquinius Superbus.

VIII.3 Alabaster ash urn from Sarteano, 2nd century BCE. Siena, Museo Archeologico. After Brunn-Körte:pl. 84.2. The scene probably represents Cacu taken captive (cf. Figs. VIII.1–2). Only one of the Vipinas brothers, here represented as nude, holds him at swordpoint and leads him away by bonds around his wrists. Artile sits and weeps, joined by a nude, standing female figure holding a scroll or tablet (Cacu's sister, Caca?) and a reclining, despondent Vanth. Head of a rearing horse in field. Far left and far right, perhaps two other Vanth figures.

Claudius mentioned the tradition that Servius was of servile birth, hence his name in Latin, but declared that he was known as Mastarna by the Etruscans. After various fortunes the army of Caelius, under the direction of Mastarna, occupied a hill in Rome, which then came to be called the Caelian, after him.

A remarkable Etruscan wall painting cycle of the 4th century BCE (Plates V-VI) confirms portions of this report by Claudius, and at the same time adds in some details to the legend of the Vipinas brothers that seem to indicate that the Etruscans had their own versions of stories told of early Rome. Found in a tomb at Vulci named after its excavator, Alessandro François, the paintings are situated adjacent to and thus likened to Greek myths and legends of the Trojan war, such as Achilles sacrificing prisoners at the tomb of Patroklos (Plate IV), and the Theban story of the brothers Eteokles and Polyneikes killing each other. On the left of the Etruscan scene (Plate V), a nude, bearded figure labeled Caile Vipinas holds out his bound hands as they are untied by another nude, bearded figure, labeled Macstrna, depicted on an adjacent wall. Under one arm Macstrna holds two swords, as if to indicate that he will use one himself and that the other will be supplied to Caile when he is released from captivity. Thus we seem to have a close parallel to the information provided by Claudius, in which the figure of Mastarna/Macstrna, demonstrates his alliance with Caile Vipinas. It is worth noting that the Etruscan name Macstrna has been analyzed by philologists as a servile name, and thus consistent with the Roman story.

Then follow, on the same wall as Macstrna, three pairs of figures involved in bloody combat. Moving to the other end of this mural, on the far right, we find that while Caile has been bound up his brother Avle (so labeled) has emerged as a victorious warrior, plunging his sword into his adversary, and two other warriors defeat their opponents as well. Evidently Macstrna and Avle Vipinas are staging a rescue of Caile, and at the same time killing off his captors. The names of the enemies suggest that they may be a force of allies from different Etruscan cities, including Volsinii (=Orvieto) and nearby Sovana. All of this seems relatively clear, and provides a background for the interpretation of the rather surprising scene that follows to the right of Avle Vipinas, on an adjoining wall.

VIII.4 Bucchero vessel from Veii, ca. 600–550 BCE. Rome, Museo Nazionale Etrusco di Villa Giulia. Photo: Soprintendenza per i Beni Archeologi del Lazio. The vessel bears an incised inscription: *mine muluv[an]ece avile vipiiennas* "Avle Vipinas dedicated me" (ET Vc 3.9). The inscription suggests that the hero Avle Vipinas was in fact a real person.

VIII.5 Bronze statuette, ca. 300 BCE. Toledo Museum of Art. Acc. 78.22, gift of Edward Drummond Libbey. Courtesy of Toledo Museum of Art. The youthful nude Hercle holds his bow and swings his club; inscribed on the right leg, *heracles mi*, "I [am] of Hercle."

VIII.6 Engraved scarab, 4th century BCE. New York, Metropolitan Museum of Art. Photo: Museum. A muscular young Hercle, naked and beardless, wrestles the Nemean lion. In field, his club and quiver.

Here is one more pair of combatants (Plate VI) with the victor labeled Marce Camitlnas, a name that is otherwise unknown. He brandishes his sword over a figure named Cneve Tarchunies Rumach, which would translate as Gnaeus Tarquinius of Rome. The story thus takes an astonishing turn, because it seems to indicate how Servius Tullius (Macstrna) came to power at Rome, by releasing Caile Vipinas and killing Tarquin and his allies, the captors of Caile. The scene takes place outdoors, as indicated by occasional bits of rocky ground, and it seems that the allies of Rome have been taken unawares, since they are mostly not armed, but rather wear mantles of civilian dress.

If this story is compared with the myth of the attack of the Vipinas brothers on Cacu, rather strangely it seems to be both a recapitulation of the theme, since Avle is shown ambushing his enemies, and an inversion of it, since Caile is shown in bondage instead of Cacu. These are the only two adventures we know of the heroes, though there are other glimpses of them in the archaeological record and in Roman writers. For example, from Veii, near Rome, comes a vase made of the characteristic Etruscan black pottery bucchero (Fig. VIII. 4), which was dedicated at a sanctuary by an individual named Avile Vipiennas, obviously the same name as that of one of the brothers.[6] It dates to the 6th century BCE, exactly the period of

VIII.7 Bronze mirror from Vulci. Vatican Museums, Museo Gregoriano Etrusco. After Rallo 2000: fig. 13. Calanice (=Herakles) prepares to take leave of Aril (=Atlas) after securing the Apples of the Hesperides. The hero wears the lion skin, with the head of the lion behind his right shoulder, mouth open. In his left hand he holds a tiny egg-shaped item, evidently one of the Apples. He carriers his signature club in his right hand. Aril supports the heavens, indicated by a large spreading amorphous shape articulated by miniature tridents. Exotic plants in the surrounding landscape.

the Vipinas brothers, since they were associates of Macstrna/Servius Tullius. Did the great Avle Vipinas visit Veii?

The heroes seem to be connected with a number of Etruscan localities. Besides Veii, we have seen that the Cacu mirror comes from Bolsena near Orvieto, and the ash urns come from Chiusi. The wall paintings at Vulci are often assumed to show a story from the history of Vulci, in which a group of soldiers under the Vipinas, from Vulci itself, defeats the Rome group. And then there is Rome, where the army of Caile settled the Caelian Hill, and where Avle also was connected with the Capitoline Hill, though largely through a fanciful etymology of the name of the hill, according to which Avle was equal to the Roman name Aulus, also spelled Olus. Arnobius (*adversus Nationes*, 6.7), writing in the late 3rd century CE, reports that on the Capitoline during excavations to lay foundations (presumably for the great Capitoline temple), a human head rolled out, thought to be the head of Olus Vulcentanus, i.e., Avle from Vulci. The Latin, *Caput Oli*, "head of Aulus," was thought to be the source of the name of the Capitoline Hill.[7] Other stories about Avle make him a king, perhaps even in Rome itself.

VIII.8 Bronze mirror, ca. 400 BCE. Berlin, Antikenmuseum. After ES:2.140. Hercle sacrifices a goat in the Garden of the Hesperides on an altar inscribed with the name of Menrva (*menruva*), the goddess who aided him in his labor. The lady who assists him shows no attributes of Menrva and is more likely one of the Hesperides. The serpent that guarded the tree emerges on left; in field a sunburst and a 6-pointed star.

There are several other prominent Etruscan heroes, known as founders of cities, who will be considered in a later chapter on legends of the founding of the Etruscans (Chapter IX). For the rest of this chapter we must survey the activities of several Greek heroes who were so important in Etruria that the Etruscans fully absorbed their mythology from Greece and often transformed it. It is very interesting that in both hero cases we shall study, Herakles and the Dioskouroi, there is a pattern rather like that of the Vipinas brothers, in which we have the theme of the twin or alter ego.

Hercle

Hercle[8] is immensely popular in Etruria and is especially recognized by his standard Greek attributes of lion skin, club, and bow and arrow (Fig. VIII.5). He carries out many of the standard Twelve Labors of Herakles/Hercules, such as the slaying of the Nemean Lion (Fig. VIII.6), which appears on an engraved sealing

VIII.9 Bronze mirror, ca. 300 BCE. Berlin, formerly Antiquarium. After ES:2.135. Hercle confronts a spring labeled Vipece, perhaps in an attempt to make it release its waters. The spring has a gargoyle spout in the shape of a lion's head. On right, an amphora tumbles downward.

stone with a scarab (beetle) on one side and the mythological theme incised in negative on the other, flat side. For some reason he was considered an especially fit subject for such stones, perhaps because they were owned by elite men who wanted to use the image to stamp their possessions and documents. But he was extremely popular on mirrors, too, i.e., he appealed to women of higher class. Labors represented there include the myth of Cerberus (Fig. VII.12),[9] and the story of Atlas and the Golden Apples of the Hesperides (Fig. VIII.7). The scene of the labor of the Apples shows the curious variation in which the name of Herakles is given as Calanice, evidently derived from Greek, Kallinikos, meaning something like "Fair Conqueror."[10] Atlas is here labeled as Aril, but other than these changes in nomenclature, the representation of the myth is quite consistent with Greek tradition. Evidently Hercle has received help from Aril in obtaining the apples, and now he leaves him behind to resume his job of holding up the heavens.

VIII.10 Bronze mirror, ca. 350 BCE. Berlin, Staatliche Museen. After ES:4.340. Hercle wrestles with the youthful Achlae (=Acheloos). The hero's standard attributes of club and bow and arrow are laid aside as he uses his hands to grab the river god by the horn on his head. Hercle wears the lion skin tied around his waist.

Another mirror shows Herakles himself in a visit to the Garden of the Hesperides (Fig. VIII.8), a variant of the story known in Greece as well in which he does not call on Atlas for help. The tree is covered with apples and fluttering birds, and the serpent guardian of the apples slithers forth from the left side of the scene. Here Hercle seems to be in the act of sacrificing a goat to his patroness Menrva, for her name is written on the altar.

More important than the Labors for our purposes is the evidence that Hercle had his own cult and mythology in Etruria. He was a worshipped god, who appears on the Piacenza Liver, in a house (no. 29) near that of Nethuns and Mariś, in a region that has been associated with water, and some have argued that this element was a key part of the worship of Hercle in Etruria. On a mirror from Vulci dating to the 4th century BCE he is shown doing battle with a lion-headed spring, named Vipece (otherwise unknown; Fig. VIII.9),[11] probably to make it release its

VIII.11 Wall painting, ca. 540 BCE. Tomb of the Bulls, Tarquinia. Photo: DAI. The scene shows a man-faced bull (Acheloos?) charging an erotic couple.

waters; the mythologem of the hero who strikes and brings waters is well known, as in the story of Moses finding water in the desert (*Exodus* 17.6). Hercle the water bringer was also responsible for creating the Ciminian Lake located in southern Etruria not far from Vulci (Servius, *ad Aen*.7.697). The tumbling amphora in this scene is a common attribute of Hercle, and he is often represented standing with one foot braced over the vessel; sometimes water pours out.

Another conquest of a water opponent may be seen in his wrestling match with the river god Achlae (=Acheloos; Fig. VIII.10), shown as beardless and youthful in a mirror that claims the only inscribed image of Acheloos from Etruria. Hercle wears the lionskin tied like an apron that covers his genital area, a fashion of dress occasionally found elsewhere in Etruscan art, though often the hero is shown with his body quite exposed (cf. Figs. VIII.5-7, 12-15). According to the Greek story, in contending with Acheloos for the hand of Deianira, Herakles tore one of the horns from the head of his opponent, and when he gave it back, received in return the magic horn of abundance of Amalthea (the *cornu copiae*). The myth obviously relates to the conquest of waters and the control of fertility.

While the cornucopiae does not seem to have enjoyed any popularity in Etruria, an Acheloos-like horned head (normally bearded, however) is seen in many contexts and over a long period, from Archaic to Hellenistic times. Considering that narrative about the horn-headed figure is so scarce, his image is surprisingly widespread, found in architectural decorations, mirror exergues, jewelry, and on armor. A particularly compelling image of the face of a man with bull's horns and ears is found on a bronze boss once deposited in a tomb in Tarquinia (Plate III).[12] It is one of six bosses, of varying sizes and decorated with the heads of lions and rams as well as the head of the bull-man. Their usage is not certain, but the emblems may have had a protective or apotropaic significance.

None of the many images of the bull-man is labeled, and it may well be that they have a significance quite outside of the Greek story of Acheloos. There is a story told by Ovid (Metamorphoses 15. 565-620) of a hero in Italy named Cipus,

VIII.12 Bronze mirror from Cascina (Valdichiana), 4th century BCE. Present location unknown. After ES:2.127. The boy Hercle is shown with his alter ego Vile, flanking Turms in the center of the composition. Hercle stands near the mouth of a spring (lower left) with his foot on an amphora. It is unclear what he holds in his hand (a cup?), and the attributes of Turms and Vile are also problematic. Turms is holding a round object, and Vile seems to hold a strigil in his left hand (but the hand is not clearly indicated.)

who found that horns had sprouted from his head. Consulting an Etruscan seer, he learned that the horns were a sign that he was destined to become king of Rome. The noble eschewed the chance to rule and to honor him the Romans engraved horns upon their city gate to commemorate the magic pair he bore. The horned heads of Etruria could thus be symbolic of royalty or rule.

In an Archaic tomb painting at Tarquinia (Fig. VIII.11; the Tomb of the Bulls)[13] there is a most surprising image of a man-faced, bearded bull, who charges a couple of males engaging in intercourse—one with a normal male dark skin, and the other, evidently a eunuch, with a light skin. The latter seems to attempt to halt the bull-man, by extending one hand as he tighly clasps a plant with the other. The bull himself registers erotic excitement. No one has succeeded in explaining this bizarre scene, but very likely it is mythological, telling some story of Acheloos or another bull-man of Etruria that has not been registered elsewhere in ancient literature or art.

VIII.13 Bronze mirror, probably from Perugia, ca. 300 BCE. Perugia, Museo Archeologico Nazionale. After CSE Italia:2.1.2a. Hercle and Vile are represented in mirroring poses, Hercle with club and lion skin and Vilae with spear, mantle, and shield.

The boyhood of Hercle was of interest to the Etruscans. An intriguing series shows him with the Etruscan equivalent of Iolaus, Herakles' squire and nephew, called Vile or Vilae, and in Etruria almost certainly his twin rather than his nephew. The two are shown as boys in the company of Turms (Fig. VIII.12; note that the child Hercle is already standing over an amphora), and are frequently depicted in twinning poses (Fig. VIII.13). The alter ego Vile may even take over one of the trials of Hercle, the strangling of the snakes, as we see in the lower extension of the Indiana mirror showing the Judgment of Elcsntre (Fig. V.19; cf. Fig. V.13, discussed earlier, the vase painting in which Hercle does strangle the serpents, and his twin Vile turns away in fear). Child Hercle himself appears in the exergue of another grand mirror depicting the Judgment of Elcsntre (Fig. V.23), where he is shown surrounded by his accoutrements of club, bow and arrow and lion skin, holding his head in dejection and sitting on what appears to be a fire. One thinks naturally of the death and apotheosis of the Greek Herakles on a pyre, but could the Etruscans have told the story of his cremation as a child?[14]

We have already noted some other extraordinary variants of the Greek myths of Herakles in Etruria, having considered in great detail the relationship of the grown

VIII.14 Bronze mirror from Civita Castellana, ca. 300 BCE. Present location unknown. After Brommer 1981:fig. 10. Hercle (far right) with the dead Thevrumines (=Minotaur) at his feet; left to right: Mine (=Minos), Menrva, Vile, and Areatha; upper exergue, unidentified boy with bird.

Hercle and Uni (Figs. V.14-17) and noted the romance between Hercle and Menrva (Fig. V.7). The myth in which Hercle is the conqueror of the Minotaur occurs more than once in Etruscan art and is not just a "mistake" by the artists.[15] The Etruscans really told that story. On a fine fourth-century mirror from Civita Castellana (Fig. VIII.14), the hero is shown with bow and arrow and lion skin, clearly labeled, discussing his conquest with Mine (=Minos), seated across from him, and in the presence of Menrva, Vile (here dressed in armor) and a matronly Ariatha. Beneath his feet lies the Minotaur, called Thevrumines (i.e., the Bull of Minos). The child holding a scroll and chasing a bird in the upper part of the scene is unlabeled and unknown, but almost certainly the vignette relates to some kind of omen.

Also rare is the narration of the salvation and healing of Prometheus, on a mirror in the Metropolitan Museum of Art (Fig. VIII.15). Here Hercle rests from

VIII.15 Bronze mirror, 3rd century BCE. New York, Metropolitan Museum of Art. After CSE U.S.A.:3.11. Prumathe (=Prometheus; seated in the center) has been freed by Hercle, on far right. The bird that gnawed his liver is lying on the ground in the middle of the scene. A youth labeled Esplace (=Asklepios, left) extends a bandage to help in healing Prumathe; Menrva meditates on the scene.

his labor in a pose very similar to that on the Thevrumines mirror, this time with his lion skin replacing the Minotaur, and the offending creature, the eagle who gnawed the liver of Prometheus, lying in a crumpled heap on the ground in the middle of the scene. Poor Prumathe is shown supported on one side by Menrva, who is often present for the deeds of Hercle, but the other attendant, the nude male youth on the left is unique. He is inscribed Esplake, evidently the equivalent of Asklepios, and he tends the patient by bandaging his wound. The combination is unknown outside of Etruria.

Then there are the myths for which the story itself is unknown, such as the Epiur scenes discussed above (Figs. IV.14-16) and the theme on a handsome relief mirror of Hercle carrying away an unknown lady called Mlacuch, whose name is closely related to the Etruscan adjective *mlaχ*, meaning "good, beautiful" (Fig. VIII.16).[16] It is of the late Archaic style and one of the earliest representations of Hercle on Etruscan mirrors. The amorous exploits of Herakles/Hercules were notorious in Greece and Rome, but this is an Etruscan addition to his list of conquests. The lady is beautifully dressed (though barefoot) and does not resist greatly, though Hercle seems to find it necessary to grip his club as he lifts her up.

VIII.16 Bronze mirror
with silver inlay, cast
in relief, ca. 480–470
BCE. London, British
Museum. After CSE
Great Britain:1.1.20d.
The youth Hercle (here
spelled Herecele) is
shown carrying Mlacuch,
a well-dressed lady
whose name is known
only in Etruria. His bow
and quiver have been
laid aside (left), but he
swings his club in his
right hand as he lifts her
up. It is disputed whether
he is rescuing or abduct-
ing her.

VIII.17 Carved scarab
ringstone, 4th century
BCE. Berlin, Staatliche
Museum, Antikensam-
mlung. Photo: Bildarchiv
Preussischer Kulturbe-
sitz. Hercle, holding his
club, sits despondently
upon an amphora, in
turn placed on a raft
of amphoras. Narrative
unknown.

It has been argued that he is in fact rescuing rather than abducting her. A curious detail is that from the lion skin he wears the head of the animal rears up and holds its mouth open as if to roar (a message of prophecy?). The knotted tail of the creature is another Etruscan motif. Hercle wears his mantle so that it wraps around his waist but leaves his genitals exposed.[17] Many attempts have been made to identify Mlacuch with some Greek heroine or other, or with a Roman goddess (the Bona Dea), or even to argue that her name comes from the Phoenician word for queen, *mlk*,[18] but no theory has won the day. Why can we not simply say that here, as with Cacu, Epiur, Pava Tarchies and Lasa Vecu, we have an Etruscan myth, the heroine of which story is a lady named Mlacuch?

Finally we may mention the myth of Hercle on the raft. It appears on more than twenty scarab stones (Fig. VIII.17) and two mirrors, both times in the mirror extension at the bottom (Figs. V.5, V. 27). Once again the amphoras play a role in a story about Hercle. The youthful hero is depicted on a raft supported by a varying number of amphoras, and sometimes appears to have improvised a sail. In one case, it looks as if he has strung up his lion skin for this purpose. The narrative is totally unknown, and we may only suggest that it shows a motif such as that of the youthful exile of the hero, who returns from the trial with increased maturity.[19]

VIII.18 Greek painted red-figure vase from Tarquinia, 500 BCE. Attributed to Oltos. Tarquinia, Museo Archeologico Nazionale. Photo: Soprintendenza per i Beni Archeologici del Lazio. Greek vessel (a) decorated with council of the gods; in center, Zeus receives wine poured by Ganymede; incised on the base (b) is an Etruscan inscription with a dedication to the *tinas cliniiaras* (=Sons of Tinia, Etruscan counterparts of the Dioskouroi, sons of Zeus).

a

b

Tinas Cliniar and Elinai

Even more common on Etruscan mirrors are the hero twins known as the Dioskouroi or Kastor and Polydeukes in Greece and as the Tinas Cliniar ("sons of Tinia") in Etruscan.[20]   An inscription on a Greek vase dedicated at Tarquinia seems to give us their Etruscan appellation (Fig. VIII.18): *itun turuce venel atelinas tinas cliniiaras*, "Venel Atelinas gave this to the sons of Tina," i.e., of Tinia. The

VIII.19 Bronze mirror, 3rd century BCE. Bologna, Museo Civico. After CSE Italia:1.1.9a. The twin Dioskouroi are shown in matching tunics and helmets, leaning away from the center in mirroring poses. Their shields are behind them. Between them stretch three horizontal lines, probably referring to the doorway lintel to their tomb, known in Greek as the *dokana*. A four-pointed star within a quincunx of dots probably refers to their shared immortality.

dedication went into a grave, an appropriate location for an object dedicated to these youths, who in Greek myth were originally one mortal (Kastor, Etr. Castur) and one immortal (Polydeukes, Etr. Pultuce) but who came to share immortality, making a bargain with Zeus that they would spend alternate days in the Underworld and in the upper air. They were very popular in early Italy, both at Rome and in Etruria, and were often regarded as savior gods. They do not appear on the Piacenza Liver, nor do they occur in the heavens of Martianus, though there is a tantalizing reference to *Iovis filii*, "sons of Jupiter" in Region 6. (There, rather than Kastor and Polydeukes, though, the expression probably refers to Pales and Favor, two rustic Italian shepherd deities.)

The twins occur over and over in a simple scheme on Etruscan mirrors, dressed in military tunics and helmets, with their shields leaning beside them (Fig. VIII.19). They may also be represented nude, with selected warriors' attributes; they may both be winged, or just one may have wings, to bring out the idea that originally only one was immortal (Fig. VIII.20). Their attributes vary, from a flourishing plant, to a swan or amphora, to an astral symbol, most typically a star

VIII.20 Bronze mirror, 3rd century BCE. Oxford, Ashmolean Museum. Drawing: Nick Griffiths. The Dioskouroi are represented both nude, but with emphasis on their dissimilarities; one is winged, wears a mantle, and carries a spear, while the other is shown with helmet, cape, and shield.

with four rays and five circles in the pattern of a quincunx (Fig. VIII.19). One other curious feature that recurs is the horizontal beams that stretch between them, evidently a remnant of the doorway to their tomb in their native Sparta, known in Greek as the *dokana*. The *dokana* and other evidence, such as the placement of the Dioskouroi beside a city gate or a tomb door, indicates clearly that they are gods of passage or door gods, who need to be treated with proper respect when one passes by them.

The great majority of their images are iconic and their actual adventures in Etruria are rather few. They appear in scenes that have to do with their ever-popular sister Elinai, who is celebrated for her egg (Fig. VI.18, where Castur holds out the egg to Tuntle as Pultuce looks on). Here it is probably the day of Elinai's birth and the egg is about to hatch, for the chariot of the dawn above announces a particular day. The border is rich with fertile vegetation and even the waters teeming with sea life may be a reflection of this moment.

Elinai is also the concern of her brothers when she is romantically involved, as on a mirror where she is shown leaning on the lap of Lamtun (=Laomedon; Fig. VIII.21), an early king of Troy, who in this variant may take the place of Tynda-

VIII.21 Bronze mirror from Perugia, ca. 350–325 BCE. Perugia, Museo Archeologico Nazionale. Drawing: Alba Frascarelli. The unusual scene shows Elinai, center, her body naked except for her slippers, a mantle wrapped around her leg and her jewelry (necklaces, diadem). She leans casually upon the lap of an enthroned, crowned mature male, labeled Lamtun, (perhaps=Laomedon, king of Troy and father of Priam; the connection is obscure). Her brothers, Castur (left) and Pultuce (right), seem to stand guard over her. Castur holds a patera that is turned so as to spill its contents. In lower exergue, a female head emerges from rich vegetation. In upper exergue, a male figure, labeled Auri, with two horses, seems to sink below the horizon; this group may represent the chariot of the moon.

reus (Tuntle). The story is unknown, but more standard fare is found in the scene cited earlier, in which Elinai and Elcsntre (Paris) are drawn together by Turan (Fig. V.25) Sometimes the three of them—Elinai, Castur, and Pultuce—stand or sit and converse (Fig. VIII.22).

The youths were known for their athletic skills, in boxing (Pultuce), horsemanship (Castur) and wrestling (both), and these themes recur in the art of Etruria and the orbit of Rome from a very early date. Most popular of all was the theme of the boxing match with Amykos, or *Amuce*, as he was called in Etruria (Fig. VIII.23).[21] The Argonauts, including Kastor and Polydeukes, encountered Amykos on a landing when they were in search of water. King of the Bebrycians and guardian of a sacred spring, he would seize strangers and offer them as human sacrifice to his father Poseidon, and the only way to avoid this fate was to defeat him in a boxing match. Polydeukes took him on and defeated him, and according to one story, tied him up to a tree in punishment, leaving the spring free for

VIII.22 Bronze mirror from Cerveteri, 3rd century BCE. Present location unknown. After ES:5.81.1. The Dioskouroi, Castur and Pultuce, are shown in standard mirroring poses (cf. Fig. VIII.19). Between them stands a naked female figure with drapery gathered between her legs; her iconography is characteristic for their sister, Elinai.

the Argonauts to go and refresh themselves. This is the most common outcome in Italy. The story of Amykos has a significant water theme, for by striking blows at the king, Polydeukes frees the spring and releases the water. Once Amykos appears outside of this tale, depicted simply as a spring with water coming forth, labeled as *Amuce*, in a scene with from left to right, Lasa, Aplu, Turan, Atunis, and Menrva (Fig. VIII.24).

Pele, Thethis, and Atlnta

The Greek hero Pele (Peleus) was frequently represented in combination with his bride Thethis (=Thetis), a motif that was cherished on Etruscan mirrors because of the connection of this couple with marriage. Sometimes he might be shown wrestling with her in order to win her over.[22] On a quite famous mirror in the Metropolitan Museum (Fig. VIII.25), the depiction has some unusual elements. The goddess bride is adorning herself for marriage and gazes into a mirror, within which is depicted her own reflection. Pele seems to have intruded into the

VIII.23 Bronze mir-
ror from Tarquinia, ca.
325–300 BCE. Tarquinia,
Museo Archeologico
Nazionale. After ES:5.91.2.
Castur and Pultuce bind
Amuce, who has been
defeated in a boxing
match by Pultuce.

boudoir scene and happens to look into the mirror as well. He registers astonish-
ment or even fear; his hair stands on end as in prophecy scenes (Figs. II.10-11)
and he flings up his arms as if in dismay. It has been suggested that he is showing
amazement over the beauty of his bride, or alternatively that he is rushing in to
throw his arms around her. I have argued instead that he is shown at the moment
that he perceives, by way of the oracular instrument of the mirror, the prophecy
about his marriage to this goddess, namely that he would have a son more famous
than himself.[23]

Thethis herself is a greatly admired figure in Etruria, appearing sometimes in
surprising places. She attends Hercle and Menrva for reasons unknown (Fig.V.7)
and attempts to restrain Menle (=Menelaus) as he tries to attack Elinai (Fig. V.27).
More recognizably Hellenic is her appeal to the supreme god on behalf of her son
Achilles (Fig. IV.1), involving a dispute with the goddess of the dawn, who made a
plea for the life of her own son.

VIII.24 Bronze mirror from Castel d'Asso, ca. 300–275 BCE. Toronto, Royal Ontario Museum. After ES:5.23. The lovers Turan and Atunis embrace, attended by Lasa and Aplu (left) and Menrva. The spring, with a human face from which the water emits, is labeled Amuce (=Amykos). It is perhaps included to indicate a locality.

Pele also could be seen wrestling with Atlnta (=Atalante; Fig. VIII.26), possibly the most popular heroine figure for the Etruscans, appearing on gems, mirrors and ash urns, as a wrestler and as a huntress. The tragic outcome of her love for Meleager has been noted in the great Athrpa mirror (Fig. V.30). In the wrestling match with Pele (in which, according to the Greek story, she was victorious) she is shown as a fit female athlete (Fig. VIII.26), wearing shorts for the sake of modesty and with her hair bound up to avoid distracting her or providing advantage to her opponent.

Pherse

Another Greek hero who occurs frequently in Etruscan representations is Pherse (=Perseus), popular for his decapitation of Medusa (Fig.V.3), often with

VIII.25 Bronze mirror, ca. 350 BCE. New York, Metropolitan Museum of Art. After CSE U.S.A.:3.14a. The goddess Thethis (=Thetis) looks intently into her mirror as she grooms herself, probably for her wedding; she is assisted by Calaina, who with her right hand offers an item of jewelry to Thethis and holds another object (a bracelet?) in her other hand. Thethis's intended spouse, Pele, sees the image in the mirror and registers his surprise. On ground, slippers and a mantle, as well as a cosmetics chest.

the assistance of Menrva.[24] The scene is usually not very etruscanized; in at least one case, however, the head of Medusa seems to be treated as oracular (II.14). The scary head of the Gorgon was ever effective as an apotropaic symbol for the Etruscans, and occurs in a wide range of media, including mirrors, terracotta antefixes, relief sculpture (Fig. X.22), wall paintings, coins and gems.

Uthuze

Odysseus was always loved in Italy, where many of his wanderings took place, and he appears in several striking depictions,[25] including a mirror in which he consults Teiresias in the Underworld (Fig. VIII.27). Here the seated Uthuze holds up his sword to threaten any other spirits who might try to approach him, as Turmś Aitaś ("The Hermes of Hades") performs his standard assignment in Greece of leading souls around (although he does not in fact do that in the section of the *Odyssey*, Book 11, in which the hero comes to consult the prophet). Teiresias is labeled as Hinthial Terasiaś, "Soul of Teiresias" and he appears with his eyes closed, to show

VIII.26 Bronze mirror, ca. 425–400 BCE. Vatican Museums, Museo Gregoriano Etrusco. After ES:2, 224. The female athlete Atlnta (=Atalante), bare-breasted but wearing trunks, wrestles with Pele (=Peleus).

that he is blind even in the Underworld. He is also shown as crippled, leaning on a crutch, and with much ambiguity about his gender, since he is shown as having the face and hair of a pretty young girl instead of the bearded head of a prophet. One wonders just what the prophecy was in this interesting variant; Turmś Aitaś seems to explain it as he turns toward Uthuze and assumes a relaxed pose, raising his right hand in a gesture that implies explanation is taking place.

Achle

After Hercle and the Dioskouroi, probably the most beloved Greek hero among the Etruscans was Achle (=Achilles), who appears in various stories, especially themes of bloodshed. A famous large wall fresco in the Tomb of the Bulls[26] at Tarquinia shows the theme of Achilles lying in wait to murder Troilos, youngest son of the king of Troy, as he ventured forth from the walls of the city to obtain

VIII.27 Bronze mirror, ca. 350 BCE. Vatican Museums, Museo Gregoriano Etrusco. After ES:2, 240. The mirror shows the prophetic theme of how Uthuze (=Odysseus) goes to the Underworld to learn his destiny from Hinthial Terasiaś ("Soul of Teiresias"). Turmś Aitaś (the Hermes of Hades) leads Hinthial Terasia_ forward to the encounter.

water at a fountain. According to a prophecy, the boy had to be sacrificed in order for Troy finally to be taken.   The theme of human sacrifice occurs in Etruscan art often, with the most compelling example probably another story in which Achilles plays a key role, the story of the sacrifice of the prisoners at the tomb of Patroklos. With this theme, we return to the François Tomb with which we started this chapter, and look at a mural situated across from the scene of the Vipinas brothers and Macstrna.   Complementing the abundant bloodshed in that scene is this grisly image of Achle decapitating a Trojan prisoner labeled Truials (Plate IV), as the pale shade of Patroklos, wrapped in his shroud and still wearing the bandages from his fatal wounds, awaits the result.   As is revealed by *Odyssey*, Book 11, and other ancient sources, the dead needed blood to feel animation, and thus the survivors had an obligation to provide it, or else some kind of substitute.   There is some evidence that the Etruscans did practice human sacrifice,[27] but of course representing the act in art might be another way to obtain the result of appeasing the dead.

VIII.28 Terracotta ash urn, 2nd century BCE. Paris, Musée du Louvre. After Briquet and Briquel 2002:67, fig. II. The battle scene shows an unknown Etruscan hero who fights using a plough. The death goddess Vanth stands on left, carrying a torch and swinging her arm out as if to affect the action.

Patroklos is labeled as Hinthial Patrukles, leaving no doubt about his status, and he is protected literally under the wing of the beautiful death spirit, Vanth, who also spreads a wing toward Achilles as she seems to entreat him not to be too cruel with the prisoner. She is joined by her partner Charu, the demon with the hammer, standing on the other side of Achilles. In our next chapter, on the Underworld, we shall have a closer look at these spirits.

The Hero with the Plough

An enormously popular theme on Late Etruscan ash urns from the area of Chiusi featured the mythologem known as "the hero with the plough" (Fig. VIII.28).[28] The scene occurs over and over, in two mechanically produced composition types (Type A has four figures; Type B has five), in terracotta ash urns of the 2nd and 1st centuries BCE. The hero is always seen from the back, with his anatomy well displayed since he wears no armor, only a mantle wrapped around his waist. He thrusts a large plough (?) at his adversaries. Unconvincing attempts have been made to link the scene with Greek heroes, such as Echetlos, who fought against the Persians at Marathon with a plough, or Kodros,[29] who sacrificed himself by going into battle without armor. Whoever he may be, the struggle of the heroic youth has been taken to reflect the political situation in Etruria in this dark, final period of Etruscan history, when a man would not have time or resources (or both) to dress in armor, and would simply take up whatever large implement he could find for fighting. If the implement is indeed a plough, the theme becomes especially poignant, referring to the miserable farmers of Etruria who fought to the last to hold on to their land. The prophecy of Vegoia discussed in Chapter II relates to this same phenomenon.

Foundation Myths and Legends

Most peoples have stories of their own founding and founders, anchoring them in a venerable past and giving them a pride in their destiny. Such stories concerning the Etruscans have survived, but they are exclusively from exterior sources (i.e., Greek and Latin authors), and there are no universally accepted representations in Etruscan art of founder heroes. Thus we may report some of the accounts of the ancients, but they are often contradictory (as is also the case for many Greek and Roman foundation stories), and in fact there is little if any evidence of what the Etruscans believed themselves about the founding of their cities and their people.

"The Origin of the Etruscans"

The prime foundation story of the Etruscan people is told by the Greek historian Herodotus, writing in the middle of the 5th century BCE (*Histories* 1.94). The passage has been taken quite seriously for what it may indicate about the historical origins of the Etruscans and their arrival in Italy, but in fact the story is set in legendary or mythological time, shortly after the time of the Trojan War, i.e., in the 12th or 11th century BCE, and thus about 700 years before Herodotus himself. The story relates how the Etruscans, normally referred to by the Greeks as Tyrsenoi or Tyrrhenoi (commonly anglicized as Tyrrhenians), originated in Lydia in Asia Minor, and were themselves originally Lydians. It was during the reign of King Atys, son of Manes, reported by Strabo, *Geography* 5.22, to be descended from Herakles and the Lydian queen Omphale. The Lydians experienced a terrible famine, and tried to find ways to divert their attention from their suffering. Under this duress they invented a number of games to occupy themselves and keep from thinking of food. They claimed to have invented dice, knucklebones and ball-games, which they later taught to the Greeks. Thus they would game for all of one day, not leaving time to think of food, and then the next day would abstain from playing and allow themselves to eat.

"They managed to live like this for eighteen years," reports Herodotus. "There was still no remission of their suffering—indeed it grew worse; so the king divided the population into two groups and determined by drawing lots which should emigrate and which should remain at home. He appointed himself to rule the section whose lot determined that they should remain, and his son Tyrrhenos to command the emigrants. The lots were drawn, and one section went down to the coast at Smyrna, where they built vessels, put aboard all their household effects and sailed in search of a livelihood elsewhere. They passed many countries and finally

IX.1 Ivory pyxis from the Pania cemetery at Chiusi, drawing, ca. 600–575 BCE. Florence, Museo Archeologico Nazionale. After *Monumenti Antichi* 1899: pl. 30. In his ship Uthuze (=Odysseus) approaches the hazard of the sea monster Skylla, here depicted with three heads.

reached Umbria in the north of Italy, where they settled and still live to this day. Here they changed their name from Lydians to Tyrrhenians, after the king's son Tyrrhenus, who was their leader."[1]

Reports of the Tyrrhenians are often interwoven with references to the Pelasgians, an even more elusive ethnic group, that is said to have sailed from the East and settled Italy before the Etruscans. The Tyrrhenians then would have taken over from them, often occupying the Pelasgian cities, according to the analysis of Pliny the Elder, writing in the 1st century CE (*Natural History* 3.5.50). Thus the founding of the Etruscan people would have taken place in two stages, with two waves of immigrants. Yet a third version of Etruscan roots was reported by Dionysios of Halikarnassos, a Greek historian writing in Italy in the time of the early Roman Empire at the end of the 1st century BCE. In his *Roman Antiquities* (1.20 and ff.), he reviewed the two other theories of the origin of the Etruscans and reported that he did not believe either report, because the Etruscans themselves stated that they had always been in Italy, i.e., were autochthonous. He notes that they called themselves by another (but perhaps not irreconcilable) name, Rasenna. Scholars of the Etruscan language have noted that the word recurs in inscriptions, and it may in fact be the Etruscan word for "The People," *rasna*.[2] Dionysios goes on to say that the theory of the Lydian origin is untenable because the Etruscan language, religion and customs were all quite different from those of the Lydians.

It is of interest that the name of the Tyrsenoi was connected with the west well before the time of Herodotus. Hesiod, the famous early Greek poet, links the name with Italy perhaps as early as 700 BCE (though some have said the passage may have been added to Hesiod's text a century later). In his *Theogony*, 1011-16, dense with mythology from the time of creation onward, Hesiod narrates, "Circe, daughter of Helios, the son of Hyperion, in shared intimacy with Odysseus the enduring of heart, bore Agrios and Latinos, the excellent and strong, who were lords of all the famous Tyrrhenians [Greek. *Tyrsenoi*] far away in a remote part of the Holy Isles."[3]

The name Latinos can, of course, be associated with the traditions of early Rome and Latium, though his brother, Agrios, "The Wild One," is otherwise unknown. It is fascinating that Odysseus should be named as an ancestor of the Tyrsenoi, for he was always a beloved hero in Etruria, represented often in art, and in fact some of the earliest depictions of his adventures occur in Italy. The encounter with the monster Skylla, who infested the Straits of Messina at the "toe" of the boot-shaped Italian peninsula appears in Etruscan art earlier than in Greece, on an ivory cosmetic jar from a tomb at Chiusi, dating to 600-575 BCE (Fig. IX.1).[4] Here Odysseus prepares to sail past the three-headed monster.

Tyrrhenos

Attempts to identify the image of Tyrrhenos in Etruscan art have been unconvincing, and we do not know what the Etruscans may have thought about his appearance.[5] There are various other mentions of this hero in ancient literature, saying that he was the son of Telephos, and thus grandson of Herakles, rather than of the Lydian Atys, and that he was himself the founder of Caere (Cerveteri), the southernmost coastal city of the Etruscans. The Greek designation for the part of the Mediterranean Sea on the west coast of Italy, the Tyrrhenian Sea, could be based on his name, or else simply derived from the Greek word for "the Etruscans," itself based on the hero's name. He is also said to have invented a kind of trumpet called "Tyrrhenian" and used by the Greeks, and also to have been an innovator in the creation of weapons, such as the javelin of the light-armed troops. One of his sons, Pisaeus, who was the eponymous founder of Pisa, was credited with inventing the battle-axe.

Tarchon

The most famous son of Tyrrhenos was Tarchon (a variant describes him as the twin brother of Tyrrhenos),[6] recognized sometimes as the chief hero of the Etruscans.

We have already seen how he played a key role in the reception of prophecy from Tages and the transmission of the *Etrusca disciplina* (Chapter II). He is known as a great founder, not only of the city of Tarquinia, but also of Mantua and eleven other major cities of the region of the Po Valley, outside of Etruria proper. (And some attribute Pisa to him, rather than to the otherwise unknown Pisaeus). He is said to have been already wise as a child, much like Tages, and to have been born with grey hair.

As noted earlier, Tarchon is probably the figure labeled as Avl Tarchunus on the mirror from Tuscania (Fig. II.2), and he is probably the prophet who listens to the child Tages on engraved gems (Figs. II.3-4). There is one other possible representation of Tarchon in art, though the work is Roman and is poorly preserved. From Cerveteri comes a marble relief of the 1st century CE showing personifications of the peoples of the various cities of Etruria (Fig. IX.2). Only three figures remain, indicating the people of Vetulonia (*Vetulonenses*), who are symbolized by a bearded, mature, nude male holding a rudder, the people of Vulci (*Vulcentani*), personified by an enthroned, dressed female holding out one hand with a Victory figure upon it, and the people of Tarquinia (*Tarquinienses*), represented by a figure in toga, with a veil pulled up over his head in the manner of a priest, and holding a scroll in his left hand. It has been suggested that this figure depicts Tarchon in his religious role as the transmitter of the Etruscan books of Tages.

There is a story told about Tarchon that has elements in common with the story of the prophet Cacu and the Vipinas brothers (Fig. II.5; Chapter II, Chapter VIII), and may well be a variant of that tale, but with more differences than similarities. It is related by Solinus, a Roman geographical writer of the 2nd century CE, quoting from Gnaeus Gellius, an annalist of the 2nd century BCE, and regards the time when Hercules founded the Ara Maxima in Rome. It tells how a warrior named Cacus,

> with Megales the Phrygian as a companion, was sent as an envoy by Marsyas the king to Tarchon the Tyrrhenian, who put him in custody. He broke his bonds and went back home. Returning with greater forces, he seized the area round Vulturnus and Campania. When he dared to appropriate even those places which the laws had granted to the Arcadian [Evander; i.e., in Rome], he was killed by Hercules, who happened to be present. The Sabines received Megales who taught them the art of augury. Hercules himself set up an altar to his own divinity that is held to be "the Greatest" among the priests.[7]

IX.2 Stone relief from Cerveteri, 1st century CE. Vatican Museums, Museo Profano Lateranense. Photo: Museum. Left to right: personifications of the people of Vetulonia, Vulci, and Tarquinia (perhaps Tarchon as a priest).

"A fine mishmash," this was called by Emeline Hill Richardson.[8]   Here Cacus, rather than a prophet, is a warrior and conqueror, and rather than having soothsaying abilities himself is attended by Megales, who knows the art of augury. Cacus, like Cacu, does get captured, but by Tarchon, not the Vipinas brothers. He breaks his bonds and resumes his career until he is killed by Hercules. We don't know what happens to Cacu after his capture. Some have tried to square the two myths and have insisted they are basically the same story, but such an exercise is really not needed. The story of Tarchon was told at a different time and in a different place from the Vipinas myth and is a perfectly legitimate myth in its own right. The two stories share certain mythologems of bondage and prophecy, but neither story is "correct" or "incorrect."

ETRUSCAN MYTH, SACRED HISTORY, AND LEGEND

Etruscan Legendary Figures in Virgil

It so happens we can track the name of Cacus to a third myth, actually better known than the scene on the Etruscan mirror or the story of Solinus. In the *Aeneid* (8.194 and ff.) the epic poet Virgil tells his own story of a half-human, murderous monster named Cacus who infested the Palatine Hill in Rome. The son of Vulcan, he was capable of breathing fire and smoke, and was a terror to all who came his way. Cacus made a fatal mistake in stealing the cattle of Hercules, and the result was that the hero trapped him in his own cave and killed him. In this version Hercules subsequently founded the Ara Maxima to himself and established the ritual for worship there.

Thus Cacus is completely transformed from the Etruscan prophet Cacu and the warrior Cacus, and has become a terrifying monster. The Vipinas brothers and Tarchon are now omitted, and so is any motif of prophecy. The only recognizable theme is the seizure of Cacus, but it is not really a capture because Hercules kills the monster immediately. It can be said that the idea of Hercules as the foe of Cacus is left over from the Solinus version, and also the founding of the Ara Maxima. But once again, it is better not to strain to put all the myths together; they come from different cultural contexts and are profoundly different. And in the powerful drama of the battle of the monster with Hercules, clearly the imagination and literary skills of the great poet Virgil played a key role in shaping mythic material.

Virgil also has a lively depiction of Tarchon as commander of Etruscan troops allied with Aeneas against Turnus in their famous epic battle. In a stirring passage (*Aeneid* 11.726 and ff.) Virgil describes how he charges into the fray, defying the warrior maiden Camilla and dispatching Venulus, one of the Rutulian warriors of Turnus. Elsewhere the poet includes other Etruscan hero/founder figures, such as Asilas of Pisa (*Aeneid* 10. 176), "the mighty seer who mediated between men and gods, and who knew the secrets held by the entrails of beasts, the stars in the sky, the voices of birds, and the flash of presaging thunderbolts."[9] We hear of Aulestes, founder of Perugia (*Aeneid* 10.207, 12.289) who brings his ships to the aid of Aeneas, but is killed by Messapus; Ocnus or Aunus, founder of Felsina (Bologna); and Capys, founder of Capua, farther south (*Aeneid* 10. 140). Both Aulestes and Ocnus are said to be the sons of the Tiber River and of Manto, daughter of Teiresias and a prophetess herself. She was sometimes said to be the source of the name for the city of Mantua (*Aeneid* 10.200), but another report was that it was named after Mantus, identified as the offspring of Dispater, father of the Underworld, or as Dispater himself (Servius, *ad Aeneid.* 10. 199).

Mezntie

Yet another legendary character found in the *Aeneid* who seems to have had a real place in Etruria is Mezentius, the cruel Etruscan tyrant of Caere (Cerveteri), who served as an ally to Turnus in his struggle against Aeneas (*Aeneid*, Books 7-10). The existence of the name in Etruria is attested by an inscription on a chalice made of impasto (675-600 BCE; Paris, Louvre), which has been read as *mi laucie mezenties*, "I belong to Laucie Mezentie."[10]

What does not seem to have been noticed is that a figure labeled Mezntie appears on an Etruscan mirror (Fig. IX.3; the name has been read previously in error as Mevntie).[11] The figure, enthroned, has been called female, but the name

IX.3 Bronze mirror, 3rd century BCE. Rome, Museo Nazionale Etrusco di Villa Giulia. Photo: Soprintendenza per i Beni Archeologici del Lazio. On left, a male figure sits enthroned dressed in flowing robes and with long sleeves, making a gesture of lament. The inscription refers to Mezntie (=Mezentius in Latin). On far right, Achle (=Achilles) arms himself, and in the middle two figures otherwise unknown: a nude female labeled Zelachtra and a nude male labeled Ethun.

Mezntie is masculine and the garb of this figure is not actually feminine. He wears long, body-fitting sleeves, probably meant to be royal, for the dress resembles the costume worn by other kingly figures on mirrors of this style.[12] The long hair need not be female, since other males in the scene also have long hair. His right hand rests upon a staff appropriate for a king, while his left hand is raised to his inclining head, as if to make a lament.

At this point interpretation breaks down, since we do not know who his female companion is—nude, standing, wreathed, wearing a high-laced shoe (a boot?)—other than to note she is labeled Zelachtra. Nor can we say more about the male next to her, labeled Ethun, nude and furnished with a sword. Both figures are known only from this mirror. On the far right is Achle (surely =Achilles), with shield, sword and mantle; his pose, with one foot raised rather awkwardly and with his two hands reaching down to his knees, is one that occurs elsewhere to show that a warrior is attaching his greaves (shin guards). Next to him is an old fellow with beard, gown (again long-sleeved?) and an exotic pointed hat, stooping over a knotted staff. The label is not sufficiently preserved to allow for interpretation.

Why would Mezntie be grieving? In the Roman story of the Etruscan king, perhaps the most notable event was the killing of his son Lausus by Aeneas (*Aeneid* 10.1092-1141). That may be the main theme of the scene here as well, but once again the original story must have been radically transformed by Virgil. For instead of the vicious warrior contemptuous even of the gods in the *Aeneid*, who rushes on to the battle field to confront Aeneas and avenge his son, thus meeting his own death, we see a sad, weakened king, surrounded by his court, including a warrior who will strap on his greaves, take up his shield and go into battle to seek vengeance. To have Achilles, who is admittedly a contemporary of Aeneas and thus of Mezentius, ally himself with the Etruscan king, provides another breathtaking example of the native myths of Etruria.

While Virgil's myths are often regarded as sophisticated poetic products of his rich imagination, it must be remembered that he was himself born at Mantua and his family name, P. Virgilius *Maro* (cf. Etruscan *maru*, the title of a magistrate), further suggests his Etruscan heritage. In addition, his text recently received confirmation from archaeology that it possibly preserved quite old mythic and legendary material. In excavations beside the Tiber River at a sanctuary excavators found a potsherd with the name Uqnuś (=Ocnus) inscribed upon it (Fig. IX.4).[13] This inscription, found on the banks of the Tiber, provides a startling echo of the genealogy of the Etruscan founder figure Ocnus, a son of the god of this river.

IX.4 Sherd of impasto pottery, end of 7th or beginning of 6th century BCE. From Rome, Area Sacra of S. Omobono. Drawing: Jacquelyn Clements. The potsherd features the inscription *uqnus*, perhaps the same name as Aucnus/Ocnus, son of the Tiber River god and legendary founder of Perugia and the Etruscan cities of the Po River Valley.

Afterlife and Underworld

T he Etruscans cared enormously about the afterlife. The archaeological record testifies to the nearly obsessive attention they gave to the burial of the dead and the provision for the continued existence of their beloved and venerated family members. It is frequently said that the Etruscans practiced ancestor worship, and therefore were ever concerned for the immortality of the deceased. This conclusion is well supported by the offerings to the dead found in the tombs and also by analogy with burial customs of the Romans, who definitely had such practices and shared with the Etruscans in the usage of certain religious rituals. In this chapter we shall consider the archaeological and literary evidence concerning such rituals and beliefs about the afterlife and Underworld and see how they relate to mythology in Etruria.

Blood and the Soul

We know that among the works attributed to Tages and studied by the Romans were the books containing the *sacra Acheruntia*, or Rituals of the Underworld (Acheron being one of the major rivers of the Underworld). We know very little about these, but one of the few references we have, from the late antique scholar Arnobius (*Adversos Nationes* 2.62), writing in the 3rd century CE, makes a statement that is significant for our purposes: "they promise this in the *Acherontic Books* in Etruria, that by the blood of certain animals, divine souls (*animae*) become endowed with certain numinous spirits and they are led away from the laws of mortality."[1] That is, the blood sacrifice was able to give immortality to dead souls. We have already mentioned, in discussing the paintings of the François Tomb at Vulci (Chapter VIII), that a similar idea appears in Homer's *Odyssey*, (11. 35 ff.), in which Odysseus slits the throat of sheep so that the blood may flow down into a pit and be drunk by the dead souls in the Underworld. When they drink the blood, they are then able to talk to Odysseus, that is, they are literally *animated*.[2] We get related information about the Etruscan soul from Servius's commentary on Virgil (*ad Aeneid*. 3.168), again of the 3rd century CE, when he states that "there are certain rites by which human souls are turned into gods . . . . these are the gods called Penates and Viales [i.e., of the Crossroads]."[3]

These little scraps of information provide some illumination for the various representations of sacrifice and bloodshed in Etruscan funerary art to which we have already referred (Plates IV-VI). The substitute for the actual pouring of blood into the earth is created by means of the *reference* to blood sacrifice, or by the representation of blood flowing. Thus the François Tomb is filled with mythologi-

X.1 Wall painting, ca. 325–300 BCE. Tomb of Orcus II, Tarquinia. Photo: DAI. In the presence of Aita and Phersipnei (on an adjoining wall of the tomb; see Fig. X.26) the Greek heroic figures Achmemrun and Hinthial Teriasals (=Agamemnon and The Soul of Teiresias) stand amid reeds populated by little silhouetted figures, probably the souls of lesser individuals in the Underworld.

cal and legendary subjects in which blood is spurting forth: the Theban brothers Eteokles and Polyneikes kill each other, Avle Vipinas dispatches his victim, Achilles slaughters prisoners. Even the motif of fighting animals in the upper zones of the decoration of the wall plays out the theme of the shedding of blood for the sake of (presumably) those buried in the tomb.

The passages from Arnobius and Servius also provide us with the information, vague and baffling, that the Penates were equivalent to immortalized human souls. These deities are evidently quite different from the Roman Penates, the household gods that inhabited the ancestral innermost chamber in a Roman home.[4] Arnobius observes (*Adversus Nationes* 3.38) that there were four different kinds of Etruscan Penates: of the sky, of the water, of the earth, and human souls. So the statement of Servius is reinforced, and we may also find the Penates in the heavens of Martianus Capella. They are located in the powerful Region 1, along with Jupiter and Janus, i.e., not in the Underworld but in the favorable northeastern zone. There are also the Shades (*Manes*) and Divine Shades (*Dii Manes*) in Martianus, in regions 11 and 13 respectively, rather where we would expect them, on the western, darker side of the cosmos.

There are many conventions for representing the soul in Etruscan art. We

X.2 Wall Painting, ca. 525 BCE. Tomb of the Jugglers, Tarquinia. Photo: DAI. A grey-haired man (the deceased?) walks forward leaning upon a knotted stick. He holds the wrist of a naked boy.

may cover quickly one of these imported from Greece, and only rarely appearing in Etruria. In the Tomb of Orcus II at Tarquinia (Fig. X.1), anonymous souls are represented as they are in Greek art of the same period,[5] as tiny silhouettes figures jumping around in the thin marsh reeds of the Underworld landscape; these little images of the soul are referred to in Greek by the term *psyche*.[6] Rather more frequent is another Greek convention, according to which heroes and heroines who died of their wounds are represented in the Underworld as wearing the bandages that covered their mortal wounds, along with a mantle or shroud. Thus appears the Soul of Patroklos in the François Tomb (Plate IV), labeled, as noted previously with the Etruscan words *Hinthial Patrukles*. Similar in appearance is the figure of *Achmemrun* in the Tomb of Orcus II, who stands to the left of the little souls (Fig. X.1); the *Hinthial Teriasals*, Soul of Teiresias, on the right, covers his head with a shroud, but has no bandages, since he did not die of battle wounds.

But these are conventions for representing only heroic figures, and Greek at that, in Etruria. The souls of Etruscans are recognizable from different conventions; these in fact are far more numerous than the isolated Greek examples. Etruscan souls may be identified on the basis of their context and activity and sometimes by their dress and attributes.

FEL : TLEŽHA : LADOALIŽA

X.3 Stone sarcophagus from Chiusi, 2nd century BCE. Chiusi, Museo Etrusco. After Pfiffig 1975: fig. 68. 2nd century BCE. The deceased journeys by horseback and encounters a monster.

The Journey to the Afterlife

Most common is the motif of the traveler to the afterlife, represented in funerary art from all over Etruria. The deceased may journey on foot, equipped with a special knotty walking stick, as in the Tomb of the Jugglers at Tarquinia (Fig. X.2), or may go on horseback, as on an ash urn from Chiusi (Fig. X.3), or in a wagon, seen on a vase from Orvieto (Fig. X.4). Sometimes there are indications that the soul must go by more than one mode of locomotion. The Orvieto vase shows the deceased riding in a wagon, flat on his back, but he carries the knotted stick that has been used (or will be) for another part of the journey. Another vessel from Orvieto shows the deceased walking with the aid of the stick (Fig. X.5).[7]

Often part of the travel is by sea, as indicated on the Chiusi ash urn, where the rider is passing a tree and heads toward a great sea monster, or *ketos*, around which are the indications of waves. Such waves are represented frequently in painted tombs, either in a naturalistic way, or as a stylized running wave pattern. The deceased may even ride *on* a *ketos*, as seen on another ash urn (Fig. X.23). This last example is interesting for its depiction of the soul as swathed in drapery, to the extent that only the eyes are visible. The motif of the swaddled soul has been noted before, on the mirror in Brussels where it forms part of the myth of Esia, and suggests that the girl is indeed deceased (Fig. V.37).

The Afterlife

What was the destination of the soul, and what was the nature of the Etruscan afterlife and Underworld?[8] It is certain first of all that the soul journeyed through a doorway or gate, as in so many myths worldwide. Tomb paintings show a doorway of the type found in a noble Etruscan house (Fig. X.6), with a frame that narrows as it moves up, topped by a broad horizontal lintel. Depictions of metal nailheads or bosses make the door even more impressive. Elsewhere the portal is shown as a powerful arched form, reinforced with bars and furnished with doorknockers (Fig. X.7).[9] Frequently the gateway features bivalve doors. It has recently been noted that the path to the Underworld goes beyond a rock, or a rocky height, and thus we are able to recognize the liminal point not in a portal, but rather a feature

X.4 Painted red-figure krater of the "Vanth" Group, 4th century BCE. Drawing of scenes running around the vessel. Orvieto, "Claudio Faina" Museum. Drawing: Jacquelyn Clements, after Manino 1980:fig. 2. On left, the deceased, holding a knotted stick, lies in a wagon drawn by mules. The hearse is followed by a chariot driven by a nude, bearded god (Aita) holding a scepter topped by a pomegranate and encircled by a serpent. Charu leads the wagon, and Vanth comes up behind, carrying a scroll of fate.

of the landscape itself. The rocky boundary appears in a good many representations of the deceased or the Underworld (Fig. X.8; X.11).[10]

At the doorway or on the shore of the waters, the soul might meet other members of the family who were there to bid farewell or possibly had gone before (Figs. X.7-8). It is also at this point, probably right outside the gates or just inside, that the soul encountered the chief escorts to the Underworld, the flamboyant demons and spirits who are known to us by several different names. Chief of these were Charu and Vanth, already mentioned in the previous chapter as attending the execution of Trojan prisoners at the tomb of Patroklos (Plate IV). It is worth noting that these spirits appear for the first time only in the Middle period of Etruscan art, from around 400 BCE, and thus the conventions we will next consider belong to roughly the second half of the time span of Etruscan civilization. Later, consideration will be given to the concepts of the afterlife before 400 BCE.

Charu and Other Demons

Charu, labeled also with the spelling *Charun* (a total of nine inscriptions are known[11] from Tarquinia, Vulci, and Volterra) has a name very similar to that of the Greek Charon, ferryman to the Underworld, but their roles are entirely different.

X.5 Painted red-figure amphora of the "Vanth" Group. Drawing of scenes running around the vessel, 4th century BCE. Orvieto, "Claudio Faina" Museum. Drawing: Jacquelyn Clements, after Manino 1980:fig. 1. On left, the deceased, walking with the help of a knotted stick, is escorted by Charu demons; one takes him by the wrist as another beats away menacing serpents. In center, an underworld chariot is pulled by great chickens, with a female figure (Phersipnei?) in the chariot. A male figure follows (Aita?), and then a nude, female figure prances along carrying a scroll upon which is written the word *vanθ*. On the far right, a non-threatening three-headed dog (=Cerberus) gnaws absentmindedly on a vulture.

The ferry to the Underworld appears only once in Etruscan art (Fig. X.8), and it is not certain that the boatman there is to be identified with the Etruscan Charu. It is true that there are demons with an oar represented occasionally in Etruria (Fig. X.9), but they wield it as a weapon rather than an instrument for guiding a boat, and nowhere is there evidence of a true equivalent of Charon.

Charu, known in well over 100 representations and arguably the most popular Etruscan mythological figure of all,[12] is quite hideous at times, for example in the François Tomb, where the demon lurks beside Achilles at the vicious slaughter of Trojan prisoners (Plate IV). There is some doubt about the gender of Charu, depicted in a garment that looks like a dress (though not like any worn by an ordinary Etruscan lady) and with a skin that is bluish or grayish; elsewhere sometimes the flesh is shown as pale and cream colored, but rarely is there the ruddy color of normal males in Etruscan art. It is true that the creature sometimes has facial hair resembling a mustache or beard or both. At any rate, for convenience we refer to Charu here with masculine pronouns, though the Etruscans may have thought of the demon as partially female or even as lacking gender.

Furthermore Charu may be plural, as is demonstrated vividly in the tomb at Tarquinia known in Italian as the *Tomba dei Caronti*, the "Tomb of the Charuns."[13] Here there are two doors to the Underworld, each flanked by a pair of the demons (Fig. X.10). All are labeled as *Charun*, with three of the four having a byname preserved in whole or in part. (The fourth one probably also had such a name, but the fresco is damaged in the area of the inscription.) Thus we have *Charun Chunchules* and *Charun Huths* (*ET* Ta 7.80-81; Fig. X.10, from left to right) as well as, perhaps, *Charun Lufe* (*ET* Ta 7.78); little is understood about their names, though Charun Huths may mean Charun Number Six (reinforcing the interpretation of the deity as a plurality), and it is also evident that the name Charun or Charu here has a generic quality, rather like the name Lasa.

These demons are well armed to protect their doors, with hammers in the one case (Fig. X.10) and in the other with axe and also sword and hammer. They are nasty fellows with serpents in their hair, and the skin is quite revolting, bluish or greenish, with one demon, Charun Huths, having blisters or sores all over the skin. All are sporting wings.

Indeed the hammer is the weapon of choice for Charu, and though most of the time he merely holds it in a menacing way, occasionally he is shown demonstrating its purpose. In a relief on the sarcophagus of the Tarquinia nobleman named Laris Pulenas, a pair of Charus swing their hammers toward the head of the central figure (Fig. X.11), probably the soul of the deceased. (Unfortunately due to the accidents of preservation, the figure is actually missing its head.) A similar usage of the hammer was maintained down into the period of the Roman Empire, when, in the gladiatorial games, a demonic character using the name of Dispater (Father Underworld) would go out into the arena and finish off the contest between two fighters. The loser, groveling in the sand, was pounded with a hammer by Dispater to make sure that he was dead.[14]

The hammer is not always used against the soul, though, but even may be used to help it out. On one of the Orvieto vessels (Fig. X.5), Charu swings the hammer towards serpents that threaten the path of the deceased. At other times, the weapon is simply set upright on the ground as a staff for the spirit to lean upon, as he greets or lounges about chatting with souls. On a red-figure vase from Vulci (Fig. X.12), he converses with a group of wounded, bandaged female souls, evidently Amazons (one of whom is called *Hinthia(l) Aturmucas*, i.e., Soul of Aturmuca, probably =Andromache, a common Amazon name), supporting himself upon the head of the upended mallet. Yet another usage of the hammer, it has been argued, was to bolt and unbolt the doors to the Underworld.

Serpents may also be part of the performance of the demons. A rather spectacular pair appears, the one brandishing serpents and wearing wings, the other

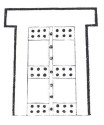

X.6 Wall painting, ca. 520 BCE. Tomb of the Inscriptions, Tarquinia. Drawing: Jacquelyn Clements. The door to the Underworld, reinforced with nail heads and closed firmly, appears on the back wall of the tomb and also on the two sidewalls.

X.7 Wall painting, 3rd century BCE. Tomb 5636, Tarquinia. Photo: DAI. Charu guards the gate to the Underworld as Vanth, with one hand on the shoulder of a young man, leads him forward toward the gate. A second, smaller figure walks in front of him, while two other males facing the opposite direction seem to offer a salute (previously deceased family members?).

X.8 Wall painting, ca. 400 BCE. Tomb of the Blue Demons, Tarquinia. After *Pittura etrusca al Museo di Villa Giulia*:fig. 110. In the center, demons escort the deceased lady to the ferry to the afterlife. Two figures, a woman and a youth, salute her (either in farewell or in greeting). On the right, two colorful demons flit about a rock that probably marks the threshold to the other world.

X.9 Sculptured walls in the Tomb of the Reliefs, Cerveteri, ca. 325–300 BCE. Photo: DAI. Underneath the main couch are depicted an anguiped demon with a steering oar and a three-headed dog, Cerberus.

X.10 Wall painting, 3rd century BCE. Tomb of the Charuns, Tarquinia. Photo: DAI. This door is flanked by two Charu demons, Charun Chunchules and Charun Huths.

swinging a mallet, on a red-figure vessel from Vulci depicting the embrace of Admetos and Alkestis, in Etruscan *Atmite* and *Alcsti* (Fig. X.13). In Etruria, the personified malevolent forces of death play a prominent role in this Greek myth. As discussed in Chapter I, this story of the wife preparing to die so that her husband may live features a very rare inscription with just a trace of Etruscan narrative.

The demons frequently act as a team, resembling nothing so much as the bevies of devils that populate Dante's *Inferno*, to many of whom that author gave personal names. For most of the assistants of Charu, inscriptions are, unfortunately, lacking, but we do know the name of one, Tuchulcha, who appears in the Tomb of Orcus II, not far from the images of Achmemrun and Hinthial Teriasals. Here once again we see how Etruscan mythological figures may dominate in a scene from Greek myth; the story relates to the unauthorized visit to the Underworld by These (=Theseus), who, when invited to sit down by Hades, became stuck fast in his place (Fig. X.14). On his lap is a board game, evidently a true game of fortune or destiny, and opposite him we see the head of his friend Peirithous, who went with him on his visit to the Underworld. As they sit they are terrorized by the demon Tuchulcha, who has the face of a vulture, serpents in the hair and wings and

X.11 Stone sarcophagus of L(a)ris Pulenas from Tarquinia, 3rd–2nd century BCE. Tarquinia, Museo Archeologico Nazionale. Photo: DAI. The casket of L(a)ris Pulenas shows a scene with Charu demons swinging hammers toward the deceased, center. On flanks, winged Vanths attend other individuals in the afterlife.

flourishes a huge serpent. The serpent here, as elsewhere in Etruscan art, features diamond shaped markings that identify it as a highly poisonous snake found in Italy today, the adder *(Vipera berus berus)*.[15] The pattern is even transferred to the wings of Tuchulcha. This monster is often referred to as male but in fact is very likely female (or neither gender), for she wears a woman's dress, has decidely pale pinkish skin (compare the standard brick-red male flesh of These),[16] and even appears to have breasts. This is the only known inscribed image of Tuchulcha.[17]

The most impressive gang of demons, only recently discovered, was found in the burial at Tarquinia fittingly named the Tomb of the Blue Demons (Fig. X.8). Here (reading from left to right) we see the aforementioned ferryboat—the only one in Etruscan art—and on the shore the interaction of several mortals. A finely

X.12 Painted red-figure krater from Vulci, 4th century BCE. Paris, Bibliothèque Nationale, Cabinet des Médailles. Photo: Bibliothèque Nationale de France. Charu is shown in a casual encounter with the souls of the Amazons Aturmuca (=Andromache) and Pentasila (=Penthesilea). The souls wear bandages over the wounds from which they died.

X.13 Painted red-figure vessel from Vulci, ca. 350 BCE. Paris, Bibliothéque Nationale, Cabinet des médailles. After Dennis 1848: frontispiece, vol. 2. Alcsti (=Alcestis) takes leave of Atmite (=Admetus) as demons threaten; Charu on left with a hammer, perhaps a twin Charu on right with serpents. Inscription: eca: ersce: nac: a_rum: fler_rce (ET Vc 7.38), translated provisionally as "She went to Acheron and made a sacrifice."

dressed lady is being propelled toward the boat by a squat, winged demon, as another, taller one seems to greet and guide her. Between him and the boat stand two mortals, an adult female and a child, who may be interpreted as still-living relatives come to say their last farewell at the boat or else, more likely, previously deceased souls greeting the new arrival. The scene is rounded off on the right by a terrifying pair of spirits, one of whom, wielding serpents with their mouths open to strike, has bright blue skin and a strange red dress. His profile is a caricature of a human visage. His winged partner, whose skin is greyish-black, flits forward, hair flying and claw-like hands reaching out to make a grab. The two hover over a liminal rock that probably marks the pale of the Underworld.

Even more recently yet another demon has come to light in a painted Etruscan tomb, located at Sarteano, near Chiusi.[18] It was opened in 2003, revealing a fine chamber painted with a banquet of eternity and an entrance corridor showing a chariot for usage in the journey to the afterlife. The hideous charioteer (Plate VII), again a red-headed demon, rushes along in the chariot pulled by bizarre lions and wingless griffins, against a shadowy background. On another wall nearby hovers a triple-headed serpent (Plate VIII) and a hippocamp, a horse-fish, also sometimes used in the journey across water to the other world.

The vivid routs of these demons show the rich imagination of the Etruscans. Not only did they depict them in their art, but they evidently would dress as snake- and torch-bearing demons on the battlefield. Livy has left a fascinating description of a battle between Romans and Etruscans from Tarquinia, occurring in 356 BCE, exactly the time when Charu and company had become popular. The Romans were thrown into panic, says Livy (7.17.3), because at the head of the Etruscan troops came rushing "priests bearing serpents and blazing torches before

X.14 Wall painting, ca. 325–300 BCE. Tomb of Orcus II, Tarquinia. Photo: DAI. These(=Theseus) and Peirithous, who in the Greek myth have come to the Underworld to abduct Persephone, are seated and playing a board game while the demon Tuchulcha stands by with menacing poisonous serpents.

them . . . [who] utterly dismayed the Roman soldiers with the extraordinary sight." This kind of dress-up must have occurred at Etruscan funerals as well, because there are frescoes from Tarquinia such as those from the Tomb of the Typhon (late third century BCE), that show a parade of nobles with attendants marching along waving serpent, torch and hammer (Fig. X.15).[19]

Vanth

The female counterpart of Charu, and almost as ubiquitous, was the goddess Vanth,[20] whom we have already seen as an important figure in the slaughter of the Trojan prisoners by Achilles (Plate IV). The origin and meaning of her name, which occurs in some nine inscriptions (from Tarquinia, Vulci, Orvieto, and Chiusi), is unknown, though the ending in *-th*, which occurs on a good many mythological names, probably means "one who" and signifies an agent. If we search for such a goddess in the scheme of Martianus, we would expect to find her in the northwest quarter of the cosmos; looking there we see only one agent deity named, in the plural, the Doorkeepers of the Earth, in Region 16. This designation is in fact sufficiently appropriate for Vanth, who is sometimes plural, is constantly depicted near doorways, is sometimes shown rising up out of the earth and is generally a liminal figure for those who are dying. The conclusion is not absolutely tidy, since there is no evidence that the root *van-* may mean "door"; on the contrary, as noted earlier, Culśanś and Culśu both seem to have names that are equivalent to

X.15 Wall painting (drawing), 3rd century BCE. Tomb of the Typhon, Tarquinia. Drawing: Jacquelyn Clements. The tomb's wall is painted with a procession to the Underworld, featuring the deceased and relatives surrounded by demons with snakes, torches, and hammers.

the Latin words for "portal" or "door," *janus* and *janua*. It could be that her name is some other Etruscan word for "Keeper," just as Latin may use *custos* to refer to someone who guards a doorway or has a wider protective role. Others have said that Vanth is a goddess of fate, and thus may be equated with the *Fata* ("Fates") in Region 13 of Martianus.

Most of the time, Vanth is an attractive female figure, a welcome contrast to her ugly partner Charu. In the François Tomb she spreads her great multicolored wings (they are red-brown, white, and blue) behind the heroes in an ominous and yet protective way, as she stands over the proceedings of the slaughter. One hand is raised in a gesture that may be interpreted as pleading, perhaps for mercy on the part of Achilles. She contrasts vividly with her partner Charu, standing on the other side of Achilles glaring balefully at the scene, his hammer at the ready. The two frequently appear together next to and around doorways, for example in the striking pair flanking the door in the Tomb of the Anina family at Tarquinia, dating to the third century BCE (Fig. X.16).[21] Here the terrifying Charu, with his scowling, hook-nosed, bestial countenance (he even has donkey's ears in this case), is balanced by the beautiful Vanth, who carries instead of the menacing hammer a torch with which she will light the way for the soul entering the dark Underworld. She is dressed in a short chiton, pulled down to reveal her breasts, but with crossing straps remaining as if to hold up the chiton. She and Charu both wear rustic boots, perhaps to signify that their work takes them into rough terrain.

The role of Vanth as an escort is quite important. She may meet souls before they get to the doorway, and escort them as they walk or ride along on horseback, wagon or chariot (Figs. X.4, X.5). In the Tomba Golini at Orvieto, the goddess attends Larth Leinies in his two-horse chariot (Fig. X.17), spreading wide her wings and holding up a scroll in one hand. The scroll also appears on the previously-discussed Orvieto vases with the journey to the Underworld (Fig. X.5), where

X.16 Wall painting, 3rd century BCE. Tomb of the Anina Family, Tarquinia. Photo: DAI. Charu, left, and Vanth, right, both winged, stand by the door waiting for the arrival of the deceased.

the word *vanθ* is written upon it. If indeed her name means "Fate" this would be a highly appropriate identification of the contents of the scroll—it may tell of the destiny of the deceased.

Another interesting attribute is the key, with which Vanth may unlock the gates she guards. This object occurs on a well-known relief from the Late Etruscan sarcophagus of Hasti Afunei, probably from Chiusi (Fig. X.18). Here the deceased is being led from the right to the left by a Vanth figure, as a number of relatives stand by, probably for the leave-taking with the deceased. The goal of the walk

ETRUSCAN MYTH, SACRED HISTORY, AND LEGEND

X.17 Wall painting
(watercolor copy), ca.
350–325 BCE. Tomba
Golini I, Orvieto. Orvieto,
Museo Archeologico
Nazionale. After *Pit-
tura etrusca a Orvieto*:
fig. 27. The deceased, a
magistrate named Larth
Leinies, journeys in a
chariot escorted by a
winged goddess with a
scroll of destiny, probably
Vanth.

of Hasti is on the left, where, beside an arched portal, a figure actually labeled Vanth stands holding under her arm a large shaft, fitted out with pegs. Very likely she has opened the door to the Underworld and now holds the key (or a bolt?). Meanwhile, through the opening door comes another figure we would surely have identified as Vanth were she not labeled otherwise: it is Culśu, whom we have met before. Here we come closest to the idea of a generic Vanth with a byname, for in every way this door goddess has the appropriate attributes: rustic boots, bared breasts, short chiton with cross straps, and torch.

Vanth sometimes takes on a more cruel aspect, carrying or wearing serpents. In the Golini Tomb I, for example she wears a girdle made up of two snakes tied together. She is frequently present at death scenes, especially the numerous violent and bloody battles represented on Late Etruscan ash urns. Like Charu, she may multiply, and thus a pair of Vanths may stand by as a battle rages, sometimes simply holding a torch, other times actively participating and even swinging a weapon (Figs. X.19-20). On a painted sarcophagus from Tarquinia dating to the 4th century BCE, a winged Vanth figure plays a distinctive role, embracing a collapsing warrior from behind as if to carry him away. It is not surprising that one scholar

X.18 Stone sarcophagus of Hasti Afunei from Chiusi, 3rd century BCE. Palermo, Museo Archeologico Regionale. After Brunn-Körte:3.54. Culśu is shown in the door to the Underworld (left), and Vanth stands ready with a key or bolt that may unlock or lock the door. On right, the deceased woman is guided by another Vanth-like figure as she embraces a man, probably her husband. Other relatives line the path, but it is uncertain whether they belong to the world of the living or the realm of

has compared these Vanths with the Norse Valkyries, whose mission was to come to the battlefield and take away the slain heroes.[22]

Vanth is also sometimes compared with the Greek Furies, and in one rare case, surely plays the role of those angry, avenging spirits. A mirror in Philadelphia shows a Greek-style myth with Orestes (*Urste*) at Delphi (Fig. VI.25), seeking purification for murdering his mother. As noted earlier, Aplu sacrifices a pig, as Urste clings to the *omphalos* of Apollo. On the left is a female figure with a snake entwined around her arm, labeled Vanth, surely enacting the part of the punishing spirits that haunted Orestes after his crime. In all Vanth appears on only two Etruscan mirrors, probably because these objects were used in daily life before they were taken to the afterlife and the grim subjects associated with death were normally considered inappropriate. (Charu never appears on mirrors.) The one other mirror where Vanth appears has the subject of Achilles with the dead Troilos; here Vanth is not in the role of a Fury, but perhaps stands by to announce the death.[23]

One more remarkable image tentatively identified as Vanth must be mentioned, if only because it is inexplicable (Fig. X.21). On the roof of the Tomb of the Vipinana family at Tuscania (ca. 300 BCE) was placed a winged female figure in the act of pulling her skirt up and back to expose her genital area. The motif has been recognized in ancient art with the term *anasyrma*, a Greek word used to describe the action of women participating in the Egyptian cults of Isis and Hathor,[24] both goddesses with Underworld connections, and known as well in connection with the cult of Demeter. The story of Baubo trying to cheer Demeter when her daughter had disappeared and gone to the Underworld perhaps helps to illuminate the significance of the gesture. Baubo, concerned because the goddess was so distraught she would not even take a refreshing drink, flung her skirt up and exposed herself. Demeter, amused, began to laugh and agreed to drink up the *kykeon*, her ritual drink.

So the image could have been used to hearten the relatives of the deceased when they visited the tomb. Yet another possibility takes into account the fact that Vanth frequently exposes the *upper* part of her body. The display of the breasts is without doubt something shocking (though not so much as the *anasyrma*), and

X.19 Terracotta ash urn from Chiusi, 3rd–2nd century BCE. Paris, Musée du Louvre. After Brunn and Körte:2.19d. Dueling warriors of unknown identity, sometimes identified as the Greek brothers Eteokles (Etruscan Evtucle) and Polynikes (Pulnice), are flanked by twin Vanths. The winged goddesses bare their breasts and legs, but their arms are covered with meshlike sleeves.

X.20 Alabaster ash urn from Todi, 2nd century BCE. Vatican Museums, Museo Gregoriano Etrusco. Photo: Museum. Winged, bellicose Vanths take part in the Greek myth of the murder of Oinomaus by Pelops.

could be related to the desire to ward off evil for the dead person much as the display of the female pudenda with the hand gesture known as the *manu cornuta* was commonly used for apotropaic effect on Etruscan ash urns.[25]

Monsters

There are many other monsters in the Etruscan Underworld. Cerberus, the three-headed dog who guards the entrance to Hades appears from time to time (Fig. X.9), and another tripartite figure, the warrior Geryon (*Kerun*) occurs in the Tomb of Orcus II. On ash urns of the latest period in Etruria, there is quite an assortment of Etrusco-Greco-Roman monsters: Gorgons with hippocamps and

X.21 Stone (nenfro) statue from Tuscania, ca. 300 BCE. Florence, Museo Archeologico Nazionale. Photo: Soprintendenza per i Beni Archeologici della Toscana. The winged figure displaying herself may be Vanth, in the role of one who shocks the visitor and thus protects the tomb. She probably flanked a doorway, with a twin on the other side of the portal.

X.22 Ash urn, 3rd–2nd century BCE. Present location unknown. After Brunn-Körte:3.141, no. 11. Winged female griffins, with the body of a lioness and the beak of a bird of prey, flank a snaky Gorgon head. Decorating an ash urn, the frightening monsters may refer to the new habitation of the deceased but also serve to keep unwanted visitors from touching the urn.

X.23 Ash urn, 3rd–2nd centuries BCE. Florence, Museo Archeologico Nazionale. Photo: DAI. The deceased soul, swathed in drapery, journeys by sea monster.

X.24 Ash urn, 3rd–2nd century BCE. Palermo, Museo Archeologico Regionale. Photo: DAI. The chest of the funerary urn, decorated with a monstrous female figure with wings, two fish tails, and a girdle of large leaves, who holds up two anchors in a threatening way. She has been equated with the monster Skylla, who protected the passage at the Straits of Messina between Sicily and the peninsula of Italy. The deceased reclines on the lid of the urn.

griffins (Figs. X.22), sea monsters (Fig. X.23), Skylla swinging an oar or a pair of anchors (Fig. X.24), and a number of other demons, with snake legs, seen also in tomb painting, for example in the two anguiped demons in the Tomb of the "Typhon" at Tarquinia (Fig. X.25a). Each of the latter is perhaps to be interpreted as a Giant (i.e., Celsclan), especially since in an adjoining scene is a goddess with vegetal appendages who has been convincingly identified as their mother, Cel Ati (Figure X.25b).[26]

We are reminded of the array of horrifying monsters assembled at the entrance to Orcus as encountered by Aeneas and described by Virgil: "there are many monstrous hybrid beasts, Centaurs stabled at the gate, Skyllas half-human. . . Gorgons, Harpies, and the shadowy shape of the three-bodied Geryon" (*Aeneid* 6. 284-89).[27]

a

b

X.25 Wall painting, late 3rd century BCE. Tomb of the "Typhon," Tarquinia. a. Anguiped monster. Photo: DAI: b. Vegetal goddess. After Brendel 1995:Fig. 319. The anguiped monster (a) is one of two who adorn the sides of a pier in the middle of the tomb, while on a third side a female with vegetal parts (b) is represented. They may be Giants, i.e., sons of Earth, and the goddess may be their mother, Cel Ati.

Aita and Phersipnei

Finally, from the Greek tradition we may mention Hades and Persephone, known in Etruria as Aita and Phersipnei (alternate spellings Eita and Phersipnai; Figs. X.26-27). Aita never appears on mirrors, though he has been recognized in vase painting,[28] while his consort appears on a mirror found in an Etruscan tomb (Orbetello), but lettered in Latin with the names of Proserpina, Venus and Jupiter (contest over the child Adonis).[29]

Aita and Phersipnei preside over the cast of characters we have observed in the Tomb of Orcus II at Tarquinia (Fig. X.26), from Achmemrun and Hinthial Teriasals to These with Tuchulcha, and Kerun. In Etruria these deities have a certain local flavor: Aita wears a cap made from the skin of a wolf, a creature which, in Italy, was often associated with death and the Underworld, and in his hand he raises aloft a serpent, rather as Charu does. Next to him sits Phersipnei, wearing an Etruscan robe, with her hair filled with snakes. Around them roll the mists of the Underworld, in the form of clouds of varying colors. The couple also appears in the Golini Tomb I at Orvieto (Fig. X.27), where they are enthroned as the principals at an Etruscan banquet; members of the Leinies family recline nearby on couches (Fig. X.28), and all are served from a table with magnificent vessels of gold and silver. The mood is nonetheless somber here, with little black clouds lining the couches and furniture, in keeping with the gloomy atmosphere we have seen in relation to Charu and Vanth and the other monsters of the Underworld.

X.26 Wall painting (watercolor copy) from the Tomb of Orcus II, Tarquinia, ca. 325–300 BCE. Photo: DAI. The rulers of the Underworld, labeled Aita and Phersipnei, sit enthroned amid rolling mists. Aita, far right, bearded and bare-chested, wears a wolfskin cap; the beautiful Phersipnei, beside him, has snakes entwined in her hair.

Rathmtr

A recent addition has been made to the iconography of the Etruscan Underworld, in the recognition of the Greek judge figure Rhadamanthys.[30] His name evidently appears as Rathmtr, on a mirror in Boston dating to the 4th century BCE. The figure is dignified, bearded, heroically seminude, as he leans upon his staff and raises a hand in a gesture of explanation to a female companion (perhaps Turan). He resembles very much the figure of Rhadamanthys in a Greek painting in the Great Tomb at Lefkadia of about the same date. There the Underworld assignment for the judge is specific; on the mirror, the theme is probably not pertaining to the afterlife, but shows Rathmtr as a wise judge or even soothsayer.

X.27 Wall painting from the Tomba Golini I, Orvieto (watercolor copy by G. Gatti), ca. 350–325 BCE. Florence, Museo Archeologico Nazionale. Photo: Soprintendenza per i Beni Archeologici della Toscana. Aita (spelled Eita) and Phersipnei (spelled Phersipnai), enthroned on the left, celebrate a banquet in the Underworld. Next to a table laden with vessels for the banquet, a youth serves drinks. Vel Leinies, a member of the family that owned the tomb, stands on the right.

The Happy Afterlife

Hades and Persephone, as we have seen, appear rarely in Etruscan art, and only at a fairly late date, in the 4th and 3rd centuries BCE. The motif of the banquet of eternity, however, is very ancient, and goes back to the earliest periods of Etruscan culture, when survivors began to tend their dead relatives by leaving bowls and cups and pitchers, along with real foodstuffs, in the graves. Excavations have revealed that actual eggs, pomegranates, honey, grapes, olives, and other appealing foods as well as drinks were put into the grave for the deceased. And in fact, there were numerous representations of the Etruscans honoring the deceased with a feast, as in the tomb paintings at Tarquinia of the 6th and 5th centuries BCE, which show individuals reclining on outdoor couches in the same way that the Leinies family dined in the presence of Aita and Phersipnei. The mood is completely different in these earlier representations, however; not only Aita and Phersipnei are missing, but so are Vanth and Charu and their assistants. Besides the banqueting there are images of athletes taking part in games and revelers dancing and drinking, often in a bright and flourishing landscape. In the Tomb of the Leopards at Tarquinia (Fig. X.29) banqueting and dancing take place among trees identifiable as bay (laurel), sacred to the gods of the Underworld because of its black berries.

The atmosphere is so happy that many have thought that the scenes represented are from real life, from the funeral feasts that were mounted to cheer and console the survivors. But others have argued that these paintings show the Etruscan afterlife as it was originally conceived and only later supplanted by the grim demonic Underworld. Once again we may turn to Virgil of Mantua for an eloquent description of the concept, as he tells how Aeneas and his companion in the Underworld came to "the Land of Joy, the pleasant green places in the Fortunate

X.28 Wall painting (watercolor copy) from the Tomba Golini I, Orvieto, ca. 350–325 BCE. Orvieto, Museo Archeologico Nazionale. Photo: Soprintendenza per i Beni Archeologici della Toscana. Vel Latithes and Arnth Leinies recline on banqueting couches as they join in the feast in the presence of Aita and Phersipnei, rulers of the Underworld. The offices they held while living are indicated by painted inscriptions above their heads. A cloudlike design around the couches represents the atmosphere of the Underworld.

X.29 Wall painting, ca. 460 BCE. Tomb of the Leopards, Tarquinia. Photo: DAI. Revelers dance in a grove, probably in the afterlife.

Woods, where are the Homes of the Blest. Here an ampler air clothes the plains with brilliant light, and always they see a sun and stars which are theirs alone. Of these bright spirits, some were taking exercise at games together on the grass of the field of play, or wrestling on yellow sand. Others were treading a rhythmic step as they danced and sang. . . . And lo, Aeneas saw others to his right and to his left about the grass, feasting and singing a joyful hymn of praise in their choir; they were in the midst of a wood of scented bay-trees"(*Aeneid* 6, 638-95).[31] The poet from Mantua captures well the spirit and numerous details of the original Etruscan afterlife, in which there was eternal pleasure for the souls in music, dancing, and feasting.

Appendix
Studying Etruscan Mythology

It is the purpose of this essay to give a concise historical and critical survey of modern writings on the mythology of the Etruscans and thus provide a guide to further reading on this subject, with special attention to the evidence obtained from art. Many studies on Etruscan myth have been published in languages other than English and thus a number of the references in this essay are in German, Italian, and French. It is hoped that the descriptions of the writings, along with translations into English of the titles, will provide a portal to these works, and that, in any case, readers will consult them for their illustrations.

The subject of mythology in Etruscan art began to receive focused attention in the 19th century with the publication of two great corpora, on mirrors—*Etruskische Spiegel* (Etruscan Mirrors; Berlin, 1840-97), in 5 volumes by E. Gerhard, A. Klügmann, and G. Körte, and on ash urns—*I rilievi delle urne etrusche* (Reliefs on Etruscan Urns; Rome, 1890-1916), in 3 volumes by E. Brunn and G. Körte. Both are rich in illustrations, which are organized according to subject matter and thus still provide a valuable starting point for mythographers and iconographers.

Gerhard was a discerning scholar of ancient myth and also published a basic work called *Über die Gottheiten der Etrusker* (On the Deities of the Etruscans; Berlin, 1847), which was utilized by George Dennis in his perceptive, reliable account in English of the "mythological system of Etruria" (*The Cities and Cemeteries of Etruria,* London, 1848, 1, l-lvi). Conscientious attention to the ancient literary sources in these older works means that they are especially useful for coverage of native deities unrecognized in Etruscan art and thus frequently omitted from current discourse (e.g., Genius, the Penates, the Lares, and other elusive group gods of the Etruscans). The discovery at Piacenza in 1877 of the famous bronze liver incised with the names of Etruscan gods led in a similar direction, in which native mythical figures were studied in the context of religion. The Swedish scholar C.O. Thulin, in *Die Götter des Martianus Capella und die Bronzeleber von Piacenza* (The Gods of Martianus Capella and the Bronze Liver from Piacenza), *Religionsgeschichtliche Versuche und Vorarbeiten* 3 (1906):1-92, wrote a basic study of the document, with his interest lying principally in haruspication, but with many comments on the various Etruscan deities listed on the liver and the way in which they related to the text of Martianus Capella, written in the 5th century CE and thought to reflect an Etruscan concept of the cosmos.

The study of mythological themes in architectural sculpture was facilitated by the appearance of the basic corpus of A. Andrén, *Architectural Terracottas from Etrusco-Italic Temples* 2 vols. (Lund, 1939-40). With the publication of a series of articles on Etruscan mirrors in the journal *Studi Etruschi* by G. Mansuelli, shortly before the middle of the 20th century, came a surge of interest in Etruscan mythology. Of particular usefulness was his survey of mythological characters and themes on the mirrors, with considerable emphasis on Greek myths found there, but also a basic survey of "Divinità e personaggi mitici etruschi" (Etruscan Divinities and Mythical Personages), *Studi Etruschi* 20 (1948-49):59-98. At the same time appeared the basic book on *Etruscan Vase Painting* by J. D. Beazley (Oxford, 1947), likewise a repository of Greek myth in Etruria, but written by a scholar whose main interest was in Greek vase painting, especially of Attica, and whose visits to Etruria were expeditions to identify Hellenic material among the provincials. His widely cited article, "Reflections on the Etruscan Mirror," *Journal of Hellenic Studies* 69 (1949):1-17, has a similar bias, as revealed by his evaluation of Etruscan mirror art: "at its best it is very Greek, often with a slightly rustic or provincial flavor that is not at all unpalatable."

In a completely different category was the seminal study by the distinguished historian of religion Stefan Weinstock, "Martianus Capella and the Cosmic System of the Etruscans," with its commentary on many of the deities [*JRS* 36 (1946): 101-29]. The text had been discussed by Thulin in relation to the Liver, but now Weinstock examined it separately and in detail. Here the approach is almost exclusively philological, with virtually no attention to the visual evidence. But Weinstock discusses many Etruscan gods otherwise ignored, and provides a context for the interaction of the gods in Etruscan myth. He situates the Etruscan view of the cosmos by means of comparisons and contrasts with Egyptian, Greek, and Iranian religious and philosophical systems.

A later significant study of the system of Martianus and of the Liver was published by L. B. Van der Meer, *The Bronze Liver of Piacenza, Analysis of a Polytheistic Structure* (Amsterdam, 1987). This work brings together many different approaches to all the problems posed by the Liver, but is especially valuable to mythographers, because of its deity by deity survey of representations of the gods named on the Liver, frequently with illustrations. In addition it lists inscriptions with the names of these deities, and illustrations of the works on which the inscriptions occur. Thus it provides a basic handbook on Etruscan gods, or at least the ones that are on the Liver (since Menrva, Turan, Aplu, and Turms—to name a few—are not on the Liver, obviously some fairly significant figures are not included).

A major contribution to the study of the gods with emphasis on their place in Etruscan ritual and religion was made by Ambros Pfiffig in his *Religio Etrusca* (Graz, 1975). He did a deity-by-deity study of all the major gods and many of the lesser known ones as well. Pfiffig also covered the Piacenza Liver and the heavens of Martianus, as well as the Etruscan themes of creation and the calendar.

Discussion of Greek myths in Etruria became a heated topic in the second half of the twentieth century, with two main camps of scholarship, in a debate focusing on the Archaic period, but not without ramifications for the later periods. A series of articles by G. Camporeale (1958, 1964, 1965, 1968, 1969, 1989) argued that the Etruscans really did not have great understanding of Greek myth, and when they used it, did not focus so much on the meaning as on the decorative potential of the material. His latest article "La mitologia figurata nella cultura etrusca arcaica," (Mythology Represented in Etruscan Archaic Culture), *Atti, Secondo Congresso Internazionale Etrusco, Florence...1985*, 1989, II, 905-24, provided a synthesis of his ideas. Working especially with engravings, paintings and reliefs on vases and small luxury objects, he noted the many "mistakes" made in Etruscan art in regard to Greek "mythological fact," referring to these with a now-famous Italian term, "banalizzazioni." Camporeale went through a litany of "errors" in Etruscan mythological scenes. The various deviations from standard Greek myths, he argued, were travesties, misunderstandings and bizarre additions, which banalized the Greek myths and deprived them of their powerful messages, leaving a prosaic and decorative representation. This theory reaches its limit in admitting that sometimes Greek vase painters made deviations, too, but it was only because they knew their vases were destined for a market of ignorant Etruscans.

On the other side was the stance of R. Hampe and E. Simon, presented in the key work, *Griechische Sagen in der frühen Etruskischen Kunst* (Greek Myths in Early Etruscan Art) (Mainz, 1964). Looking especially at painted vases and bronze relief sculpture, they argued that the variants of Greek myth found in Etruria actually showed a profound knowledge of the material, based on experience of the Greek figurative arts and literature. According to this theory, the Etruscan usage of myth was rational and selective, and showed the integration of Greek material into Etruscan culture, sometimes including details or whole compositions that were not directly testified in Greek art but were absolutely consistent with Greek tradition. Thus Simon was able to interpret every detail of a well-known but baffling decoration of an amphora in The Metropolitan Museum of Art, New York, as showing the goddesses of the Judgment of Paris *before* their famous squabble, while they were reclining at the feast of the wedding of Peleus and Thetis. She subsequently published numerous innovative readings of representations of Greek myth in Etruscan art (gathered in *Schriften zur Etruskischen und italischen Kunst und Religion* (Writings on Etruscan and Italic Art and Religion) (1996), not without sometimes arousing the objections of other scholars.

Ingrid Krauskopf, in her study of the Theban cycle in Etruria (*Der Thebanische Sagenkreis und andere Griechische Sagen in der Etruskischen Kunst* (The Theban Cycle and other Greek Myths in Etruscan Art) (Mainz, 1974), reviewed the debate carefully, and then contributed her analysis and exceptionally good documentation, based on vases, gems, tripods, and several other sculptural monuments, noting that the Theban saga was more popular in Etruria than in Greece itself. She observed that sometimes (as in Greece), the myths were not narrated "correctly," and in addition there were in Etruria versions of the Theban myths quite unknown in Greece. Some years later Krauskopf made another major contribution to the study of Etruscan myth, with her monograph on *Todesdämonen und Totengötter im vorhellenistischen Etrurien, Kontinuität und Wandel* (Death Demons and Gods of Death in Etruria before the Hellenistic Period, Continuity and Change) (Florence, 1987).

Another important review of Theban mythology in Etruria was published by J. P. Small, *Studies Related to the Theban Cycle on Late Etruscan Urns* (Rome, 1981), a thorough catalog of Hellenistic material that complements Krauskopf's study, which had emphasized the Archaic and Classical periods and had little coverage of the urns. Small found surprising evidence that some of the urns, long labeled as Eteocles and Polynices, may in fact show another—Roman—story, Aeneas and Turnus. She subsequently published an article-length study on this idea, along with other studies that indicated a very different way of thinking about myth in Etruria. Rather than looking to Greece, she explored the possibilities of ties with Rome, and at the same time stressed the importance of native myth. Her *Cacu and Marsyas in Etrusco-Roman Legend* (Princeton, 1982) is a full-length study of a theme that is non-Greek and points in new directions. At the same time, Anne Weis was publishing her article on the mythological theme of the figure tied to a barren tree, "The Motif of the *Adligatus* and Tree: A Study in the Sources of Pre-Roman Iconography," *AJA* 86 (1982):21-38, found widely in Italy and indicating, according to her, the ambient of an artistic and cultural common language in Central Italy in the 4th century BCE. Most recently, studies by T. P. Wiseman have helped to illuminate the nature of myth in early Italy. His book, *The Myths of Rome* (2004), is a stimulating compendium that includes essays pertaining to the myths of early Rome, Praeneste, and Etruria.

The mythology of Praeneste, a city where a language closely related to Latin was spoken and written, presents a unique body of material that runs parallel to Etruscan myth and sometimes overlaps it, but which is so unusual that it deserves a comprehensive study in its own right. Mirrors and bronze cistae (cylindrical cosmetic chests) engraved with scenes of local and foreign origin reveal the rich repertory of Praenestine myth. The pioneeering study of mirrors by G. Matthies, *Die Praenestinischen Spiegel* (Strassburg, 1912), and the corpus of cistae by G. Bordenache Battaglia, A. Emiliozzi Morandi, F. Coppola, and F. Jurgeit, *Le Ciste prenestine* (Rome, 1979-1990), are among the essential studies. M. Menichetti has interpreted Praenestine myth in terms of its social and political significance for the aristocracy, especially in relation to early Rome: *Quoius forma virtutei parisuma fuit—:ciste prenestine e cultura di Roma medio-repubblicana* (Whose beauty was equal to his virtue: Praenestine Cistae and the Culture of Middle-Republican Rome) (Rome, 1995).

Monograph studies of categories of artifacts provided organization of materials so that their rich mythological content could be addressed. P. Zazoff, *Etruskische Skarabäen* (Etruscan Scarabs) (1968), assembled a corpus of engraved gems, showing how they featured their own particular selection of subjects appropriate for seal stones, especially single-figure representations of heroes such as Hercle, Achle and the Thebans.

A Guide to Etruscan Mirrors (1982), edited by N. T. de Grummond, included a unit on "Greek Gods and Heroes on Etruscan Mirrors," by Richard De Puma, and a unit on "Etruscan Mythological Figures," by Cheryl Sowder, with an alphabetical treatment of Etruscan gods and spirits (from Achvizr to Zipna), which remains the most convenient and reliable short guide to these little-known figures.

In the late 20th century, several corpora provided spectacular new tools for studying all of this material. The iconographical lexicon of classical mythology, *Lexicon Iconographicum Mythologiae Classicae*, 8 vols. (1981-99), with its many illustrated and in-depth articles on purely Etruscan figures, as well as regular features of coverage of Greek mythological figures in Etruria, is of surpassing importance. The scientific corpus of Etruscan mirrors, *Corpus Speculorum Etruscorum*, the first fascicles of which appeared in 1981, turns out new volumes at a steady pace (26 issued at the time of writing). To study the inscriptions on the mirrors and other Etruscan artifacts and monuments, one may now consult the authoritative corpus of Helmut Rix, *Etruskische Texte* (Etruscan Texts), 2 vols. (Tübingen, 1991). Special sections on inscriptions on mirrors and gems are helpful for using philology to interpret mythology (II, 345-68). A recent work by L. B. Van der Meer was inspired by the appearance of this work, *Interpretatio etrusca, Greek Myths on Etruscan Mirrors* (1995), in which the author uses only mirrors with inscriptions to sort out various categories or themes in mirror iconography: immortality, healing, divination, rescue, birth, victory.

For the study of political imagery in Etruscan mythology, one may consult F.-H. Pairault Massa, *Iconologia e politica nell'Italia antica, Roma, Lazio, Etruria dal VII al I secolo a.C.* (Iconology and Politics in Ancient Italy: Rome, Latium and Etruria from the 7th to the 1st Century B.C.E.)(Milan, 1992), an intellectual distillation derived from Pairault Massa's many years of experience with the problems of Etruscan iconography (see the bibliography, esp. 97-98). The work ranges widely in time and space and draws on art historical theory for its methodology. The approach stresses the importance of the total context of a work, including its patron and social and political programs and the fact that images in art vary as they move through time. She frames her work by relying heavily on the model of the political history of early Italy that has been constructed in numerous publications by M. Torelli (for a concise summary in English and bibliography, see Torelli, "History: Land and People," in *Etruscan Life and Afterlife: A Handbook of Etruscan Studies*, ed. L. Bonfante, Detroit, 1985, 47-65.) Menichetti has contributed to this dialogue as well, with his *Archeologia del Potere, Re, immagini e miti a Roma e in Etruria in età arcaica* (The Archaeology of Power: Kings, Images and Myths at Rome and in Etruria in the Archaic Period) (Rome, 1994).

A resurgence of interest in Etruscan religion will no doubt have repercussions for the study of myth. Of great importance is the publication of papers given at the colloquium *Les étrusques, les plus religieux des hommes, État de la recherche sur la religion étrusque* (The Etruscans, the Most Religious of Men, State of Research on Etruscan Religion) (Paris, 1997), ed. F. Gaultier and D. Briquel. One of its most compelling features is an 88-page bibliography, which includes a full listing of conferences and exhibitions on the Etruscans during the second half of the 20th century. Sections with papers on the Etruscan pantheon and on gods from outside Etruria are especially relevant. The book is in French, with those papers by scholars from outside of France translated; there are no papers by anglophones. In a nearly contemporary publication, J.-R. Jannot addresses mythical themes frequently in his *Devins, dieux et démons, regards sur la religion de l'Étrurie antique* (Soothsayers, Gods and Demons, Observations on the Religion of Ancient Etruria) (1998). A synthetic work in English on *The Religion of the Etruscans*, based on a conference in at Florida State University (editors Nancy T. de Grummond and Erika Simon 2006) and contains many important essays by leading scholars in the field.

To study Greek myth in art, T. H. Carpenter, *Art and Myth in Ancient Greece* (London, 1991), remains an essential handbook guide to the Greek representations that serve as comparanda for the Etruscan material. Alan Shapiro's *Myth into Art* (1994) is essential for its rigorous comparison of the respective treatments of myth in art and literature. Two important recent publications that deal mainly with Greek myth in art but point to new directions of methodology that may be relevant for the study of Etruscan mythological art as well are: J. P. Small, *The Parallel Worlds of Classical Art and Text* (Cambridge, 2003), and S. Woodford, *Images of Myth in Classical Antiquity* (Cambridge, 2003). Small, in particular, articulates a simple but previously unrecognized principle that radically affects the way we interpret scenes of myth in art: artists do not illustrate texts, as scholars often assume, but rather stories. They may derive their ideas about a myth from a number of sources—other works of art, oral tradition, or texts that were read but not memorized and regarded as incontrovertibly correct. The implications for the study of Etruscan myth are clear: scholars should stop trying to judge Etruscan representations of myths on whether they are consistent with Greek texts.

Notes

PREFACE

1. Examples of this approach are so numerous that they scarcely need to be cited. One particularly conspicuous example is van der Meer 1995, which in spite of its title, *Interpretatio etrusca: Greek Myths on Etruscan Mirrors*, has as one of its central tasks the locating of possible precedents in Greek vase painting for the scenes that appear on Etruscan mirrors. Van der Meer confines himself to examining mirrors that have inscriptions, actually a quite small percentage (10%) of the known Etruscan mirrors, but these lend themselves especially well to tracking down Greek names and words to use for comparisons. See the review of the work by Schwarz 1997.

2. See the discussion in the Appendix, 236-37.

3. The most popular myth of the death of Achilles has the hero die of an arrow shot into his foot by Paris on the battlefield at Troy, a story linked to the idea of the "Achilles heel." A remarkably different version is that told by a late mythographer according to which Achilles was ambushed or run through at the shrine of Apollo Thymbraios while negotiating to marry Polyxena, daughter of the king of Troy. Is this later myth "false"? For the stories, see Gantz 1993, 626 and 659. There are many other examples; Peter Green observed (2000, 184) "just how rich, varied and complex from the beginning such alternative versions[of the Trojan cycle] were."

4. Knauer 2002, 295.

5. See de Grummond 1985; *Les étrusques et l'Europe.*

6. One thing this book is not intended to do is to give an overview of Greek mythology in Etruria; I have left out some of my own personal favorites in Etruscan art because they have a lower priority for the objectives of the work. There are of course numerous publications on the topic and those who are interested can find an abundance of material. See Beazley 1947; Camporeale 1965, 1968, 1969, 1985; Richardson 1976; De Puma 1982; Pairault Massa 1992; van der Meer 1995; Krauskopf 1997.

7. E.g., Torelli 1986, Pairault Massa 1992, Menichetti 1994.

8. There are some rather important cases in which we are unsure of the Etruscan name. In particular I have used the Latin form Tages for the principal Etruscan prophet; see Chapter II.

9. In this study there is not space to review the battles over defining the words "myth" and "mythology." The possibilities have been so much discussed that one author, William G. Doty, was able to isolate more than 50 different attempts at defining myth. See his discussion for a thorough and thoughtful examination of the problem (Doty 1986: 9-11).

10. Eliade 1991, 3-4.

11. Doty 1986, xiv.

12. To put the matter a little more simply, we are dealing with stock parts that may be combined to create a particular theme.

13. The Etruscans adopted the alphabet used by the Greeks (taken in turn from the Phoenicians) for writing down their language, which was—it should be noted—totally unrelated linguistically to Greek or Phoenician. For the conventions referenced see the chart in *TLE*, p. 13. I also follow the practice of not capitalizing any words within an Etruscan inscription. More advanced conventions, observed by the leading experts on the Etruscan language, utilization of which might cause confusion here, may be found in the recent excellent corpus of Etruscan inscriptions compiled by H. Rix, *ET* 37-39. Also basic for the study of the Etruscan language: *CIE*

and Bonfante-Bonfante 2002.

14. Text revised from material originally presented as a paper, "A View of Etruscan and Praenestine Myth," at the conference "The Etruscans Now" held at The British Museum, December, 2002.

15. For handy reference on Greek gods and myths, the following are highly recommended: Carpenter 1991 (concise bibl. on Greek myth in art, pp. 247-49); Gantz 1993 (though entitled *Early Greek Myth*, the work is rich in references to later material as well); Shapiro 1994; Simon 1998. For Roman myth in art and literature, the best starting point is Wiseman 2004; always useful is Simon 1990.

16. Their names are: Marcia Anderson, Angela Aslanska, John Beeby, Kelly Burleson, Sara Chumbley, Jamieson Donati, David Gagliano, Katherine Harrell, Lorraine Knop, Veronica Pagan, Andrew Pappas, Drew Philbeck, Linnaea Preissler, Jamie Proctor, Katie Rask, Jacquelyn Simmons, Heather Walker, and Elizabeth Wilson.

Chapter I

1. Mallory 1989, 7 and 87-94, gives concise coverage of terminology and theories on the Indo-European populations in Italy. On the early presence of the Etruscans, see Ridgway 2002, esp. 15-16, and Haynes 2000, 4. The earliest known inscription in the Etruscan language occurs around 700 BCE: Cristofani 1979, 378. The nature of Etruscan writing and language is discussed, pp. 10-11.

2. On representations of the human figure, see Haynes 2000, 7-8. The best bibliography on Etruscan art is that provided by F.R. Serra Ridgway in Brendel 1995, 481-513. On writing, see note 20.

3. Hencken 1968, 41-42, fig. 10 and pl. 50; Hencken 1968a, 117-18, and fig. 106.

4. The figures have a special charm, especially the motif of "two seated figures" on Villanovan ash urns that face one another and clasp hands, or bow to each other, or raise their arms up high, etc. Hencken 1968a, 29, notes the suggestion that they represent figures at a funeral feast; in any case it is difficult to extract any narrative from their relationship.

5. Fugazzola Delpino 1984, 164-66; Elliot 1995, 20. On wolves, see further note 6.

6. Cristofani-Martelli 1983, 284-85. On the special significance of wolves in Italy, see Richardson 1977. The Lady of the Beasts first occurs in Anatolia (Turkey) in the 6th millennium BCE, seated and flanked by felines: Roller 1999, 30-32 and fig. 1. Cf. the Near Eastern representations of the goddess with owls and lions: Neumann 1963, pl. 126 and 270-78 for a discussion of the wide territories of the Lady of the Beasts. In Greece the mistress of animals of the 7th and 6th centuries BCE controls felines, deer, fish and birds: Carpenter 1991, 44, and fig. 75. A Greek vase from Boeotia (Simon 1998, 135 and fig. 139) sometimes said to show wolves with the goddess features instead stylized lions (the tail is far too long for a wolf). This Lady of the Beasts or Mistress of Animals became known to the Greeks as Artemis, but this need not mean that the Etruscans called the goddess by that name or understood her as such.

7. Martelli 1987, 261. Menichetti 1994, 48. Bonfante 2003, 47-48.

8. The lyre player scene and the dragon scene are often studied together. Martelli 1987, pls. 37, 38, and 41, with notes on the plates, 261-62 and 264. Menichetti 1994,48-50. Martelli 2001. Bonfante 2003, 47-48. On the lyre-player, see also Simon 1995.

9. Marazov 1998, 160.

10. Massa-Pairrault 1994. Torelli 2000, 608 (no. 212). Bonfante-Bonfante 2002, 134 and 136 (with full bibl.). For a possible image of Medea with cauldron on an Etruscan mirror, see Neils 1994, 190 and fig. 17.2 (youthening of Jason?).

11. It has been conjectured that Taitle's connection with Metaia could lie in the fact that they

both had special knowledge and magic power. Bonfante-Bonfante 2002, 136.

12. Szilágyi 1992, 1998, esp. 190, 695-696. See also 44, 156-157, 189-191, 214, 247-248, 300-301, 364-65, 480-82.

13. Szilágyi 1992, 1998, 45 (bound man), 214-215 (Master of Birds).

14. Richardson 1976.

15. See the discussion of lightning and its bearers in Chapter IV.

16. *CSE*, U.S.A. 1.26. For more on Usil, see chapter VI, esp. Fig. VI.36, which shows the god of the sun with the god of the sea and the goddess of the dawn.

17. Haynes, 2000, 261.

18. Discussed below, p. 152.

19. It is interesting that objective drawings made recently for the *CSE* such as this one are much more useful for studying Etruscan styles than those made for *ES* in the 19th century, which tended to smooth out "irregularities" and make the images look more "classical" Greek. In selecting images for illustration in this volume, I have whenever possible used a modern drawing instead of the old one in *ES*. As a note of caution, there are still many items in the 19th-century corpus that have not been restudied and it has been necessary to utilize those drawings.

20. The estimate is based on the number of inscriptions in *CIE*. Some of these are discounted by specialists, however, as "graffiti" of one or two letters that do not qualify as readable "texts." Cf. Bonfante-Bonfante 2002, esp. 57-59.

21. Puhvel 1987, 4, 20, 33-42; specifically on the Etruscans as non-Indo-European, 145-146.

22. The connection is not at all far-fetched. Etruscan trade with northern Europe began as early as the Villanovan period: *Les Etrusques et l'Europe* 1991, 158-67. The Etruscan version of the alphabet seems to have been transmitted across the Alps, where it was adapted in a wide area to the runic scripts of the Germanic peoples: Bonfante-Bonfante 2002, 117-20.

23. *TLE* 399 and *ET* Vt S.2. Another possible translation takes the final verb to mean "drank milk" rather than " was adopted." Bonfante-Bonfante 2002, 155. For a fuller explanation of this surprising scene, see p. 83. For another example of an illustration with a text, see Fig. X.13 and the caption.

24. Pallottino 1975, 225. The word was noted by classical authors as *aesar*: Suetonius, Augustus 97, Dio Cassius 56.29. Cf. the Icelandic account of Snorri Sturluson, in which the principal group of Norse gods is known as the "Aesir": *Prose Edda* 1954, 27-28, etc.

25. The best recent study of the Zagreb linen book is that of Roncalli 1985, 17-64. Cf. Bonfante-Bonfante 2002, 58, 183.

26. Van der Meer 1987.

27. Discussed fully in Chapter III.

28. De Grummond 1982; concerning subject matter, see especially chapter VII, on "Etruscan Mythological Figures" by Cheryl Sowder (100-28). For recent thoughts see de Grummond 2002a. Carpino 2003 contains much useful iconographical discussion. Van der Meer 1995 deals with thematic representations on mirrors (almost exclusively inscribed).

29. Richter 1968 is useful. There are two basic works in German: Zazoff 1968 and Martini 1971.

30. Basic and exhaustive catalogue by Steingräber 1986.

31. For fuller discussion and documentation of Hercle, see Ch. VIII.

32. Elliott 1995. Cf. the discussion of Aita (=Hades), who wears the wolf-skin cap, in Ch. X. Sometimes the creature is not a wolf, however, but may look like a horse or a monster.

33. Rackham 1967 for the translation.

34. Brunn-Körte 3, 21.

35. Elliott 1995 argues convincingly for the possibility of theatrical performances involving wolf masks and skins.

36. Simon 1984, 155.

37. Page 1990, 16, 63,65. The ending is not happy, for Fenrir swallowed Odin and then was himself slain by Vidar, son of Odin.

38. See the discussion of the debate in the Appendix: Studying Etruscan Mythology, p. 237

39. L. Kahil, "Helene," *LIMC* 4 (1988): 501.

40. Appendix 237.

41. Pallottino 1975, 192.

42. Pallottino 1975, 204-208.

43. See 161-63 below.

44. Thomas 1991, 10. The idea conveyed by the name of this book, *A Cultural History of Gesture*, is exciting, but unfortunately the title is misleading, since the work features a series of essays delivered as papers, not really integrated into a continuous history.

45. Morris et al. 1979. I thank Elizabeth T. Wilson for calling this study to my attention. I learned a great deal from her Master's Paper on "Etruscan Gestures: An Analysis of Four" (Florida State University, 2005). She deals with four gestures, especially in Etruscan tomb painting: the horned hand, the hand to the forehead (grief), the outstretched palm, and the seizing of the wrist.

46. For the gesture, the vertical horned hand, see Morris 1979, 120-34.

47. Boegehold 1999, 22.

48. It is interesting to note that the pointing finger is used by prophetic figures from the Bible in Renaissance and Baroque art, for example, in renderings of St. John the Baptist by Leonardo da Vinci (Paris, Musée du Louvre), Guido Reni (London, Dulwich College Picture Gallery), and others.

49. Boegehold 1999, 25, calls the gesture "alerting the audience." His quotes from Quintilian and Apuleius provide quite precise descriptions of how an orator may get the attention of his listeners. Again, there are good parallels from art of later periods. The figures in the Vienna Genesis (Vienna, Library) and the Joshua Rotulus (Vatican Museums) regularly hold up one hand with two fingers extended to show that they are speaking.

50. Jucker 1956.

51. Boegehold 1999, 18-20. In some cases in Etruria, it is clear that the gesture is used to turn the head to give attention to someone or something.

52. Nagy 1996, 2002; coverage and extensive illustration of this kind of material in Wiman 1990, 93-179.

53. Bonfante 1980.

54. Nagy 1996, 52; or more generously, "light-hearted," Bonfante 1980, 148. She suggests that the whole group may reflect performances of Greek tragedy in Etruria, for, as has often been pointed out, some of the groups are set in front of a stylized architectural framework that resembles a temple front. The main problem with seeing these mythological figures as theatrical, however, is the frequent nudity of both males and females, which, given all we know of the Etruscans, could scarcely have been acceptable on stage.

55. Scenes with the Dioskouroi and Lasa (Figs. VII.25, VIII.19) may also be characterized as "emblematic." I have excluded such specimens almost totally from this work, since the emphasis here is on myths that do have narrative content.

56. De Jorio 2000. This fascinating work, with its superb introduction by Adam Kendon, is an important document in the history of gesture. It surprised and disappointed me that I found little in the Neapolitan system that helped to elucidate Etruscan gesture. Of the 29 gestures il-

lustrated in plates 19-21, I found only two that were relevant for the Etruscans: the horned hand (pl. 19.2), which seems to occur only in Etruscan funerary art and does not, to my knowledge, occur in mythological scenes, and the gesture of "indicating" (pl.19.5), which fits very well with the gesture of a person explaining a prophecy.

57. Doty 1986, esp. 42-47, for the theories about myth and behavior models espoused by Durkheim and Malinowski.

58. On Etruscan religion: Pfiffig 1975. The best short account is in Pallottino 1975, ch. 7. See also Torelli 1986. For fuller and up-to-date discussions see de Grummond and Simon, 2006.

59. Carpino 2003, 46-48, probes the question of the meaning of the egg for the Etruscans. Cf. 125-28 below.

60. Steuernagel 1998.

61. Pairault Massa 1992, Menichetti 1994.

62. Beard, North, and Price 1998, vol. II, ch. 7, for many examples. Fontenrose 1978, 244-354.

63. Colonna 1992.

64. See Dumézil 1966, 18-31, for a critique of the concept of *numen* devised by H. J. Rose; Beard, North, and Price 1998, vol.II, 3, with the concise objection that the word *numen* rarely occurs before the period of the Empire, and only then did it acquire the meaning of "divine power."

65. Pallottino 1975, 140.

CHAPTER II

1. See Massa Pairault 1985, esp. 59-65, de Grummond, 2000b and de Grummond 2006. For examples of the work of the haruspices, who interpreted the sacred writings and various signs from the gods, see Dumézil 1966, 2, esp. 606-608; Beard, North and Price 1998, 2, Ch. 7, "Divination and Diviners," contains many instances of prophetic actions in early Rome, not necessarily Etruscan, but surely under Etruscan influence.

2. Wood 1980, 325-44. Small "Tages," *LIMC* 7 (1994): 832-33, with bibl.

3. Ovid, *Metamorphoses*, 15.553-559; John the Lydian, *de Ostentis*, 2.6.B, Festus 492.6.8.

4. For Tarchon, see Chapter IX.

5. Pallottino 1975, 123-25.

6. A "charter myth" need not originate *before* the rituals or social order to which it pertains. Rather it is normally told as a justification of an existing order: Malinowski, 1992, 87, 113. The fact that the earliest documentation of the story belongs to the 4th century BCE need not be a hindrance to describing this theme as a charter.

7. Bonghi Jovino 2001.

8. The onset of an epileptic seizure was popularly attributed to divine visitation, a notion reported (and scorned) in the Hippocratic text, *The Sacred Disease*, 1-4.

9. The interpretation of the mirror from Tuscania given here is based on the article by Pallottino 1979. There is some disagreement about the interpretation, for which see Torelli 1988 and Pairault Massa 1992, 143-44, and n. 10 below.

10. Some have argued that the ending of Tarchunus is a genitive, implying that we have here Avl, the "son of Tarchon" (Torelli 1988, 113). Such an individual could represent the phenomenon of mythological doubling, in which the adventures of one character are rerun in a second similar character (cf. the Etruscan kings of Rome, Tarquinius Priscus and Tarquinius Superbus). The form *Tarχun, which would be the nominative, does not occur in Etruscan, and we cannot be sure that the Romans had such a form before them when they spoke of Tarchon. In any case, the Romans were prone to drop an Etruscan genitive ending, as in the Vipinas brothers, who

became Vibenna in Latin.

11. For the equivalence of Veltune and the Etruscan god Vertumnus, referred to as the "principal god of Etruria" by the Romans, see the full discussion in Chapter IV below.

12. Torelli 1988, 111. The ending of the name is in the locative case, which suggests that this is a place name.

13. Torelli 1988, 113. Pairault Massa 1992, 144.

14. De Grummond 2000b, 30, note 8 with bibl.

15. Torelli 2000, 529 and 637 (Cat. no. 325).

16. Basic reference: Small 1982. Review of bibliography Luschi 1991, esp. 105 (note 1).

17. On Orvieto, see especially Pallottino 1975, 116. Stopponi 1991, 88.

18. Cf. the discussions, pp. 21, 100, 151.

19. Small 1982, 7-9.

20. M. Harari, "Vegoia," *LIMC* 8 (1997): 183-84. See also Chapter III, n. 1.

21. R. Lambrechts, "Lasa," *LIMC* 6 (1992): 217-25. Rallo 1974.

22. De Grummond 2000b and 2002b.

23. V. Saladino, "Kalchas," *LIMC* 5 (1990): 931-34.

24. Guthrie 1952. De Grummond 2000b: 39-42. A new study by Richard De Puma 2001 reviews the previously published Etruscan and Greek examples of the mythologem studied here and adds two important mirrors to the relevant corpus. See also de Grummond forthcoming b.

25. Guthrie 1952, 35-39. De Grummond forthcoming b. A word of caution: it is always possible that the head on these vases, never labeled, is in fact not that of Orpheus. The single labeled specimen of the head of Orpheus is the one on the Etruscan mirror (Fig. II.10), which is used to "prove" the identity of the head on the Greek vases.

26. De Grummond 2002b.

27. Page 1990, 24, 27. The story occurs in the *Heimskringla* of Snorri Sturluson.

28. Colonna and Michetti, "Uni," *LIMC* 8 (1997): 161.

29. Canciani, "Albunea," *LIMC* 1 (1981): 481.

30. Camporeale, "Umaele," *LIMC* 8 (1997): 158-59.

31. Van der Meer 1995, 86, unaccountably states that the word *urphe* appears on the rock beneath Umaele's foot. No such inscription exists on this mirror. Cf. Rix 1992, Vs S. 19 and *CIE* 10875. Van der Meer's treatment of Umaele, 86-93, is marred by numerous errors.

32. Lysaght 1986, 199. This is also said to be the pose of a druid when prophesying.

CHAPTER III

1. Harris 1971, 31-40, w. extensive bibl. Pfiffig 1975, 157-59. See also Chapter II, n. 20.

2. On the shadowy figure of Arruns of Clusium, sometimes equated with Arruns Veltymnus, see Heurgon 1959, 41-42, and 1964, 228, 230, 233, 294 (n. 37).

3. Heurgon 1959. Harris 1971, 35-37.

4. Author's translation, from text in *Agrimensores* 1848, I, 350. See also de Grummond and Simon 2006, 30-31, 191-92.

5. Censorinus, *De Die Natale* 17.5-6. Plutarch, *Sulla* 7.4-11. Servius, *Buc.* 9.46. For discussion, see Pfiffig 1975, 159-61.

6. Edlund-Berry 1992 gives the best overview of what we know about Etruscan calendars.

7. For the Brontoscopic Calendar of Nigidius Figulus, see Turfa 2006b. The quotes from the calendar are taken from pp. 182-183.

8. Cicero, *De Div.* 2.18.42. For a full discussion, see Pallottino 1975, 144-46, and van der Meer 1987, 27-29.

9. Pallottino 1975, 144-46, 261 (n. 15); van der Meer 1987, 19-20. Maggiani 1982, 61-62.

10. Pliny, *NH* 2.138-139. Servius, *ad Aeneid.* 1.42.

11. For Laran, the Etruscan god of war, see pp. 138-40; Satre occurs on the Piacenza Liver (discussed below, pp. 47-51; see also Fig. III.1 and notes on the illustration.) Basic discussion of Satre as Saturnus: Pfiffig 1975, 312-13. Pliny (*NH* 2.138-39) also names Summanus as a deity who throws lightning but it is evident from other writers and from inscriptions that Summanus is a name given to Jupiter in his aspect as a god during the night: Pfiffig 1975, 316.

12. The best review of the passage is Weinstock 1946. See also Torelli 1986, 208-10 , van der Meer 1987, 22-26, and de Grummond and Simon 2006, 3-4, 199-200.

13. Author's translation from text in Weinstock 1946, 102.

14. Pfiffig 1975, 115-127, Maggiani 1982, Torelli 1986, 210-13, and esp. van der Meer 1987.

15. Scholars vary somewhat on the numbering of the regions of the Liver. The scheme used by Maggiani 1982, fig. 1, is most convincing.

CHAPTER IV

1. Basic bibliography on Tinia: Pfiffig 1975, 231-36; van der Meer 1987, 30-37. G. Camporeale, "Tinia," *LIMC* 7 (1997):40-421. Simon 2006, 45-46, 51, 52, 60.

2. De Grummond 2004, 353-54, for inscriptions from the sanctuary of Tinia at the Belvedere, Orvieto, that make dedications to *apa*.

3. *Prose Edda* 1954, 31. Odin's name, if transliterated into Etruscan, would be Utin.

4. *Prose Edda* 1954, 27, 29-30. See also Chapter I, n.24.

5. See the discussion in Seneca, *Quaestiones Naturales* 2.41.1-2. I have profited greatly in my study of Etruscan lightning and thunder from the unpublished Master's paper of Lorraine Knop, "Lightning in Etruria: Its Manifestation in Art and Myth" (Florida State University, 2005), and from the translation of the Brontoscopic Calendar of John the Lydian made by Turfa 2006b.

6. Richardson 1983, 1, 358-59, for basic publication of the statuette, 21.8 cm. high, dated 500-450 BCE. Simon 1990, 111, dates the work to the late 6th century.

7. E.g., Carpenter 1991, Figs. 95b, 96, 99, 100. Carpenter comments, however, on the "variation" in the lightning: "the shape of this weapon may vary—sometimes ornate and flower-like, sometimes a simple missile" (39).

8. *ET* Af 8.1-8.8. Bonfante-Bonfante 2002, 183-85, lists eight border markers, but there are only three, each marked on multiple sides with the same inscription for a total of eight inscriptions: Carruba 1976.

9. Krauskopf 1987, 55-56. Elliott 1995, 24, 32 (n. 19).

10. Hostetter 1986, 20-27.

11. Simon 2006, 51.

12. *ES* 5, no. 21 (222-23). Because the story is without parallel, the authenticity of the mirror, now lost, has been doubted; it has been noted that it shows a composition known in reverse from a scene on a mirror in Bologna that depicts the bandaging of Philoktetes. Carpino 2003, 31, 114. Stylistically the mirror is quite consistent with works created at Vulci in the fourth century BCE, and I see no reason to question its authenticity.

13. Discussed more fully in Chapter V.

14. For Thalna and the other goddesses (spirits) mentioned in this section, see Chapter VII.

15. De Grummond 1982, 184.

16. Rebuffat-Emmanuel 1973, 54-59. See above, p. 15 for discussion of the scene in the lower zone with Helen.

17. E. Mavleev, "Epiur," *LIMC* 3 (1986):810-12. Liepmann in *CSE* Bundes republik Deutschland 2.5 and 2.18.

18. See Chapter VII.

19. Pallottino 1975, 115, 125, 126. Stopponi 1991, 88. Capdeville 1999, 110-115.

20. The excavators are Simonetta Stopponi and Claudio Bizzarri of the University of Macerata. See Stopponi 2002.

21. Author's translation.

22. On Favor, whom I believe to be equivalent to Etruscan Thuf, see de Grummond, 2005.

23. *Ovid* 1986.

24. Radke 1965, 257-58. She does not seem to have been represented in art.

CHAPTER V

1. The topic is complex and charged with emotion. A sensible account was already made by Pomeroy 1975, 1-15. A recent review of scholarship on the goddess takes a deconstructive position regarding the model of the universal great mother: Roller 1999, esp. 9-18. It is not surprising that a reaction has set in against the work of Jung and his disciples, who visualized an archetypical mother already potent in prehistoric times (Neumann 1963), and against the theories of Marija Gimbutas (1989, with full bibliography of her works, 359).

2. The possible exception is the goddess Cel, whose name means "Earth" in Etruscan. But cf. my reservations, p. 106.

3. Colonna, "Athena/Menerva," *LIMC* 2(1984): 1050-74.

4. Pfiffig 1975, 298. Turfa 2006a, 98.

5. Cristofani, "Maris I," *LIMC* 6 (1992), 358-60.

6. We shall say a good bit more about Mariś in discussion of the male gods below, Chapter VI, which may help to elucidate these two problematic mirrors. My own arguments on the identity of Mariś are given at length in de Grummond forthcoming a.

7. Concise review of the myth: Gantz 1993, 235-37.

8. See Carpino 2003, 15 and 107 (n. 35, with bibl.)

9. Roncalli 1965, 28-33, 69-77. Haynes 2000, 217-19.

10. Colonna 1985, 128-29. Serra Ridgway 1990, 522, reviews the varying theories about the string of some 20 cell-like rooms that run alongside Temple B at Pyrgi, conjectured to have been used by the hierodules of Uni-Astarte; but perhaps rather than for prostitution they served as shelters for pilgrims or as ritual dining rooms.

11. Colonna and Michetti, "Uni," *LIMC* 8 (1997): 159-71, esp.159. Radke 1965, 153, regards the name Uni as a loan word from Latin.

12. Simon 1982. Colonna and Michetti, "Uni," *LIMC* 8 (1997): 170 (no. 92)

13. Homer 1951.

14. De Grummond, 2000b, 53-54, w. bibl.

15. Simon 2006, 51.

16. *Pittura etrusca a Orvieto* 1982, 91-93.

17. Brendel 1995, 219-20, figs. 146-47. Simon 2006, 51.

18. E.g., Diodoros 4.9.6. For a survey of texts and images, see Gantz 1993, 378. Cf also *CSE* Italia 1.1.15, p. 38, and Rasmussen 2005, 36.

19. Serra Ridgway 1996, I, 79-80.

20. This identification was suggested to me by Elizabeth Heuer, who is preparing an article on her idea. cf. Ramussen 2005, 30, on Hebe on the Volterra mirror.

21. On Turan Ati (on a mirror), see de Grummond 2004, 355. Concerning Eros: A warrior labeled as Erus, embracing a winged goddess named Zinthrepus on a mirror from the area of Volterra (ES 5. 121) shows no basis for being identified as the son of Aphrodite: Krauskopf, "Erus," *LIMC* 4 (1988): 14.

22. Bloch and Minot, "Aphrodite/Turan," *LIMC* 2 (1984): 169-76.

23. *TLE* 854.

24. On the mirror, see Bonfante 1977. On Althaia, see Gantz 1993, 328-30. Simon 2006, 52, argues that the figure is indeed intended to allude to the story of the Greek Althaia, mother of Meleager, and is included here as an "anti-theme" to the peace of the gods shown by the concord of the goddesses; the "war" within her family would be called to mind. Other Etruscan mirrors do show blending of themes on a single disc, but normally they occupy distinct areas of the mirror. Only rarely are characters from different myths placed side by side in the same frame: cf. V. 30 (Turan and Atunis and Meliacr and Altlenta) and VII. 22 (Hamphiare and Aevas). My own suspicion is that in this case Althaia is a figure in Etruscan myth whose name happens to resemble that of a Greek character.

25. Nagy 1996 and 2002.

26. Nagy 2002, 8. The nude figure on the left has a bit of drapery in her left hand, suggesting that the gesture fits the mythologem by indicating display of beauty.

27. Carpino 2003, 74-77, reviews the possibility that the mirror, currently in Paris, Petit Palais, is a forgery. She finds convincing stylistic parallels for all significant elements in the composition, and suggests that the scene itself is authentic. She gives the possibility that the mirror may have been made in modern times but copied from an ancient design.

28. Lambrechts 1978, 34. For the three versions known, see Lambrechts 29-34, ES 2.207.4 and ES V.104.2.

29. In fact, the reasons for the usage of obscenity in myths of the world are seldom patent. See Malinowski 1992, for discussion of myth and obscenity. For more on the motif of exposing oneself, see Fig. X.21 and the discussion in the text, p. 184. Cf. also Fig. VIII.11, and text, p. 184, for a strange erotic encounter.

30. Bloch and Minot, "Aphrodite/Turan," *LIMC* 2 (1984): 175 (no. 41). The identification is conjectural. The barring female may also appear as clothed and wingless.

31. Feruglio 1998, for the initial publication of the mirror and for a discussion of the *iynx*. I am grateful to JoAnn Delmonico Luhrs for sharing with me her thesis (Bryn Mawr College, 2004) on "Brides, Prostitutes and the *Iynx*: Symbols of Eros," from which I learned much about the *iynx*.

32. De Grummond 1982, 108-109. Sensitive reading in von Vacano 1960, 7-13. Zimmer 1987, 30.

33. Pfiffig 1975, 61-63. On the use of magical nails in Greece, see Boardman-Kurtz 1971, 216-217; none of the usages listed seem parallel to the Etruscan custom.

34. Simon 2006, 54, rightly interprets the scene as a mistress of animals with leaping wolf puppies, rather than as Helen with the Dioskouroi carrying animals from the hunt, as per Cristofani-Martelli 1983, 285.

35. Colonna 1985, 73 and 77, and Colonna 2006, 155, argues, however, that the great temple at Tarquinia, the Ara della Regina, was dedicated to this goddess. See also the discussion below, pp. 131-32, on her connection with the Portonaccio temple at Veii.

36. Bonfante and Bonfante 2002, 165 (no. 47). The meaning of the epithet *spulare* for Aritimi is unknown. The lack of provenance discourages conjecture.

37. Colonna 1994, 368-69.

38. De Grummond 2004, 359-67, presents arguments for a lunar aspect.

39. Colonna 1976-77. De Grummond 2004, 354-55. The statues, now lost, included both males and females, evidently all votaries, carrying assorted offerings; it is not possible to argue that one or more of the female figures represents Cel herself. Basic documentation on Cel: van der Meer 1987, 73-75.

40. Rupp 2002.

41. Bloch and Minot, "Eos/Thesan," *LIMC* 3 (1986):789-97.

42. Bloch, "Thesan," *LIMC* 3 (1986), 789-90. Colonna 1994, 351.

43. Serra Ridgway 1990, 523. Simon 1990 152-57.

44. Serra Ridgway 1990, 523. Simon 2006, 47, and Krauskopf 1997, 31-32, connect the rooster god with Morning Dew. On the so-called 20-celled structure, see note 10, p. 248.

45. De Puma 1994.

46. Carpino 2003, 17-21, with numerous examples. It is time to be cautious about the notorious pastiche of a terracotta sculpture akroterion from Cerveteri showing a striding goddess carrying a child (Carpino, pl. 21); it was wrongly dated and interpreted by Goldberg 1987, who failed to deal critically with the rather obvious and inconsonant additions to the piece. Now stripped down to its authentic core (*Die Welt der Etrusker* 1988, 170 and pl. p. 128), the sculpture no longer shows the head of the child or the head, wings and winged shoes of the goddess; nor can we be sure that the support for the akroterion was crescent-shaped. In short, it is not possible to discuss the identity of the figures.

47. Vermeule 1979, 21, 163.

48. The basic publication is a group of articles from a conference in Orvieto, 1984, published in *Annali della Fondazione per il Museo* "Claudio Faina" 3 (1987).

49. Bruni 1986, 33 (with refs.), lists seven examples. One shows the figure crouching in a basin (no. III.16, pl. 19). An additional two specimens were recently exhibited: Andreae, Hoffmann and Weber-Lehmann 2004, 104, nos. 114 and 116; no. 116 is described, however, as a *Jungling*, "youth."

50. Colonna 1987 analyzes other finds at the sanctuary, noting the presence of Hercle and a Pan-like figure (=Faunus), with overtones of the fertility cult of the Lupercal at Rome. The goddess associated with Faunus and Hercules is the Bona Dea ("Good Goddess"); the Etruscan goddess could thus be her counterpart in Etruria, though the Bona Dea does not seem to have been a deity of the dead. Cf. Scullard 1981, 116-17, 199-201.

51. Inscriptions from Graviscae (Turfa 2006, 97, with bibl.) suggest that the Greeks equated Demeter with Vei, but there does not seem to be a parallel in the iconography of Demeter for the nudity of the Cannicella goddess. For votive offerings to Vei in the shape of a uterus, see Turfa 2006a, 101.

CHAPTER VI

1. I have argued a new identification for Mariś that makes him, too, a son of Tinia, albeit a rather surprising one. See pp. 140-44 below and at greater length de Grummond, forthcoming a.

2. Cristofani, "Fufluns/Dionysos," *LIMC* 3(1986):531-40. Bonfante 1993.

3. Livy 1976.

4. We have the names of four maenadic females in Etruscan art—Himaca, Munthuch, Thalna (see E. de Grummond 2000-2001) and possibly Vesuna (discussed below). Of satyrs, the following names are known: Achsun, Aulunthe, Chelphun, Hathna, Mastei, Puanea, and Sime. All the names but one (Mastei) come from Etruscan mirror inscriptions. Mastei appears on an Etruscan black-figure amphora in Dresden: *Welt der Etrusker* 1988, 151-52. For Achsun, see Zimmer 1987, fig. 16. For others see the entries by Sowder in de Grummond 1982, 109, 110, 113, 122.

5. Simon 2006, 49. Turfa 2005:234-35.

6. See the discussion on Castur (Kastor) in Chapter VIII.

7. Krauskopf, "Eros (In Etruria)," *LIMC* 4 (1988): 1-2. Theories about Aminth are discussed

by Sowder in de Grummond 1982, 108. The little figure has no bow and arrow and there is no connection with Turan that might help to identify him as her son. It is sometimes said that this is a statue, placed on a base, but I think it more likely from the action of the spirit that he is a "real" figure involved in the plot of the story. For the inconography of Jason in Etruria, see J. Neils, "Iason," *LIMC* 5 (1990): 629-38. I find uncomvincing the identification of this scene (631) as the theme of Jason praying to Amor to cause Medea to fall in love with him.

8. Radke 1965, 335. Small, "Vesuna," *LIMC* 8 (1997):236. Van der Meer 1997. Her name appears only here in Etruscan, but she is known from inscriptions in Umbrian and Volscian (Latin-related languages of ancient Italy), where she seems to have been a vegetation goddess.

9. De Grummond 2000b, 80.

10. Krauskopf, "Eros (In Etruria)," *LIMC* 4 (1988):1-2. Here, too, are lacking attributes and a context to support the identification; Svutaf has no bow and arrows and does not appear with Turan.

11. *ES* 5.35 and commentary pp. 44-47. Small, "Vesuna," *LIMC* 8 (1997): 236 with refs.

12. Harari, "Turms," *LIMC* 8 (1997): 98-111.

13. Gantz 1994, 319-21, for the various permutations (two eggs instead of one; Helen in one egg, three children in the other, etc.)

14. Carpino 2003, 42-48.

15. Harari, "Turms," *LIMC* 8 (1997):102 (no.50). Heres in *CSE* Deutsche Demokratische Republik 1.13 (33).

16. On the World-Egg of the Orphics, see Guthrie 1952, esp. 92-95. On the egg of Helen: L. Kahil, "Helene," *LIMC* 4 (1988): 503-504.

17. Pieraccini 2003, 173. Carpino 2003:47-48.

18. Gantz 1994, 288-97, for the two abduction episodes.

19. Krauskopf, "Aplu," *LIMC* 2 (1984):335-63.

20. Krauskopf, "Aplu," *LIMC* 2 (1984):336.

21. Colonna 1994, esp. 359.

22. Brendel 1995, 238-44.

23. *ET* Ve 3.11, 3.29, 3.33, 3.34, 3.45.

24. The statue is under new reconstruction at the time of writing. There is no question that the deer was present.

25. Van der Meer 1987, 136-39, for inscriptions. Tirelli 1981, for many illustrations of possible images of the sun.

26. Colonna 1994 and Colonna 2006, 135-40.

27. Van der Meer 1987, 133-35. There is no *LIMC* article on Tiv.

28. Camporeale, "Auri," *LIMC* 3 (1986):54-55.

29. cf. my arguments in the article in preparation, "The Sacred Day on Etruscan Mirrors," for *Etruria e Italia Preromana, Studi in onore di Giovannangelo Camporeale.* I am extremely grateful to Alba Frascarelli for furnishing me with her new and authoritative drawing of the mirror from Perugia (Fig. VIII.12), which makes it certain that the reading of the inscription is *auri* instead of *aur* (as already surmised by Camporeale: note 28 above). Tirelli 1981 assembles the images she hypothesizes to be the Etruscan god of the sun; for my argument, see especially pl. 16b, in which a youth drives two horses, with a crescent moon indicated next to the horses.

30. Van der Meer 1987, 124-126.

31. Jucker 1956.

32. Gantz 1993, 75-76.

33. Hemelrijk 1984 is the essential work on the hydrias from Cerveteri; the workshop that produced these vases was under strong Ionian Greek influence and the artists may have been

Greeks in part or wholly. They seem etruscanized, however, in their view of society, and the myths that reflect their views are therefore appropriate to include here.

34. Simon, "Ares/Laran," *LIMC* 2 (1984):498-505.

35. The reading given by Maggiani 1982, 57, is undoubtedly correct (cf. caption for Fig. III.1, House 26), but the sense of the inscription may be as understood by van der Meer 1987, 114, that a reference is intended to Lar or Laran.

36. Simon 2006, 58.

37. Discussed in detail in De Grummond, forthcoming a.

38. See pp. 74-75 above.

39. Schilling 1991a.

40. Colonna 1980 has argued that the Etruscan name Farthan and related words occurring in various inscriptions refer to reproduction or begetting, and has used the term Genius as a translation for a god named Farthan. There need be no conflict with the argument made here: I suggest that the Roman concepts of Genius as 1) a personal attendant deity and 2) as a begetter simply received two different names in Etruria: Mariś and Farthan.

41. Pfiffig 1975, 285.

42. Zazoff 1968, 81, no. 136.

Chapter VII

1. Basic references on Janus: Simon 1990, 88-93; Schilling 1992b. Taylor 2000.

2. *ET* Co 3.4. Bonfante and Bonfante 2002, 166 (source 48). On Culśanś see generally: I. Krauskopf, "Culśanś," *LIMC* 3 (1986): 306-308; Pfiffig 1975, 246-47; van der Meer 1987, 75-82.

3. Maggiani 1988.

4. Taylor 2000, 38.

5. Maggiani 1988.

6. De Grummond 2000, 259-61. It has been argued that the mirror shows a story that appears in Dracontius, *Romulea* 10, 177-336, but there are many significant differences: G. Camporeale, "Aminth," *LIMC* 1 (1981): 665.

7. Thorough coverage with bibliography in van der Meer 1987, 90-96. Maggiani and Pallottino both thought that Nocturnus and Cilens were equivalents; van der Meer argues that Cilens=Fata (Martianus Region 13). Unfortunately there is no single Roman goddess named Fata, but rather this designation is surely the plural of the neuter *fatum*, the normal way to refer to the Fates in Latin.

8. Basic for Selvans, and including references to Silvanus: Pfiffig 1975, 297-301; van der Meer 1987, 58-66; Simon 1990, 200-205; Schilling 1992d. On Silvanus, see Dorcey 1992.

9. De Simone 1997, 199-200.

10. Now in the J. Paul Getty Museum, Malibu; 4th century BCE; key references and illustration in Bonfante and Bonfante 2002, 167.

11. On the context of boundaries and the role of Selvans, see Edlund-Berry 2006, esp. 116-18.

12. Radke 1965, 279-82.

13. Cristofani 2000, 286.

14. Minto 1927,475-76. He makes an apt comparison with the pagan seers in Dante's *Inferno*. XX.13, who are depicted as having twisted their heads backwards so that they could not see where they were going. Dante includes two Etruscan prophets, Aruns of Luni and Manto (XX.46, 55).

15. De Grummond 2005.

16. Van der Meer 1987, 105-107, and de Grummond 2005.

17. On the subject of personifications among the Romans see especially Axtell 1907.

18. Sowder in de Grummond, 1982, 124. Camporeale 1960; Camporeale, "Thalna," *LIMC* 7 (1994): 900-902.

19. Dumézil 1970, 43-44, gives other references in Latin. He argues (unconvincingly) that it was not the case that Romans were uncertain about gender, but rather that they just wanted to be sure they were covering all possibilities, as in writing a letter "Dear Sir or Madam." For a review of Etruscan deities showing ambiguity of sex, see Cristofani 1997. His discussion, however, resists the idea that these deities can change sex: he argues that Thalna is masculine, that Achvizr is masculine in only one case, and that when Alpan and Evan (both more frequently feminine) appear as masculine on the same mirror it is a mistake of the engraver. But since Cristofani wrote his article an additional male Thalna has appeared, Fig.VII.10, and another male Achvizr may be added, Fig. VII.20. This kind of variation appears frequently and consistently in regard to Etruscan divinities; thus it is no longer tenable to say that the artists were "mistaken."

20. *CSE* USA. 3.20.

21. C. Weber-Lehmann, "Thanr," *LIMC* 7 (1994): 908. Maras 2001.

22. Sowder in de Grummond 1982, 117-18. Lambrechts, "Mean," *LIMC* 6 (1992): 383-85.

23. Sowder in de Grummond 1982, 118-19, 181-182. Lambrechts, "Munthuch," *LIMC* 6 (1992): 688-89.

24. Sowder in de Grummond 1982, 106-107. Van der Meer 1987, 82-87. Lambrechts, "Alpan," *LIMC* 1 (1981): 573-76.

25. Sowder in de Grummond 1982, 106. R. Lambrechts, "Achvizr," *LIMC* 1 (1981): 214-16.

26. Sowder in de Grummond 1982, 115-116. Camporeale, "Leinth," *LIMC* 6 (1992): 249-50.

27. Sowder in de Grummond 1982, 113. Krauskopf, "Evan," *LIMC* 4 (1988): 126-27.

28. Sowder in de Grummond 1982, 116. Lambrechts, "Malavisch," *LIMC* 6 (1992): 346-49.

29. De Grummond 1982, 181-83. Bonfante 1990, 34, for the theory that Malavisch is really Helen.

30. Attributed to the Meidias Painter; see Burn 1987, 40-44, 96.

31. Useful discussion of the Meidian personifications in Burn 1987, 32-33. See also individual entries in Shapiro 1993.

32. I. Jucker in *CSE* Schweiz 1. 17 (p. 39).

33. For a third example of Zipna tending a mirror, see *CSE* Schweiz 1.28.

34. Ambrosini 1995.

35. Ambrosini 1995, 191-92, based on an earlier argument by Mansuelli but with new details and synthesis.

36. I. Krauskopf, "Sethlans," *LIMC* VII (1994): 654-59, lists only this work as showing the combination of Sethlans and Turan. Yet another problem is posed by the number of divisions of the wheel or cycle held by Sethlans. The Etruscan examples of the wheel of Ixion cited by Ambrosini 1995, 187, have six or eight spokes.

37 Authoritative presentation in Rallo 1974. See also Lambrechts, "Lasa," *LIMC* 6 (1992): 217-25; van der Meer 1987, 109-12.

38. Rastrelli 1993. Haynes 2000, 343-45.

CHAPTER VIII

1. The basic reference on the Vipinas brothers is Small 1982. See further the refrences in notes 5-7 below.

2. Campbell 1949. See the wide range of theories on the hero (von Hahn, Rank, Lord Raglan) covered by Dundes 1990, esp.188-89.

3. Not included in any of the hero theories in Segal 1990; I give here my own ideas of this common motif in the hero myth. The alter ego is not necessarily a twin, though a twin may fill this role by showing that he is less important than his brother.

4. Examples could be multiplied. I omit twins from Mesoamerica, but cannot resist mentioning Frodo and Sam, created by the great folklorist J.R.R. Tolkien for the *Lord of the Rings*.

5. Heurgon 1989, 46-49, gives a review, with bibliography, of Latin evidence for the Vibenna or Vivenna brothers, as they were called. For the bronze tablets recording the speech of Claudius, a transcription of the text, a translation into Italian, and a commentary see Buranelli 1987, 238-42 (entry by Ivan Di Stefano Manzella)

6. Buranelli 1987, 234, no. 93 (entry by F. Boitani); see also 234-35, no. 94 (entry by Gilotto) for a later vessel (in red figure decoration) with the name of Avle Vipinas.

7. For discussion and other references to the legend see Dumézil 1970, 41-42. Pfiffig 1975, 147-48.

8. Schwarz, "Hercle," *LIMC* 5: 196-253.

9. Zazoff 1968, 91, no. 167.

10. Rallo 2000, 232-48 for a thorough review of the mirror. On Calanice see esp. 238, note 19. The word *kallinikos* was used in a poem in praise of Herakles by Archilochos, writing around 700 BCE; an astonishing confirmation of the usage of this name in Etruria occurs on a partially-preserved impasto cup from Tarquinia (late 8th/early 7th century BCE): *mi kalan*...For a relief mirror with Calanice and Castur freeing Prumathe, see Carpino 2003, 48-55. On the myth in Greece, see Gantz 1993, 410-413.

11. McDonough 2002. Vipece may be cognate with the Latin *vibex*, meaning "mark of a blow." The name has also been read as Philice. On the theme of Hercle at the spring and possible Greek influences on the Etruscan renditions, see Massa Pairault 2000, 183-86.

12. Buranelli 1992, 56-59. See also H.P.Isler, "Acheloos," *LIMC* 1 (1981): 12-36, esp. 12.

13. Steingraber 1986: 353-55.

14. Hermansen 1984 151, touches upon the idea that the flames may be used to revive someone who has died.

15. Brommer 1981, 4 and 9.

16. Carpino 2003, 9-16. *CSE* Great Britain 1.1.20. For the possibility that the figure represented here may be equivalent to the Roman Bona Dea (= "Good Goddess")and may have been worshipped at the Cannicella sanctuary in Orvieto, see Colonna 1987, 19-22 and Ch. V., note 50, above.

17. This last detail is less clear in a new drawing of the mirror (Fig. VIII.16) than in the drawing reproduced in *ES* 4.344, but photos old and new (e.g., Carpino Pl. 1, and description, p. 10) support the reading here.

18. Carpino 2003, 13, lists the various theories.

19. Zazoff 1968, 122-23. Sometimes the figure on the raft appaears to be a Silenus. Up-to-date review in Turfa 2005, 238 with bibl.

20. De Puma, "Tinas Cliniar," *LIMC* 3 (1986): 597-608. De Grummond 1991.

21. Richardson 1984.

22. De Grummond 2000a.

23. De Grummond 2002b, 69. For the prophecy see Gantz 1993, 228.

24. De Puma in de Grummond, 1982, 99. Zazoff 1968, 192. Lambrechts 1978, 27.

25. See further discussion of Odysseus p. 202 below, and Fig. IX.1.

26. Steingräber 1986, 353-55.

27. Bonfante 1984.

28. Szilagyi, "Echetlos," *LIMC* 3 (1986): 677-78. Briguet and Briquel 2002, 66-82. The article in *LIMC* makes no attempt to count the number of examples surviving. The recent catalog of Etruscan ash urns in the Louvre produced 12 in that collection alone. The newly reorganized Museo Archeologico at Santa Maria della Scala in Siena features a display of 21 such urns all in a row.

29. Echetlos was represented in a painting in the Stoa Poikile in Athens, but otherwise no representations of him are known in Greek art. Further, the warrior in the Etruscan scenes does not fight against Persians, rather soldiers in Greek or generic dress. The hero of Marathon remains remote to Etruria of the 2nd century BCE. Kodros does not fit the iconography because he did not fight with a plow, but rather with a scythe. In fact, in the one known image of Kodros in armor, he is depicted with a spear: Simon, "Kodros," *LIMC* 6 (1992), 86-88. For a recent discussion of the problem of the subject matter, see Turfa 2005, 268-69.

Chapter IX

1. Herodotus 1996, 40.

2. Bonfante-Bonfante 2002, 51.

3. Hesiod 1988, 33.

4. De Grummond 2000, 262-63.

5. Harari, "Tyrsenos," *LIMC* 8 (1997): 155-56 discusses the possibilities.

6. Small, "Tarchon," *LIMC* 7 (1994): 845-46.

7. Small 1982, 45.

8. Richardson 1964, 222.

9. Virgil 1956, 256.

10. Haynes, 2002, 67, 69. Full bibliography in Bonfante and Bonfante 2002, 44, note 139. The name Laucie is suggestive as well, reminding of the son of Mezentius, Lausus.

11. J.P. Small, "Mevntie," *LIMC* 6 (1992): 566. The letter which I read as *z* is almost identical to the first letter of the name above the nude, standing female read by scholars as Zelachtra (*ET* OI S.22). For further discussion of the mirror, see I.Krauskopf, "Ethun," *LIMC* 4 (1988):38, and also G. Camporeale, "Achle," *LIMC* 1 (1981): 209 (no. 164). Fuller arguments will be presented in my study, in preparation, "Mezentius in Etruria." I thank Lorenzo Galeotti for discussing the mirror with me and for providing a photo of the newly cleaned mirror.

12. King Oeneus on a mirror with Atalanta and Meleager: *CSE* France 1.1.14; Priam: *ES* 5.118.

13. Colonna 1976, 375 (no. 129).

Chapter X

1. Author's translation.

2. Cf. Burkert 1985, 59-60, on the power of blood in Greek religion.

3. Author's translation.

4. Dumézil 1970, 353-55.

5. Vermeule 1979, 9 and fig. 4; the little silhouette souls of the Greeks are normally winged.

6. Vermeule 1979, 30-31. It is a mistake to call these by the name *eidolon,* which refers to a full-size replica of the deceased person. See also Bremmer 1983, 78-80.

7. For both vases see Manino 1980.

8. Krauskopf 2006 presents a concise essay and an exhaustive bibliography. For a refreshing review of the elements of the Etruscan Underworld and the positive nature of many of these

motifs, see Serra Ridgway 2000.

9. Schaeffer 1994, for a nuanced reading of the many representations of arched doors in Etruscan funerary art. She believes that these doors are representations of the entrance to a tomb. Krauskopf 2006, 67 and 69 (note 11) reviews the arguments and weighs in for the interpretation of the door as leading to the Realm of the Dead.

10. Roncalli 1996 and 1997.

11. Jannot 1997, 140, lists eight inscribed images, and 144, a dedication to him on a Greek vase.

12. Unsurpassed is the monograph of De Ruyt 1934.

13. Jannot 1997 lays out the evidence on the multiplied images of Charu and Vanth.

14. De Ruyt 1934, 186, 191, 234, and 246 for ancient sources on Dispater.

15. Hostetler 2002.

16. Steingräber 1986 is the best source for color reproductions of Etruscan paintings. For the color of the arm of Tuchulcha, see pl. 131.

17. Harari, "Tuchulcha," *LIMC* 8(1997): 97-98. Because of the vulture face, Tuchulcha is sometimes confused by modern scholars with the Greek death demon Eurynomos, mentioned by Pausanias (10.28.1) as being present in the Underworld painted by Polygnotos in the Lesche of the Knidians at Delphi (5th century BCE). But that creature, whose flesh was blue-black, "like that of flies hovering around meat," did not have vulture features; he was merely seated on a vulture's skin.

18. Minetti 2005.

19. Steingräber 1986, 352.

20. Weber-Lehmann, "Vanth," *LIMC* 8 (1997): 173-83.

21. Serra Ridgway 2000, 307-309.

22. Richardson 1964, 243. On Valkyries, cf. Page 1990, 61-62.

23. *ES* 5.110.

24. Hathor brought good humor to the great god Re by exposing herself to him. On Demeter and Baubo, see T. Karaghiorga-Stathacopoulou, "Baubo," *LIMC* 4 (1988): 87-90. Plutarch, *De Iside*, 378d. cf. Herodotus 2.60.

25. Weber-Lehmann 1997 identifies the figure in X.21 as a Siren, making comparisons with these creatures, represented with bird's feet and musical instruments, sometimes lifting up their skirts. The absence of parts such as feet and objects held in the hands of the Tuscania figure prevents a a conclusion about this interesting theory.

26. Rupp 2002, for the argument about this "vegiped" goddess. For the latest review of anguipeds, vegipeds and also piscipeds, see Serra Ridgway 2003, esp. 12-13.

27. Virgil 1956, 155-56.

28. Krauskopf, "Aita/Calu," *LIMC* 4 (1988): 394-99.

29. De Grummond 2004, 361-63. The mirror is made in the style of those from Latin Praeneste. For Phersipnei on other monuments, see Mavleev, "Phersipnei," *LIMC* 7 (1994): 329-32.

30. De Puma 1998.

31. Virgil 1956, 166-67.

Bibliography

Agrimensores 1848. *Die Schriften des römischen Feldmesser*, ed. K. Lachmann, vol. I. Berlin.

Ambrosini, L. 1995. "Sethlans con la ruota di Issione su uno specchio inciso da Corchiano." *StEtr* 61:181-203.

—1996. "Una coppia di specchi del gruppo 'delle Lase' con un nuovo tipo di raffigurazione." *StEtr* 63-94.

Andreae, B., A. Hoffman, and C. Weber-Lehmann 2004. *Die Etrusker. Luxus für das Jenseits*. Munich: Hirmer Verlag.

Axtell, H. L. 1907. *The Deification of Abstract Ideas in Roman Literature and Inscriptions*. Chicago, IL: University of Chicago Press.

Beard, M., J. North, and S. Price 1998. *Religions of Rome*. 2 vols. Cambridge: Cambridge University Press.

Beazley, J. D. 1947. *Etruscan Vase Painting*. Oxford: Oxford University Press.

Becatti, G. 1947. *Meidias, Un manierista antico*. Florence: Sansoni.

Boardman, J., and D. Kurtz 1971. *Greek Burial Customs*. Ithaca, NY: Cornell University Press.

Boegehold, A. L. 1999. *When a Gesture was Expected, A Selection of Examples from Archaic and Classical Greek Literature*. Princeton, NJ: Princeton University Press.

Boethius, A. 1978. *Etruscan and Early Roman Architecture*. Harmondsworth: Penguin.

Bonfante, L. 1973. "Roman Costumes, A Glossary and Some Etruscan Derivations." In *Aufstieg und Niedergang der römischen Welt* I.4. 584-614. Berlin: Walter de Gruyter.

— 1975. *Etruscan Dress*. Baltimore, MD: Johns Hopkins University Press.

— 1977. "The Judgment of Paris, the Toilette of Malavisch, and a Mirror in the Indiana University Art Museum." *StEtr* 45:149-68.

— 1980. "An Etruscan Mirror with 'Spiky Garland' in the Getty Museum." *J. Paul Getty Museum Journal* 8:147-54.

— 1984. "Human Sacrifice on an Etruscan Funerary Urn." *AJA* 88:531-39.

— 1990. *Etruscan*. London: British Museum.

— 1993. "Fufluns Pacha: The Etruscan Dionysus." In *Masks of Dionysus*, ed. T.H. Carpenter and C.A. Faraone, 221-35. Ithaca, NY: Cornell University Press.

— 2003. "The Greeks Overseas." In *The Greeks beyond the Aegean: From Marseilles to Bactria*, ed. V. Karageorghis, 43-55. New York: Alexander S. Onassis Public Benefit Foundation.

Bonfante, L., and G. Bonfante 2002. *The Etruscan Language: An Introduction*, rev.

ed. Manchester: Manchester University Press.

Bonghi Iovino, M. 2001. " '*Area sacra*/complesso monumentale' della Civita." In *Tarquinia etrusca, una nuova storia*, ed. A.M. Moretti Sgubini, 21-29. Rome: "L'Erma" di Bretschneider.

Bonnefoy, Y., ed. 1992. *Roman and European Mythologies*, trans. W. Doniger et al. Chicago, IL: University of Chicago Press.

Bremer, J. 1983. *The Early Greek Concept of the Soul.* Princeton, NJ: Princeton University Press.

Bremer, J., and H. Roodenburg, eds. 1991. *A Cultural History of Gesture*. Ithaca, NY: Cornell University Press.

Brendel, O. J. *Etruscan Art.* New Haven, CT: Yale University Press.

Briguet, M.-F., and D. Briquel 2002. *Musée du Louvre, Les urnes cinéraires étrusques de l'époque hellénistique*. Paris: Réunion des Musées Nationaux.

Brommer, F. 1981. "Theseus und Minotauros in der etruskischen Kunst." *RM* 88:1-12.

Bruni, S. 1986. *I Lastroni a scala*. Rome: Giorgio Bretschneider.

Brunn-Körte=Brunn, E., and G. Körte 1872-1916. *I rilievi delle urne etrusche*. 3 vols. Berlin: G. Reimer.

Buranelli, F., ed. 1987. *La Tomba François di Vulci*. Rome: Quasar.

— 1992. *The Etruscans, Legacy of a Lost Civilization*, trans. w. intro. N.T.de Grummond. Memphis, TN: Wonders.

— 2004. "Die Kopien des Gemäldezyklus der Tomba François von Carlo Ruspi im Museo Gregoriano Etrusco des Vatikan." In *Die Etrusker*, ed. B. Andreae, A. Hoffman, and C. Weber-Lehmann, 168-75. Munich: Hirmer Verlag.

Burkert, W. 1985. *Greek Religion*. Cambridge, MA: Harvard University Press.

— 1992. *The Orientalizing Revolution, Near Eastern Influence on Greek Culture in the Early Archaic Age*. Cambridge, MA: Harvard University Press.

Burn, L. 1987. *The Meidias Painter*. Oxford: Clarendon Press.

Campbell, J. 1949. *The Hero with a Thousand Faces*. Bollingen Series 17. Princeton, NJ: Princeton University Press.

Camporeale, G. 1960. "Thalna e scene mitologiche connesse." *StEtr* 28:233-62.

— 1965. "Banalizzazioni etrusche di miti greci." In *Studi in onore di L. Banti*, 111-23. Rome: "L'Erma" di Bretschneider.

— 1968. "Banalizzazioni di miti greci, II." *StEtr* 36:21-35.

— 1969. "Banalizzazioni di miti greci, III." *StEtr* 37:59-76.

— 1989. "La mitologia figurata nella cultura etrusca arcaica." In *Atti, Secondo Congresso Internazionale Etrusco, Firenze . . .1985*, II, 905-24. Rome: G. Bretschneider.

Capdeville, G. 1999. "Voltumna ed altri culti del territorio volsiniese." *Annali della Fondazione per il Museo "Claudio Faina"* 6:109-35.

Carpenter, T. 1991. *Art and Myth in Ancient Greece*. London: Thames & Hudson.

Carpino, A. 2003. *Discs of Splendor, The Relief Mirrors of the Etruscans*. Madison, WI: University of Wisconsin Press.

Carruba, O. 1976 "Nuova lettura dell'iscrizione etrusca dei cippi di Tunisia." *Athenaeum* 54:163-73.

Cianferoni, C. G. 2001. *The World of the Etruscans*. Florence: Nuova Grafica Fiorentina.

CIE = Corpus Inscriptionum Etruscarum

Colonna, G. 1976. "La diffusione della scrittura." In *Civiltà del Lazio primitivo*, 372-76. Rome: Multigrafica Editrice.

— 1980. "Note di lessico etrusco (*farthan, huze, hinthial*)." *StEtr* 48:161-80.

— ed. 1985. *Santuari d'Etruria*. Milan: Electa.

— 1987. "I culti del santuario della Cannicella." *Annali della Fondazione per il Museo 'Claudio Faina'* 3:11-26.

— 1994. "L'Apollo di Pyrgi." In *Magna Grecia, etruschi, fenici: Atti del trentatreesimo convegno di studi sulla Magna Grecia, Taranto, 8-13 ottobre 1993*, 345-75. Taranto: Istituto per la storia e l'archeologia della Magna Grecia.

— 1996. *L'Altorilievo di Pyrgi, Dei ed eroi greci in Etruria*. Rome: "L'Erma" di Bretschneider.

— 1997. "Divinités peu connues du panthéon étrusque." In *LPRH*: 167-84.

— 2006."Sacred Architecture and the Religion of the Etruscans." In *Religion of the Etruscans*, ed. N. T. de Grummond and E. Simon, 132-68. Austin, TX: University of Texas Press 2006.

Cristofani, M. 1979. "Recent Advances in Etruscan Epigraphy and Language." In *Italy before the Romans*, ed. D. Ridgway and Francesca R. Serra Ridgway. London: Academic Press, 1979.

—1986. "Faone, la testa di Orfeo e l'immaginario femminile." *Prospettiva* 42, 2-12.

— 1995. *Tabula Capuana*. Florence: Leo S. Olschki Editore.

— 1997. "Masculin/féminin dans la théonymie étrusque." In *LPRH*: 209-19.

— 2000. *I Bronzi degli etruschi*. Novara: Istituto Geografico De Agostini.

Cristofani, M., and M. Martelli 1987. *L'Oro degli etruschi*. Novara: Istituto Geografico De Agostini.

CSE = Corpus Speculorum Etruscorum

Dalley, S. 1989. *Myths from Mesopotamia, Creation, the Flood, Gilgamesh and Others*. Oxford: Oxford University Press.

de Grummond, E. 2000-2001. "Maenads and Meaning: Antefixes from Tarquinia in American Collections." *Bulletin, Museums of Art and Archaeology, University of Michigan* 12:7-30.

de Grummond, N.T., ed. 1982. *A Guide to Etruscan Mirrors*. Tallahassee, FL: Archaeological News.

— 1986. "Rediscovery." In *Etruscan Life and Afterlife, A Handbook of Etruscan Studies*, ed. L. Bonfante, 18-46. Detroit, MI: Wayne State University Press.

— 1991."Etruscan Twins and Mirror Images: The Dioskouroi at the Door." *Yale University Art Gallery Bulletin* 10-31.

— 2000a. "An Etruscan Mirror in Tokyo." In *Aspetti e problemi,* ed. M. D. Gentili 69-77. Rome: Aracne, 2000.

— 2000b. "Mirrors and Manteia: Themes of Prophecy on Etruscan Mirrors." In *Aspetti e problemi.*, ed. M. D. Gentili, 27-67. Rome: Aracne, 2000.

— 2000c. "Gauls and Giants, Skylla and the Palladion: Some Responses." In *From Pergamon to Sperlonga, Sculpture and Context*, eds. N.T. de Grummond and B. Ridgway, 255-77. Berkeley, CA: University of California Press.

— 2002a. "Etruscan Mirrors Now." *AJA* 106:307-11.

— 2002b. "Mirrors, Marriage and Mysteries." *JRA* 47:63-85.

— 2004. "For the Mother and for the Daughter: Some Thoughts on Dedications from Etruria and Praeneste." In *Charis. Essays in Honor of Sara A. Immer-*

wahr, ed. Anne P. Chapin, *Hesperia* suppl. 33:351-70.

— 2005. "Roman Favor and Etruscan Thuf(ltha): A Note on Propertius 4:2.34." *Ancient West and East* 4.2: 296-317.

— 2006. "Prophets and Priests." In *The Religion of the Etruscans*, ed. N. T. de Grummond and E. Simon, 22–44. Austin, TX: University of Texas Press.

— forthcoming a. "Maris, the Etruscan Genius." In *Across Frontiers: Etruscans, Greeks, Phoenicians and Cypriots. Studies in Honour of David Ridgway and Francesca R. Serra Ridgway.*

— forthcoming b. "A Barbarian Myth? The Case of the Talking Head." In proceedings of the conference "Barbarians of Ancient Europe" held at University of Richmond, March 2003.

— de Grummond, N. T., and E. Simon, eds. 2006. *The Religion of the Etruscans.* Austin, TX: University of Texas Press.

de Jorio, A. 2000. *Gesture in Naples and Gesture in Antiquity*, trans. with intro. by A. Kendon. Bloomington, IN: Indiana University Press.

Dennis, G. 1848. *The Cities and Cemeteries of Etruria.* 2 vols. London: John Murray.

De Puma, R. D. 1982. "Greek Gods and Heroes on Etruscan Mirrors." In *A Guide to Etruscan Mirrors*, ed. N. T. de Grummond, 89-100. Tallahassee, FL: Archaeological News.

—1994. "Eos and Memnon on Etruscan Mirrors." In *Murlo and the Etruscans, Art and Society in Ancient Etruria,* ed. R. De Puma and J. P. Small, 180-89. Madison, WI: University of Wisconsin Press.

— 1998. "The Etruscan Rhadamanthys?" *Etruscan Studies* 5:37-49.

— 2001. "An Etruscan Mirror with the Prophesying Head of Orpheus." *Record, Princeton University Art Museum* 60:18-29.

— De Puma, R. D., and J. P. Small, eds. 1994. *Murlo and the Etruscans: Art and Society in Ancient Etruria.* Madison, WI: University of Wisconsin Press.

De Ruyt, F. 1934. *Charun, Démon étrusque de la mort.* Rome: Institut Historique Belge.

De Simone, C. 1997. "Dénominations divines étrusques binaires; considérations préliminaires." In *LPRH:* 185-207.

Dorcey, P. F. 1992. *The Cult of Silvanus: A Study in Roman Folk Religion.* Leiden: E. J. Brill.

Doty, W. G. 1986. *Mythography: The Study of Myth and Rituals.* Tuscaloosa, AL: University of Alabama Press.

Dumézil, G. 1970. *Archaic Roman Religion*, trans. P. Krapp. 2 vols. Baltimore. MD: Johns Hopkins University Press.

Dundes, A. 1990. "The Hero Pattern and the Life of Jesus." In *In Quest of the Hero,* 179-223. Princeton, NJ: Princeton University Press.

Edlund-Berry, I. E. M. 1992. "Etruscans at Work and Play: Evidence for an Etruscan Calendar." In *Kotinos, Festschrift für Erika Simon*, 330-37. Mainz: Von Zabern.

— 2006. "Ritual Space and Boundaries in Etruscan Religion." In *The Religion of the Etruscans,* ed. N. T. de Grummond and E. Simon, 16-31. Austin, TX: University of Texas Press.

Eliade, M. 1991. "Toward a Definition of Myth." In *Roman and European Mythologies*, ed. Yves Bonnefoy. Chicago, IL: University of Chicago Press.

Elliott, J. 1995. "The Etruscan Wolfman in Myth and Ritual." *Etruscan Studies* 2: 17-33.

Emmanuel-Rebuffat, D. 1997. "Hercle aux Enfers." In *LPRH*: 55-67.

ES = Etruskische Spiegel 1840-97. E. Gerhard, A. Klügmann, and G. Körte, *Etruskische Spiegel* 5 vols. Berlin: G. Reimer.

ET = Etruskische Texte (=Rix 1991).

Les Etrusques et l'Europe 1992. Paris: Editions de la Réunion des musées nationaux.

Feruglio, A. E. 1998. "Uno specchio della necropoli di Castel Viscardo, presso Orvieto, con Apollo, Turan e Atunis." In *Etrusca et italica: Scritti in ricordo di Massimo Pallottino*, 299-314. Pisa: Istituti Editoriali e Poligrafici Internazionali.

Fontenrose, J. 1978. *The Delphic Oracle, Its Responses and Operations, with a Catalogue of Responses*. Berkeley, CA: University of California Press.

Fugazzola Delpino, M. A. 1984. *La Cultura villanoviana*. Rome: Edizioni dell'Ateneo.

Gantz, T. 1993. *Early Greek Myth, A Guide to Literary and Artistic Sources* 2 vols. Baltimore, MD: Johns Hopkins University Press.

Gentili, M.D., ed. 2000. *Aspetti e problemi della produzione degli specchi figurati etruschi*. Rome: Aracne.

Gimbutas, M. 1989. *The Language of the Goddess*. San Francisco, CA: Harper.

Goldberg, M. 1987. "The 'Eos and Kephalos' from Caere, Its Subject and Date." *AJA* 91:605-14.

Green, P. 2000. "Pergamon and Sperlonga: A Historian's Reactions." In *From Pergamon to Sperlonga, Sculpture and Context*, eds. N.T. de Grummond and B. Ridgway, 166-90. Berkeley, CA: University of California Press.

Guthrie, W. K. C. 1952. *Orpheus and Greek Religion*. Princeton, NJ: Princeton University Press.

Harris, W.V. 1971. *Rome in Etruria and Umbria*. Oxford: Clarendon Press.

Haynes, S. 2000. *Etruscan Civilization, A Cultural History*. Los Angeles, CA: J. Paul Getty Museum.

Hencken, H. 1968a. *Tarquinia and Etruscan Origins*. London: Thames & Hudson.

Hencken, H. 1968b. *Tarquinia, Villanovans and Early Etruscans*. Cambridge, MA: Peabody Museum of Harvard University.

Herodotus 1996. *Herodotus, Histories*, tr. A. De Sélincourt, w. intro. by J. Marincola. Harmondsworth: Penguin Books.

Hesiod 1988. *Hesiod, Theogony, Works and Days*, trans. M. L. West. Oxford: Oxford University Press.

Heurgon, J. 1959. "The Date of Vegoia's Prophecy." *JRS* 49:41-45.

Heurgon, J. 1964. *Daily Life of the Etruscans*, trans. J. Kirkup. London: Weidenfeld & Nicolson.

Homer 1951. *The Iliad of Homer*, trans. R. Lattimore. Chicago, IL: University of Chicago Press.

Hostetter, E. 1986. *Bronzes from Spina* I. Mainz: von Zabern.

Hostetler, K. 2002. "Serpent Iconography: A New Analysis of the Etruscan Demons of the Underworld." Paper delivered at the British Museum Conference: "The Etruscans Now":http://www.open.ac.uk/Arts/classtud/etruscans-now/papers/hostetler.htm

Jannot, J.-R. 1997. "Charu(n) et Vanth, divinités plurielles?" In *LPRH:* 139-66.

— 1998. *Devins, dieux et démons. Regards sur la religion de l'Étrurie antique.* Paris: Picard.

— 2000. "The Etruscans and the Afterworld." *Etruscan Studies* 7:81-99.

Jucker, Inez. 1956. *Der Gestus des Aposkopein.* Zurich: Iuris-Verlag.

Knauer, E.R. 2001."Observations on the 'Barbarian' Custom of Suspending the Heads of Vanquished Enemies from the Neck of Horses." *Archäologische Mitteilungen aus Iran und Turan* 33:283-332.

Krauskopf, I. 1987. *Todesdämonen und Totengötter im vorhellenistischen Etrurien: Kontinuität und Wandel.* Florence: Leo S. Olschki.

— 1997. "Influences grecques et orientales sur les représentations de dieux étrusques." In *LPRH:* 25-36.

— 2006. "The Grave and Beyond in Etruscan Religion." In *Religion of the Etruscans*, ed. N. T. de Grummond and E. Simon. 66-89. Austin, TX: University of Texas Press.

Lambrechts, R. 1978. *Les miroirs étrusques et prénestins des Musées royaux d'art et d'histoire à Bruxelles.* Brussels: Musées royaux d'art et d'histoire.

LIMC = Lexicon Iconographicum Mythologiae Classicae

LPRH = 1997. *Les Étrusques, Les plus religieux des hommes, XII*^es *Rencontres de l'École du Louvre*, eds. F. Gaultier and D. Briquel. Paris: La documentation française.

Luschi, L. 1991. "Cacu, Fauno e i venti." *StEtr* 57:105-17.

Lysaght, P. 1986. *The Banshee. The Irish Supernatural Death Messenger.* Dublin: Glendale Press.

Maggiani, A. 1982. "Qualche osservazione sul fegato di Piacenza." *StEtr* 50:53-88.

— 1988. "Argos, Janus, Culsans. A proposito di un sarcofago di Tuscania." *Prospettiva* 52:2-9.

—1992. "Iconografie greche e storie locali dell'arte etrusco-italica tra IV e III secolo a.C." *Prospettiva* 68:3-12.

Malinowski, B. 1992. *Malinowski and the Work of Myth*, ed. I. Strenski. Princeton, NJ: Princeton University Press.

Mallory, J.P. 1989. In *Search of the Indo-Europeans, Language, Archaeology and Myth.* London: Thames & Hudson.

Manino, L. 1980. "Semantica e struttura della figura demonica nel pittore orvietano della 'Vanth." *Annali della Fondazione per il Museo "Claudio Faina"* 1: 59-72.

Mansuelli, G.A. 1948-49. "Studi sugli specchi etruschi. IV: La mitologia figurata negli specchi etruschi." *StEtr* 20:59-98.

Maras, D. F. 2001. "La dea Thanr e le cerchie divine in Etruria: Nuove acquisizioni." *StEtr* 64: 173-97.

Marazov, I., ed. 1998. *Ancient Gold: The Wealth of the Thracians.* New York: Harry N. Abrams.

Martelli, M. 1987. *La Ceramica degli etruschi.* Novara: Istituto Geografico De Agostini.

Martini, W. 1971. *Die Etruskische Ringsteinglyptik. RM-EH* 18. Heidelberg: F. H. Kerle.

Massa-Pairault, M. –F. 1985. "La divination in Etrurie. Le IVe siècle, période critique." *Caesarodunum*, Suppl. 52:56-112.

— 1994. "Lemnos, Corinthe et l'Étrurie. Iconographie et iconologie à propos d'une olpè de Cerveteri (VII siècle av. n.è.). *PP* 279:437-68.

— 2000. "Problemi ermeneutici a proposito degli specchi. Esame di alcune scene connesse con il mito di Eracle." In *Aspetti e problemi*, ed. M. D. Gentili, pp. 181-207. Rome: Aracne 2000.

McDonough, C. 2002. "Hercle and the Ciminian Lake Legend: Source Study for an Etruscan Mirror." *CJ* 98.1:9-19.

Morris, D., et al. 1979. *Gestures, Their Origin and Distribution*. London: Jonathan Cape.

Menichetti, M. 1994. *Archeologia del potere: Re, immagini e miti a Roma e in Etruria in età arcaica*. Milan: Longanesi.

Minetti, A. 2005. "La Tomba della Quadriga Infernale di Sarteano." *StEtr* 70:135-59.

Minto, A. 1927. "Curiosità archeologiche." *StEtr* 1:475-76.

Nagy, H. 1996. "The Judgment of Paris? An Etruscan Mirror in Seattle." In *Etruscan Italy, Etruscan Influences on the Civilizations of Italy from Antquity to the Modern Era*, ed. J. Hall, 45-63. Provo, UT: Brigham Young University and Museum of Art.

— 2002. "Two Etruscan Mirrors in West Coast, USA, Collections, Thoughts on Production." Paper delivered at British Museum Conference "The Etruscans Now": http://www.open.ac/uk/Arts/classtud/etruscans-now/papers/nagy.htm.

Neils, J. 1994. "Reflections of Immortality: The Myth of Jason on Etruscan Mirrors." In *Murlo and the Etruscans*, ed. R. D. De Puma and J. P. Small, 190-95. Madison, WI: University of Wisconsin Press, 1994.

Neumann, E. 1963. *The Great Mother, An Analysis of an Archetype*. Bollingen Series 47. Princeton, NJ: Princeton University Press.

Ovid 1986. *Ovid, Metamorphoses*, trans. A.D. Melville. Oxford: Oxford University Press.

Page, R.I. 1990. *Norse Myths*. London: British Museum.

Pairault Massa, F.H. 1992. *Iconologia e politica nell'Italia antica, Roma, Lazio, Etruria dal VII al I secolo a.C.* Milan: Longanesi.

Pallottino, M. 1975. *The Etruscans*, trans. J. Cremona, ed. D. Ridgway. Bloomington, IN: Indiana University Press.

— 1979. "Uno specchio di Tuscania e la leggenda etrusca di Tarchon." In *Saggi di Antichità* 2:679-707. Rome: Giorgio Bretschneider.

Pfiffig, A.J. 1975. *Religio Etrusca*. Graz: Akademische Druck- u. Verlagsanstalt.

Pieraccini, L. 2003. *Around the Hearth: Caeretan Cylinder-Stamped Braziers*. Rome: "L'Erma" di Bretschneider.

Pittura etrusca al Museo di Villa Giulia 1989. Rome: De Luca Edizioni d'Arte.

Pittura etrusca a Orvieto 1982. Rome: Edizioni Kappa.

Pomeroy, S. 1975. *Goddesses, Whores, Wives and Slaves: Women in Classical Antiquity*. New York: Schocken.

Prose Edda 1954 *The Prose Edda of Snorri Sturluson, Tales from Norse Mythology*, trans. Jean I. Young. Berkeley, CA: University of California Press.

Puhvel, J. 1987. *Comparative Mythology*. Baltimore, MD: Johns Hopkins University Press.

Radke, G. 1965. *Die Götter Altitaliens*. Münster: Verlag Aschendorff.

Rallo, A. 1974. *Lasa iconografia e esegesi*. Florence: Sansoni.

— 2000. "Motivi ispiratori greci nella decorazione di alcuni specchi etruschi." In *Aspetti e problemi*, ed. M. D. Gentili, 225-48. Rome: Aracne, 2000.

Rasmussen, T. 2005. "Herakles' Apotheosis in Etruria and Greece." *AntKunst* 48:30-39.

Rastrelli, A. 1993. "La decorazione fittile dell'edificio sacro in località I Fucoli presso Chianciano Terme." *Ostraka* 351-67.

Rebuffat-Emmanuel, D. 1973. *Le miroir étrusque d'après la collection du Cabinet des Médailles*. Rome: "L'Erma" di Bretschneider.

Richardson, E. H. 1964. *The Etruscans: Their Art and Civilization*. Chicago, IL: University of Chicago Press.

— 1976. "The Gods Arrive." *ArchNews* 5:125-33.

— 1977. "The Wolf in the West." *Journal of the Walters Art Gallery* 36:91-101.

— 1983. *Etruscan Votive Bronzes, Geometric, Orientalizing, Archaic*. 2 vols. Mainz: P. von Zabern.

— 1984. "The Tree and the Spring: The Story of Amycus and the Dioscuri." *ArchNews* 13:57-67.

Richter, G.M.A. 1968. *Engraved Gems of the Greeks, Etruscans, and Romans* I. London: Phaidon.

Ridgway, D. 2002. *The World of the Early Etruscans*. Jonsered: Paul Aströms Vörlag.

Ridgway, D., and Francesca R. Serra Ridgway, eds. *Italy before the Romans: The Iron Age, Orientalizing, and Etruscan Periods*. London: Academic Press, 1979.

Rix, H. 1991 *Etruskische Texte*, 2 vols. Tübingen: Gunter Narr Verlag.

Roller, L. 1999. *In Search of God the Mother: The Cult of Anatolian Cybele*. Berkeley, CA: University of California Press.

Roncalli, F. 1965. *Le Lastre dipinte da Cerveteri*. Florence: Sansoni.

— 1985. *Scrivere etrusco*. Milan: Electa.

— 1996. "Laris Pulenas and Sisyphus: Mortals, Heroes and Demons in the Etruscan Underworld." *Etruscan Studies* 3:45-64.

— 1997. "Iconographie funéraire et topographie de l'au-delà en Étrurie." In *LPRH*: 37-54.

Rupp, W. 2002. "The Vegetal Goddess in the Tomb of the Typhon." Paper delivered at the British Museum Conference: "The Etruscans Now": http://www.open.ac/uk/Arts/classtud/etruscans-now/papers/rupp.htm

Rutter, N.K., and B.A. Sparkes, eds. 2000. *Word and Image in Ancient Greece*. Edinburgh: Edinburgh University Press.

Scheffer, C. 1994. "The Arched Door in Late Etruscan Funerary Art." In *Murlo and the Etruscans: Art and Society in Ancient Etruria*, ed. R.D. DePuma and J. P. Small, 196-210. Madison, WI: University of Wisconsin Press.

Schilling, R. 1992a. "Genius." In Bonnefoy 1992: 127-28.

— 1992b. "Janus." In Bonnefoy 1992: 129-30.

— 1992c. "Roman Gods." In Bonnefoy 1992: 68-77.

— 1992d. "Silvanus." In Bonnefoy 1992: 146.

Schwarz, S. 1997. "Greek Myths on Etruscan Mirrors." *JRA*: 326-29.

Scullard, H.H. 1981. *Festivals and Ceremonies of the Roman Republic*. Ithaca, NY: Cornell University Press.

Segal, R. 1990. "Introduction: In Quest of the Hero." In *In Quest of the Hero*, vii-xli.

Princeton, NJ: Princeton University Press.

Serra Ridgway, F. R. 199. "Etruscans, Greeks, Carthaginians: The Sanctuary of Pyrgi." In *Greek Colonists and Native Populations*, ed. U. P. Descoeudras, 511-30. Oxford: Oxford University Press.

— 1996. *I Corredi del Fondo Scataglini a Tarquinia, Scavi della Fondazione Lerici*. Milan: Comune di Milano.

— 2000. "The Tomb of the Anina Family: Some Motifs in Late Tarquinian Painting." In *Ancient Italy in its Mediterranean Setting, Studies in Honour of Ellen Macnamara*, ed. D. Ridgway et al. 301–16. London: Accordia Research Center.

— 2003. "L'Ultima pittura etrusca: stile cronologia, ideologia." *Orizzonti, Rassegna di archeologia* 4:11-22.

Shapiro, H.A. 1993. *Personifications in Greek Art, The Representation of Abstract Concepts 600-400 B.C.* Bern: Akanthus.

— 1994. *Myth into Art*. London: Routledge.

Simon, E. 1982. "Era ed Eracle alla Foce del Sele e nell'Italia Centrale." *AttiMGrecia* ser. 3.1: 209-17.

— 1984. "Le divinità di culto." In *Gli etruschi: una nuova immagine*. 152–67. Florence: Giunti Martello Editore.

— 1990. *Die Götter der Römer*. Munich: Hirmer Verlag.

— 1995. "Nachrichten aus dem Martin-von-Wagner Museum. Orpheus unter Kriegern." *AA*: 483-87.

— 1998. *Die Götter der Griechen*. Munich: Hirmer Verlag.

— 2006. "Gods in Harmony: the Etruscan Pantheon." In *Religion of the Etruscans*, ed. N. T. de Grummond and E. Simon, pp. 45-65. Austin, TX: University of Texas Press.

Small, J.P. 1976. "The Death of Lucretia." *AJA* 80:349-60.

— 1982. *Cacus and Marsyas in Etrusco-Roman Legend.* Princeton, NJ: Princeton University Press.

— 2003. *The Parallel Worlds of Classical Art and Text*. Cambridge: Cambridge University Press.

Sowder, C. 1982. "Etruscan Mythological Figures." In *A Guide to Etruscan Mirrors*, ed. N. T. de Grummond, 100-28. Tallahassee, FL: Archaeological News, 1982.

Sprenger, M., and G. Bartoloni 1977. *Etruschi, l'Arte*. Milan: Editoriale Jaca Book.

Steingräber, S., ed. 1986. *Etruscan Painting: Catalogue Raisonné of Etruscan Wall Paintings*. English edition, ed. D. and F. Ridgway. New York: Johnson.

Steuernagel, D. 1998. *Menschenopfor und Mord am Altar: Griechischen Mythen in etruskischen Gräber*. Wiesbaden: L. Reichert.

Stopponi, S. 1991. "Etruscan Orvieto and Perugia." In *Gens Antiquissima Italiae, Antichità dall'Umbria a New York,* 85-94. Perugia: Electa Editore Umbria.

— 2002. "Recent Archaeological Investigations at Campo della Fiera at Orvieto." Paper delivered at the British Museum Conference, "The Etruscans Now": http://www.open.ac/uk/Arts/classtud/etruscans-now/papers/stopponi.htm

Szilágyi, J.G. 1992, 1998. *Ceramica etrusco-corinzia figurata*. Pt. I (1992) and Pt. II (1998). Florence: Leo S. Olschki Editore.

Taylor, R. 2000. "Watching the Skies: Janus, Auspication and the Shrine in the Roman Forum." *MAAR* 45:1-40.

Tirelli, M. 1981. "La rappresentazione del sole nell'arte etrusca." *StEtr* 49:41-50.

TLE = 1968. *Testimonia Linguae Etruscae*, ed. M. Pallottino. 2nd ed. Florence: La Nuova Italia.

Torelli, M. 1986. "Lineamenti del pantheon e della disciplina." In *Rasenna, Storia e civiltà degli etruschi*, 198-216. Milan: Scheiwiller.

— 1988. "Etruria principes disciplinam doceto. Il mito normativo dello specchio di Tuscania." *Studia Tarquiniensia* (*Archaeologia Perusina* 9):109-18.

— 1997. "Les Adonies de Gravisca. Archéologie d'une fête." In *LPRH*:233-91.

— ed. 2000. *Gli Etruschi*. Milan: Bompiani.

Turfa, J.M. 2005. *Catalogue of the Etruscan Gallery of the University of Pennsylvania Museum of Archaeology and Anthropology*. Philadelphia, PA: University of Pennsylvania Museum of Archaeology and Anthropology.

— 2006a. "Votive Offerings in Etruscan Religion." In *Religion of the Etruscans*, ed. N. T. de Grummond and E. Simon, 90-115. Austin, TX: University of Texas Press.

— 2006b. "The Etruscan Brontoscopic Calendar." In *Religion of the Etruscans*, ed. N. T. de Grummond and E. Simon, 173-90. Austin, TX: University of Texas Press.

Van der Meer, L.B. 1987. *The Bronze Liver of Piacenza, Analysis of a Polytheistic Structure*. Amsterdam: J.C. Gieben.

— 1995. *Interpretatio etrusca: Greek Myths on Etruscan Mirrors*. Amsterdam: J.C. Gieben.

— 1997. "Religion ombrienne et religion étrusque." In *LPRH*: 223-31.

Vermeule, E. 1979. *Aspects of Death in Early Greek Art and Poetry*. Sather Classical Lectures 46. Berkeley, CA: University of California Press.

Virgil 1956. *Virgil, The Aeneid*, trans. W. F. Jackson Knight. Harmondsworth: Penguin.

Von Vacano, O.-W. 1960. *The Etruscans in the Ancient World*. Bloomington, IN: Indiana University Press.

Weber-Lehmann, C. 1997. "Die sogenannte Vanth von Tuscania: Seirene Anasyromene." *JdI* 112:191-246.

Weinstock, S. 1946. "Martianus Capella and the Cosmic System of the Etruscans." *JRS* 36:101-29.

Die Welt der Etrusker, Archäologische Denkmäler aus Museen der Sozialistichen länder. Berlin: Henschelverlag.

Willis, R., ed. 1996. *World Mythology*. New York: Henry Holt.

Wiman, I.M.B. 1990. *Malstria—Malena. Metals and Motifs in Etruscan Mirror Craft*. Göteborg: Paul Aströms Förlag.

Wiseman, T.P. 1995. *Remus, A Roman Myth*. Cambridge: Cambridge University Press.

— 2004. *The Myths of Rome*. Exeter: University of Exeter Press.

Wood, R.E. 1980. "The Myth of Tages." *Latomus* 39:325-44.

Zazoff, P. 1968. *Etruskische Skarabäen*. Mainz: von Zabern.

Zimmer, G. 1987. *Spiegel in Antikenmuseum*. Berlin: Staatliche Museen Preussischer Kulturbesitz.

Index

INDEX